UNFLINCHING
COURAGE

Also by Senator Kay Bailey Hutchison

American Heroines: The Spirited Women
Who Shaped Our Country

Leading Ladies: American Trailblazers

UNFLINCHING COURAGE

Pioneering Women
Who Shaped Texas

Senator Kay Bailey Hutchison

HARPER PERENNIAL

NEW YORK • LONDON • TORONTO • SYDNEY • NEW DELHI • AUCKLAND

HARPER ● PERENNIAL

FIRST HARPER PERENNIAL EDITION PUBLISHED 2014.

Designed by Leah Carlson-Stanisic

Library of Congress Cataloging-in-Publication Data has been applied for.

ISBN 978-0-06-213071-6 (pbk.)

14 15 16 17 18   OV/RRD   10 9 8 7 6 5 4 3 2 1

This book is dedicated to my children, Kathryn Bailey Hutchison and Houston Taylor Hutchison. I hope the nineteenth-century pioneers who faced obstacles with unflinching courage and in so doing built our great state and nation will be an inspiration to them and to their generation.

Contents

VIII: Master Builders:
A Tale of Two Cities and Two Centuries   291
1850s–1950s

Epilogue   317

Appendix: Family Trees

Acknowledgments

No one can write a book alone; there are so many archivists, librarians, editors, researchers, and experts' brains to pick that it invariably becomes a collaboration.

My research writer, Howard Cohn, is the easiest person with whom to work. He does excellent research and I trust his judgment. My editor, Claire Wachtel, was eager to publish the stories of early pioneer women, and her commitment to ensuring that the role of women is preserved in American history has been proven through the years. She has edited the fabulous books Cokie Roberts has written, and this is the third one she has done with me that adds to the chronicles that will be read by future generations documenting how America's exceptionalism developed.

Howard and I started our journey to uncover the women who aren't widely known but contributed so much to the building of Texas, and to add to those who were already in the history books.

Noted Texas historians gave generously of their time. Ted Fehrenbach is the father of Texas historians in this generation. We gained insight from him and potential sources to further explore. Don Carleton, director of the Dolph Briscoe Center for American History at the University of Texas; Frances Vick, historian, author, and former president of the Texas State Historical Association; and the late Archie McDonald, preeminent East Texas historian, author, and professor at Stephen F. Austin State University, all gave us valuable suggestions, on subjects and research sites. Linda Reynolds, director of the East Texas Research Center at Stephen F. Austin State University, copied many papers and letters from which we gained additional knowledge of several women profiled in the Texas Revolution chapter. Carolyn Spears, curator at the Stone Fort Museum, took time to show me Anna Raguet Irion's wedding dress and that of her daughter Harriet Raguet Taylor, which have been beautifully preserved and stored in the Stone Fort Museum, on the campus of Stephen F. Austin State University in Nacogdoches.

One set of letters referenced by Archie and Linda included correspondence of Thomas J. Rusk that I was able to trace to the El Paso Public Library. It was there, through the generous help of the Border Heritage librarian, Marta Estrada, and the library information specialist, Claudia Ramirez, that I found the original suicide letter written by Senator Rusk to his children, explaining his despondency.

J. P. (James Perry) Bryan and Stephen C. Cook, descendants of Emily Austin Bryan Perry, gave me more family information that added depth to her profile.

Luci Johnson, while giving my children and me a tour of the LBJ Ranch in the Lyndon B. Johnson National Historical Park, introduced me to the story of Eliza Bunton Johnson, her great-grandmother, who became a wonderful addition to the Trail Drives and Ranches chapter.

When I wrote to my friends Tres Kleberg and Jamey Clement, descendants of Henrietta King, to ask for more information about her, they and Helen Kleberg Groves were immensely helpful.

Dr. Linda Sundquist, who wrote the definitive biography of Mary Shindler, helped me find some of her literary works and personal writing that highlighted her amazing life.

Dianne Garrett Powell, whose family gave the University of Texas at Arlington historic Texas maps and documents, among them the Irion family papers that include letters from my great-great-grandfather, Charles S. Taylor, added confirmation of some of the most interesting facets of Anna Raguet Irion's life. Dianne is a past president of the Texas State Historical Association.

Betty Sharp Adcock, another descendant of Dr. Frank Sharp, sent me a copy of the obituary of Martha Hall Sharp that documented her early death in Tennessee, while visiting her family after her move to San Augustine.

Barbara Tucker Mitchell, my second cousin, also provided great help with the family tree of the Sharp family, from the historical records in San Augustine County.

Former lieutenant governor of Texas Bill Hobby and his children, Paul Hobby and Laura Hobby Beckworth, gave me several citations, which greatly enriched the chapter about Oveta Culp Hobby.

Pattye Greer, my longtime friend and a former member of the Stephen F. Austin State University Board of Regents, was immensely helpful in locating the photograph of Polly Rusk.

David Zepeda, of the Briscoe Center, contributed invaluable maps to illustrate the life of Jane Long, the Austin Family, the major battles of the Texas Revolution, and the cattle trails to points north.

Finally, Melinda Poucher helped edit the chapters as they were written and has a future career as a major writer or editor, if she chooses that route. She caught many a mistake or repetition that I missed. I couldn't have done it without her, and . . . it was she who thought of the title!

Introduction

The Spirit of Texas has been cussed and discussed through-out its storied history. Texans are ruggedly independent, fiercely loyal, colorful, fun-loving, and entrepreneurial.

There could be a thousand different reasons given for the unique Texas persona, but I believe it boils down to two major features of our history. First, Texas, alone among the states, fought single-handedly for its independence. Like the Americans who rebelled against oppressive British rule, Texans rose up against the Mexican dictator Santa Anna. The building of a new republic in 1836 marked the beginning of an independent streak that has been passed through the generations. What began as a republic led to statehood in 1845.

The second way our ancestors evinced their Texas spirit was by conquering the harsh land. As the famous Texas historian T. R. Fehrenbach noted, "the Anglo frontier in Texas was not a frontier of traders, trappers and soldiers, as in most other states. It was a frontier of farming families, with women and small children, encroaching and colliding with a long-ranging, barbaric, war-making race." Though Indian wars were common in other states, in Texas they lasted for more than forty years, and the torture doled out by Comanche tribes in particular spared no one. In their attempts to run the settlers out of their hunting and grazing lands, the Indians not only attacked the men, they also made examples of the women, the children, and the elderly.

The nineteenth century put its stamp on the Texas mystique. The early half was dominated by the revolution and the second half by the settling of the unforgiving land.

Contributions by women to the building of the state were crucial to the resulting spirit. To call those pioneer women rugged and resilient would be an understatement. Many of them came from southern states and genteel backgrounds. They were educated and had grown up in comfortable surroundings. They entered an untamed frontier with virtually no comforts or amenities. They followed their husbands, who sought to make their own way mostly because of the cheap or free land. They lived in crude log cabins or even mud huts, had little furniture, and made the most of their utensils, clothes, and necessities. They were threatened by weather, revolution, and Indian raids, and a few even endured arduous trail drives, herding cattle to markets thousands of miles away.

But they stuck it out. They showed resilience and unflinching courage. These women were full partners, often giving birth to ten or twelve children, many of whom died young in a region where doctors were scarce. They used their educations in art, literature, and music to create a society from this rugged existence. Their positive attitude lent a lively character to the new Texas. It was common for the families to meet for "balls," where guests would bring food, amateur musicians would play, and all would dance the night away.

After visiting her cousin Stephen in 1831, historian Mary Austin Holley observed:

> It is not uncommon for ladies to mount their mustangs and hunt with their husbands, to ride long distances on horseback, to attend a ball with their silk dresses . . . in their saddlebags. Hardy, vigorous constitutions, free spirits, and spontaneous gaiety are thus induced, and contin-

ued a rich legacy to their children, who, it is to be hoped, will sufficiently value the blessing not to squander it away in their eager search for the luxuries and refinements of polite life. . . . Many a wife in Texas has proved herself the better half, and many a widow's heart has prompted her to noble daring.

Another noted Texas historian, Frances Vick, believes the independence of these women was partially due to the Spanish laws that set the precedent for women's property rights. Widows inherited half of estates and daughters generally inherited equally with their brothers. Community property has long been the law in Texas, so even in divorce, women were entitled to half their marital property. These laws gave women wealth from which they could build vast fortunes and holdings. Many became independent business, farm, and ranch owners, establishing their individual identities.

In "Cowboys and Southern Belles," an essay in *Texas Myths*, Sandra L. Myres includes this quote from Necah Furman:

This geographic vastness, the state's frontier heritage, and its crass individualism contributed to the development of its predominantly masculine character . . . [and its] particular brand of regional chauvinism has produced a woman soft on the outside but with a backbone of steel.

When I talked to T. R. Fehrenbach about my effort to focus on the role of women in shaping the culture of Texas, he affirmed my premise. He said grandmothers ruled in the early families and wives often kept the household and business accounts. If widows or daughters inherited ranches on the frontier, they ran them and were dealt with as equals. The frontier era may have ended in the 1880s or '90s, but the frontier mentality lasted for many more years.

I decided to write this book because I grew up hearing the

stories of Texas's past. My great-great-grandfather, Charles S. Taylor, was one of the leaders of the Texas Revolution, having been an elected delegate to the 1836 convention that produced the Texas Declaration of Independence. He served in many positions through the years, first appointed by President Sam Houston and later elected chief justice of Nacogdoches County. My great-great-grandmother, Anna Mary, was his helpmate. They had thirteen children. She participated in the Runaway Scrape, the exodus from Texas during its revolutionary war. Our family has lived in Nacogdoches since the first Taylors called it home in 1832. My mother and her three sisters grew up in the house my grandparents built a few blocks from the original Charles S. Taylor home site. We visited there as children, playing with our cousins and listening to the stories of the families that settled Texas more than 175 years ago—many of whom have intertwined and stayed right there in Nacogdoches. Now I am making memories for my children in the same house, hoping to instill in them a love for Texas and the positive can-do attitude that has made Texas what it is today.

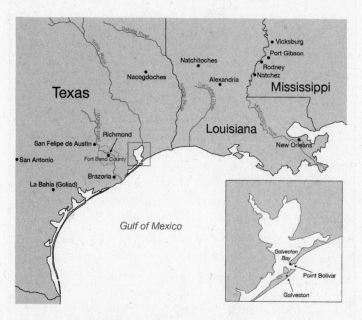

Detail map of Mississippi, Louisiana, and East Texas showing Wilkinson/Long family homes.

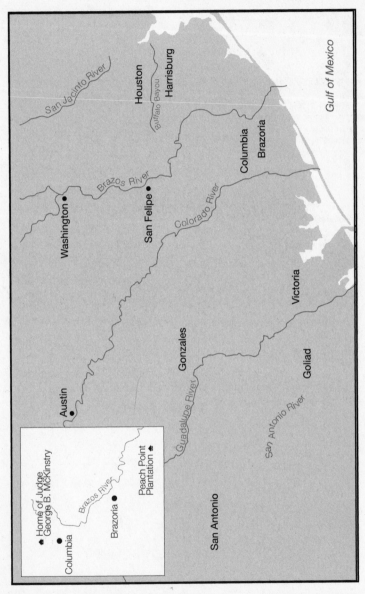

Detail map of Texas in 1836. Inset shows locations of Austin family homes.

TEXAS

Battle of
the Alamo

Battle of
Gonzales

Battle of
San Jacinto

Battle of Goliad

Battle of Gonzales (October 2, 1835)

Battle of Goliad (October 10, 1835)

Battle of the Alamo (February 23 – March 6, 1836)

Battle of San Jacinto (April 21, 1836)

Gulf of Mexico

Major battles of the Texas Revolution.

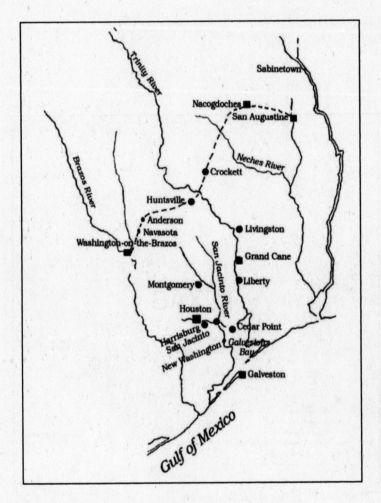

East Texas map showing Houston and Lea family homes.

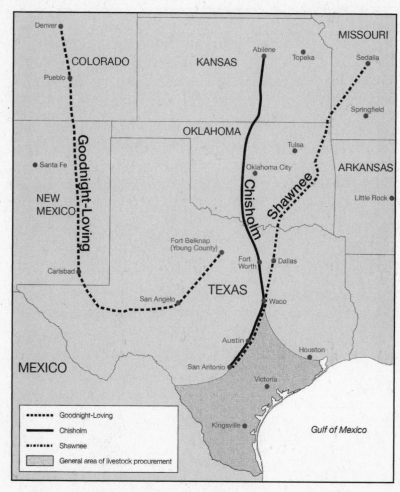

Major cattle trails from Texas to Missouri, Kansas, and Colorado.

Prologue:
Overview of
Nineteenth-Century
Texas

In the early nineteenth century, immigrants from the United States began making their way to the Spanish province of Coahuila and Texas (a Mexican state after 1821) in small numbers, homesteading and establishing trading posts in the eastern part of the region, near San Augustine and south of the Red River. Although Spain prohibited foreign settlement and trading with the Indians, the newcomers were mostly ignored as long as they stayed out of politics. At about the same time, Cherokees and other Indian tribes, forced from their ancestral homelands in North Carolina, Tennessee, and Georgia by encroaching settlers, moved west to Texas as well.

After the 1819 Adams-Onís Treaty established the Louisiana-Texas boundary at the Sabine River, some Americans maintained that Louisiana territory included Texas and took steps to wrest control of the region from Spain. Their goal was most likely its eventual incorporation into the United States. James Long, a physician turned merchant, gathered about three hundred volunteers for an unauthorized military expedition (known as a filibuster) into Texas, where he occupied Nacogdoches and declared an independent republic.

Within a few months, Long and his followers were driven out of Texas by Spanish troops, but he returned with another army in 1820. He was captured in 1821, when he tried to ally himself with the triumphant Mexican Revolution against Spain, and imprisoned in Mexico, where he was shot and killed under mysterious circumstances the following year.

Long's volunteers were motivated less by patriotism than by their leader's promise of generous grants of one league of land (4,428 acres) to each soldier. Many other Americans, especially those who had suffered financial losses in the economic collapse known as the Panic of 1819, were also attracted by the prospect of free land in Texas. One of them was Moses Austin, who after losing a fortune in Missouri lead mines secured an empresarial grant from the governor of Texas to settle three hundred American families in Texas. In 1821, before he had the chance to put his plan into action, Moses Austin died, but his son Stephen Fuller Austin stepped in to fulfill his father's dream of restoring the family's fortunes and good name.

Between 1825 and 1831, Stephen F. Austin received four additional contracts from the Mexican government to settle a total of two thousand American families in Texas. He had little difficulty finding takers for grants of a league and a *labor* (177 acres) to new settlers, in return for nominal fees to be paid over six years or more. There were other empresarios (land agents), including Martin de León (the only native Mexican), Green DeWitt, and Haden Edwards, but Austin's active role in promoting Anglo-American immigration and negotiating with successive governments in Mexico earned him the title of "Father of Texas." As early as 1830, more than ten thousand settlers had immigrated to Texas from the United States. Most were subsistence farmers, but an increasing number of planters arrived as well, growing cotton and sugarcane on large tracts of land with slave labor.

Because large land grants in Texas were available at little or no cost, planters often relied on slave labor to raise cash crops like cotton. Austin himself, though he personally regarded slavery as a "curse of curses," justified slave labor as the only means of turning Texas into a rich agricultural economy. To satisfy Mexican prohibitions against slaveholding, laws were enacted to permit new immigrants to bring their slaves with them or to convert bondsmen into indentured servants who became, in all but name, chattel to be bought and sold at the whim of their owners.

Despite periodic friction between Texans and the Mexican government—chiefly over issues such as taxes and local control—most Anglo-Texans were satisfied with their rights under the liberal Mexican Constitution of 1824 and desired only the loosening of restrictions on immigration and separate statehood within the Mexican federation. However, in 1834, General Antonio López de Santa Anna seized dictatorial powers as president, and Stephen F. Austin, who had gone to Mexico City to petition for reforms and Texas statehood, was arrested and confined there from January 1834 to July 1835. When he finally returned to Texas in August 1835, the people were calling for independence from Mexico, and Austin, who had previously favored diplomacy over military action, supported that call.

During October and November 1835, a series of minor military encounters between Texas volunteers and Mexican forces resulted in the withdrawal of the Mexican military from everywhere in Texas except San Antonio. In November, a convention of elected delegates (called a Consultation) held in San Felipe stopped short of declaring independence during its two weeks of meetings, stating instead that Texas would maintain allegiance to Mexico as long as that country was governed by the Constitution of 1824—the very constitution that Santa Anna had already suspended. In Austin's view, the rhetorical ploy sent a signal to the dictator's federalist opponents in Mexico and bought time for Texas to prepare for war before separating from the mother country.

After the Consultation appointed Austin a commissioner to the United States, where he was to help secure loans and credits for munitions, solicit volunteers, and lobby for support for Texas independence and eventual annexation, he was succeeded as commander of the Texas army by Edward Burleson. On December 5, Burleson and Ben Milam led three hundred men into San Antonio, where four days later, General Martín Perfecto de Cos, Santa Anna's brother-in-law, surrendered and agreed to lead his troops back across the Rio Grande. For the moment, no Mexican troops remained in Texas, and most of the Texans, including General Burleson, went home. But a few proposed invading Mexico, in search of spoils and an alliance with federalists across the border. Sam Houston, who was now commander in chief of the "regular army" (which had no troops), went to Goliad, southeast of San Antonio, where he was able to convince most of the would-be invaders to abandon their ill-considered plans.

Determined to teach the upstart Texans a lesson, Santa Anna led an army of at least two thousand men across the Rio Grande on February 16, 1836, headed to San Antonio. At the same time, 550 cavalry, under the command of General José Urrea, entered Texas along the Gulf coast. Santa Anna's first goal was to retake San Antonio. The city was of no military significance, and in January Houston had ordered Colonel James Neill to evacuate the Alamo there, but Neill and James Bowie decided that the old mission, with its high, two-foot-thick walls and reinforced with cannon seized from Cos, was impregnable and decided to defend it. With only 150 men to defend a perimeter nearly a quarter-mile around, however, the Texans could not hold off Santa Anna's numerically superior forces for long. The Mexican general could easily have starved the defenders out, but he craved a dramatic, decisive victory, and on March 6 ordered his troops to storm the fort and take no prisoners. The 182 or 183 Texan volunteers defended the Alamo to the last and were killed, either during the fighting or immediately afterward, having exacted the price of six hundred dead and wounded from Santa Anna's troops.

News of the Mexican invasion sowed widespread alarm throughout the region. Many of the able-bodied men who had not already volunteered left to join the army, and the remaining civilian population—women, children, the elderly, and slaves—hastily fled eastward to get out of the path of the approaching armies. Their flight, which became known as the "Runaway Scrape," ultimately involved nearly all of the region's settler population, who also feared that Indians and rebellious slaves might take advantage of their defenselessness by raiding or killing them. The flight, which began even before Santa Anna had besieged San Antonio, swung into high gear when word of the Alamo massacre circulated.

On March 1, fifty-nine delegates convened at Washington-on-the-Brazos to decide the future of Texas. Sam Houston, a delegate from Refugio, convinced the delegates not to adjourn in order to go to the defense of the Alamo but to remain and address the matters before them. The next day, the delegates signed the Texas Declaration of Independence, a document composed mainly by George C. Childress and patterned on the American declaration of sixty years earlier. It stated, among other claims, that Mexico no longer protected the lives, liberty, and property of the people of Texas; that it had degenerated from a constitutional federal republic to a military dictatorship; that the people's petitions had been ignored and their representatives imprisoned; that the welfare of Texas had been ignored; and that public education, trial by jury, freedom of religion, and other essentials of good government had been neglected. The declaration also charged that the Mexican army had invaded the region to exterminate its citizens and that its government was "weak, corrupt, and tyrannical."

Before leaving Washington-on-the-Brazos to take command of the army at Gonzales, Houston also persuaded the remaining delegates to write a constitution for the new republic and choose an interim president, vice president, and cabinet. When he set off on March 6, Houston did not know that the Alamo had already fallen. Shortly after he arrived in Gonzales, however, he learned that three Mexican armies, under Generals Vicente Filisola, Antonio Gaona, and José Urrea, were moving across Texas along roughly parallel routes, with the aim of extirpating the settlements and snuffing out the hopes of the new republic.

Outnumbered and outgunned, Houston had no choice but to retreat, in order to protect the civilian refugees in their eastward flight and to gain time in which to recruit and train an army. He ordered James Fannin, in command of four hundred troops at Goliad, to fall back to Victoria, but owing to Fannin's delay and tactical missteps in carrying out the order, some 350 of his men were captured at the battle of Coleto on March 19 and 20, and massacred, on Santa Anna's orders, a week later.

Criticized on all sides for avoiding a confrontation with the enemy, Houston struggled to train his troops even as many of them, disillusioned by his refusal to attack or even to reveal his plans, deserted or turned disobedient. At San Felipe, when the general ordered a further retreat twenty miles upriver to Jared Groce's plantation, where he spent two weeks drilling the army and instilling a measure of military discipline, two officers, Moseley Baker and Wiley Martin, declined. Unwilling to risk a mutiny, Houston assigned the Baker and Martin companies to guard the Brazos River crossings at San Felipe and Fort Bend. President David G. Burnet joined the chorus of critics as well, writing, "The enemy are laughing you to scorn. You must fight them. You must retreat no further. The country expects you to fight. The salvation of the country depends on your doing so."

Houston bided his time until April 16. Then, learning that Santa Anna had crossed the Brazos at the head of an army of one thousand men, roughly the size of his own force, and left his remaining troops with General Filisola on the opposite side of the river, he hurried his men toward Buffalo Bayou—a march of fifty-five miles through rain and mud—in order to establish his position in the shelter of the trees lining the bayou and force Santa Anna to defend the exposed prairie west of the San Jacinto River. Although General Cos arrived on the morning of April 21 with an additional 550 troops, Houston's surprise attack overwhelmed the enemy, killing more than 630 Mexican soldiers and capturing 730. Santa Anna managed to escape during the battle, but he was captured the next day and agreed to terms that sealed the Texans' victory and guaranteed their independence. The Treaties of Velasco ended the war, required the Mexican armies to withdraw south of the Rio Grande, and bound Santa Anna to persuade the Mexican government to recognize Texas as an independent republic whose border with Mexico was the Rio Grande.

Mexico never ratified the Velasco agreement, but as a practical matter, the independence of the republic was assured when U.S. president Andrew Jackson announced on March 3, 1837, his last day in office, that he had named Alcée La Branche American chargé d'affaires to Texas. Recognition, however, did not solve all of the new republic's problems. Other nations—notably Britain and France—withheld recognition, and the United States dragged its feet on the question of annexation, which left Texas with $1.25 million in debt, no access to credit markets, and a cash-poor populace averse to paying taxes. The Texas Congress issued redeemable, interest-bearing paper money, but the notes declined in value when the government proved unable to get on a more secure financial footing. Texas's chronic financial problems would not be solved until 1850, when the U.S. Congress voted to appropriate $10 million to permit Texas to pay off the national debt left over from its years as an independent republic.

Except for a short-lived occupation of San Antonio by a force led by General Adrián Woll in September 1842, Mexico did not violate Texas territorial integrity again until after annexation, when Mexican troops crossed the Rio Grande in April and May

1846 to confront U.S. cavalry and infantry under General Zachary Taylor. The first confrontation ended tragically in the unauthorized Mier expedition (carried out by discontented Texan
militia and volunteers), when 176 Texan fighters who had been
taken prisoner after crossing into Mexico escaped and were
recaptured. Santa Anna ordered the execution of every tenth
man, as well as Ewen Cameron, their leader. In what became
known as the Black Bean Episode, the victims were selected by
having each man draw a bean from a clay jar containing 159
white beans and 17 black ones. The second incursion, by six
hundred Mexican soldiers in April 1846, led to the Mexican
War, which ended with the signing of the Treaty of Guadalupe-
Hidalgo in February 1848. This treaty settled the question of
territorial sovereignty between the United States and Mexico
and opened the South Texas frontier to settlers and ranchers of
both Mexican and Anglo backgrounds.

At the close of the Mexican War, the greatest danger to
Texas settlers in sparsely populated areas was not the armies
or outlaws on the other side of the Rio Grande. Indians, especially Comanches, Kiowas, and a supporting cast of nomadic
tribes with shifting allegiances, posed a continual threat to life
and property, and their stealthy, hit-and-run tactics of raiding
were more difficult to anticipate or to repel. Of the hundreds
of Indian raids carried out over the more than half century
between the earliest Anglo settlements and the mid-1870s, the
most notorious may well have been the Comanche-led attack
on Fort Parker in May 1836. Attacking the compound of the
extended Parker clan in Robertson (present-day Limestone)
County in broad daylight, a band that may have consisted of as
many as five hundred warriors murdered three of the Parker
men and took five women and children captives, one of whom,
Cynthia Ann Parker, married Chief Peta Nocona and became
the mother of Quanah Parker, the last major Comanche chief.

As president of the Republic of Texas, Sam Houston attempted to establish friendly relations with the Indian tribes

in Texas through treaties, but he was unable to effect a permanent peace, and other Texas leaders, such as Mirabeau B. Lamar and Thomas J. Rusk, favored a more aggressive approach. To further complicate matters, leaders of some Indian tribes, among them Chief Bowl of the Cherokees, undermined the chances for peaceful accommodation with the Texans by forming alliances with Mexican and pro-Mexican Tejano groups who planned to overthrow the Texas Republic by force after treaties guaranteeing their rights to lands in Texas were annulled. Although few Indians actually agreed to join forces with the Mexican loyalists, only a small number of tribes—notably the Alabamas and Coushattas, who had assisted the Texans during the 1836 revolution—were allowed to live in peace. Even Chief Bowl, who accepted an order to leave Texas in 1839 (but did not sign a formal agreement to do so), was killed, wearing the sword he had been given by Sam Houston, along with his Cherokee compatriots and their allies, by troops under the command of Thomas Rusk and Edward Burleson. When Houston condemned the attack, one of the soldiers tried to assassinate him with an axe.

Other attempts at negotiation ended as badly. When a group of Comanche chiefs proposed peace negotiations in 1840, they were told to bring all of their white captives with them, but they arrived at the Council House in San Antonio with only a few Mexican children and Matilda Lockhart, a girl of sixteen. When the commissioners, William Cooke and Hugh McLeod, told the Comanche chiefs that they would be held hostage until the remaining captives materialized, fighting broke out that ended only after thirty-five Comanches and seven Texans were dead. Attempts to exchange the twenty-seven Comanches taken prisoner for the white captives came to naught. According to one report, most of the captives were tortured to death to avenge the deaths of the Comanches and the mistreatment of the peace negotiators.

Further retaliation followed the so-called Council House

Fight in August 1840, when Chief Buffalo Hump led five hundred warriors on a killing and raiding spree through the Guadalupe Valley towns of Victoria and Linnville. As the attackers withdrew, two hundred Texan volunteers pursued them, killing about one hundred Comanches, and two months later, another group of Texans, assisted by Lipan Apaches and Tonkawas, surprised the raiders in their central Texas village, killed 130 of them, and recovered some of the plunder from the Victoria and Linnville raid. Thus was the tenor of Anglo-Indian relations set in the republic. Although periodic attempts to establish trade and negotiate treaties were made, including one that Houston, as president, signed in 1844 with all the powerful tribes in the republic, hostilities ceased entirely only years later, when the Indians ceded the land to the Anglos and relocated to reservations.

Blessed with vast expanses of fertile soil, especially in its eastern half and along the Gulf coast, Texas before and after its 1845 annexation evolved into an agricultural economy that resembled other regions of the Old South. Most farmers, who did not own slaves, grew corn and vegetables, raised pigs and cows, and hunted and foraged for fish, game, fruit, and wild plants with which they fed their households. A minority were slaveholders, who in addition to growing the same crops and raising the same livestock as their smallholding neighbors, also produced cash crops, overwhelmingly cotton. A few planters, centered in Brazoria County, grew and processed sugarcane.

Compared to farming, cattle raising attracted relatively few people in Texas before the Civil War. Those who did raise cattle tended to own smaller tracts of land than later ranchers, and because most land was unfenced, their herds often grazed on uninhabited public land. At the time, the market for their cattle was primarily in Louisiana; the fabled cattle drives to midwestern and northern destinations were as yet mainly in the future. Cities were also slow to develop in Texas, in part because the climate and abundance of arable land favored agriculture, and also because the distances posed obstacles to the dependable transportation systems urban and commercial centers require. The region's many rivers were often too shallow to make them reliably navigable, and the relatively flat topography also meant that their waters could not be harnessed to generate electrical power.

During the Civil War, Texas, unlike most of the rest of the Confederacy, remained relatively untouched by the fighting. But more than half of Texans eligible for the draft served during the war, the majority as volunteers, which meant that the families of the wealthy suffered the losses of fathers and sons, husbands and brothers, along with the less affluent. Approximately one-fourth of these men—some fifteen thousand—who served in nearly every theater of the war, died in battle or from wounds or disease. Among the volunteers were about two thousand Unionists who joined the United States Army. To the women who remained behind fell the tasks of caring for their families unaided, managing farms and plantations, and waiting for news from the front. One mark of women's success in running their farms and plantations during the Civil War is the fact that more than three hundred thousand bales of Texas cotton were exported, much of it along various routes (one running through the King Ranch), to Mexico and thence to other foreign shores, despite a Union blockade of major Texas ports.

Families in frontier settlements also contended with more frequent Indian raids during the war, because the scarcity of able-bodied men made the raiders more intrepid. Some troops and special regiments were assigned to patrol the most vulnerable areas, but the Comanches, Kiowas, and other tribes quickly adapted to the patrols' routines and preyed on the settlers with relative impunity. Nor were Indians the only plunderers on the frontier of settlement: Deserters and other marginal individuals who took refuge in isolated areas on the fringes of the settlements also stole from the unprotected settlers.

In the years after the Civil War, the population of Texas

mushroomed, doubling in the decade between 1870 and 1880, to 1.6 million, and nearly doubling again by the turn of the twentieth century, when the state's population passed 3 million. Most of the new immigrants came from the Old South, where postwar recovery was slower than in Texas. As the line of settlement pushed westward, Indian raids continued, and pressure increased on the federal government to reach accommodation with the Comanches, Kiowas, Cheyennes, Arapahoe, and other tribes behind most of the violence. Preferred tactics included a combination of military action and peace policies that encouraged the Indians to abandon their nomadic way of life and move onto reservations. In 1874, after a protracted campaign in which soldiers and rangers, aided by Indian scouts, pursued Indian warriors in northwestern Texas and on both sides of the Rio Grande, a series of battles known as the Red River War culminated in an encounter in the Palo Duro Canyon. Only a few Indians were killed in the attack, but their horses and supplies were seized, and by mid-1875, nearly all the Indians had returned to their reservations or were in custody.

Just as crucial to the military campaign to force the Indians into submission was the destruction of the great buffalo herds by hunters responding to increased demand for the animals' hides. Buffalo had roamed over an expanse that stretched from the Rocky Mountains to the Mississippi River, as far north as Minnesota and south to Louisiana. Their hides had long been prized as robes, but in the 1870s they began to be used in industry as well. Armed with powerful Sharps rifles, hunters would aim for the leader of a herd, and when the lead animal fell, the others would stop running and could be killed at will until they regrouped and started moving forward again. Skinners stripped the hides from the carcasses and left the meat to rot or be devoured by scavengers.

It is estimated that in the course of the decade from 1870 to

1880, roughly three thousand buffalo hunters killed more than 3.5 million of the creatures that have been called "the most economically valuable wild animal[s] that ever inhabited the American continent."

With the decline of the buffalo herds, and unable to poach the livestock of settlers and ranchers, the Comanches and other Indians, denied their traditional source of "food, clothing, shelter, bedding, saddles, ropes, shields," had little choice but to submit to the reservation system.

Some large ranches existed in Texas even before the decimation of the buffalo herds and the sequestering of the roving Indian tribes, but they were the exceptions rather than the rule. A few, notably the ranching partnership of Richard King and Mifflin Kenedy in South Texas, managed to ride out the Civil War, when Union control of the Mississippi River closed off access to markets outside the state. With the end of the war, the markets to the north, east, and west clamored for Texas beef, ushering in a period of cattle drives to stockyards and transshipment points thousands of miles from Texas ranches. The ranches themselves, which grew in size and number, spread across the state, and many evolved into multistate operations. Although the railroad came late to Texas, from the 1860s onward cattle drives followed the Chisholm Trail and others north to railheads in Kansas City, Missouri; Abilene and Dodge City, Kansas; and Denver and Pueblo, Colorado. Other drives ended as far afield as California, Wyoming, Montana, Chicago, or even the east coast.

Two industries that were crucial to the development of large-scale ranching in Texas also helped to foster the growth of its cities in the last third of the nineteenth century: banks and railroads. The access to credit supplied by the former and the latter's introduction of swift, reliable transportation made it possible for cities like San Antonio, Dallas, Houston, and Fort Worth to evolve into manufacturing, trading, meatpacking, and financial centers. The railroads rapidly made up for the time lost during the Civil War, expanding from fewer than five hundred miles of track to more than eight thousand in less than twenty years. The Houston & Texas Central Railroad, for example, linked that city to Dallas in 1872, paving the way for the emergence of both urban centers as commercial and industrial hubs. The first businesses to prosper were industries that processed the region's agricultural products. Dallas thus emerged as a leader in flour milling in the 1870s and '80s. By the end of the latter decade, lumber milling, centered in the area east of Houston, overtook grain processing as the state's leading industry.

Before the outbreak of the First World War, construction of a fifty-mile-long deepwater ship channel between the Port of Houston and Galveston Bay turned Houston into the country's most important shipping point for raw cotton. Earlier, in 1901, the discovery of immense oil deposits at Spindletop, near the East Texas city of Beaumont, ushered in the state's first oil boom. As new oil fields were tapped, Houston was poised to develop into an important oil-refining hub as well, thanks to the port's ability to handle the large tankers that transported crude and processed petroleum. These and related developments helped traditional Texas pursuits, such as agriculture and livestock raising, evolve into viable modern forms as well and paved the way for the emergence of new enterprises—among them communications, energy, and aerospace.

Part I

MY HERITAGE

1810–1883

Anna Mary Taylor
Mary Shindler
Martha Hall Sharp

Eva Rosine and
Anna Mary Ruoff

Mary Shindler

The Taylor-Shindler and Hall-Sharp family trees appear in the appendix.

Texas is paradise for men and dogs,
but hell for women and horses.

-VARIOUS SOURCES AND VERSIONS

Much has been written about the men who led the way and persevered until they found success in this tough land. Fewer chronicles exist about the circumstances faced by the women who ventured to Texas, stood by those men, and helped shape the unique spirit of Texas.

I grew up hearing the stories of the Texas Revolution from my mother, Ella Kathryn Sharp Bailey. Her roots were in Nacogdoches, the oldest town in Texas, where so much of the struggle occurred and history was made. Her ancestors were active participants in the revolution and helped shape the emerging republic and later state of Texas. Her childhood home, which is still in our family, is one block from the Old Stone Fort, where the town meetings and elections were held in the 1820s and '30s.

The fort sits on the grounds of Stephen F. Austin State University and is a constant reminder on today's bustling campus of the roots that were planted 175 years ago. It is where Mother's great-grandfather, Charles S. Taylor, was elected a delegate to the Convention of 1836.

In our family gatherings there was always talk of "the old days" and the people who grew up together and their ancestors. So many Nacogdoches families are intertwined with the early settlers who intermarried through the generations. Strong women also ran through the stories. My grandmother was widowed in 1930; of her four daughters, two were still living at home: my mom, age eighteen, and my aunt, age eleven. The Great Depression left her to manage with no income. She owned land, but there was no market for it. My mother said that though her mother had no business experience, she just kept cobbling things together and managed to send both younger daughters to college.

So I start this book of unflinching courage with the earlier women of my family, who passed their strength and ingenuity through the generations of Taylor, Shindler, and Sharp women. From participants in the Runaway Scrape, to those who lost children and husbands and were left in dire financial difficulties, to the first woman elected to the United States Senate from Texas, resilience is the common thread.

My family is only one of the many whose women contributed to the building of Texas and its indomitable spirit. Most women of the nineteenth century could have had an easier life if they had stayed in the East. But they chose the more difficult road for the biggest rewards—the accomplishment of building a country that became the greatest state in America.

Anna Mary Taylor

Anna Mary Taylor was born Anna Maria (later changed to Mary) Ruoff on March 16, 1814, in Wurttemberg, Germany, to Johann and Anna Maria Ruoff. Her parents moved from Germany to Louisiana when she and her sister Eva Catherine Rosine were young girls.

In New Orleans, Johann and Anna Maria contracted yellow fever, and family records show that they died there in the early 1830s. The Ruoff children were raised by Monsieur and Madame Placide Bossier in Natchitoches, Louisiana. On a trip to that city, Adolphus Sterne, a merchant and landowner from Nacogdoches, Texas, met Eva Catherine Rosine Ruoff. Adolphus was smitten and the couple married in 1828. Their home in Nacogdoches became a social center for the bustling town and a boardinghouse for those passing through.

Charles Stanfield Taylor was born in 1808 in England, orphaned at an early age, and raised and educated in law by his uncle. When he came of age, he took his inheritance and came to America, landing in New York and sailing shortly thereafter to Louisiana. In 1828 he bought a horse in Natchitoches to ride to Nacogdoches, a journey of about one hundred miles. The horse died on the journey and he walked into Nacogdoches carrying his bags. He stayed at the Adolphus Sterne boardinghouse and began exploring opportunities in this new territory that was still part of Mexico. In June of that year, Eva Sterne's sister, Anna Mary, visited from Louisiana and met Charles at the Sterne home. Two years later, on May 28, 1830, Charles and Anna Mary were married in the Sternes' parlor.

Charles became a prominent lawyer and was elected to local office in 1832, the first of many official positions he held. The

Taylors' first child, Evariste, was born in March 1832. Marie Rosine followed in July 1833, George in November 1834, and Texana in January 1836.

Charles continued in public service, serving as alcalde (chief executive, judge, and head of the town council) and land commissioner for the government of Mexico. As resistance to the heavy taxes imposed by the Mexican government was building, Charles's loyalty to the Mexican government ebbed. He joined Thomas Rusk, Sam Houston, and many other Texans in protest. When delegates were elected to the Texas Convention at Washington-on-the-Brazos to write a declaration of independence, both Rusk and Charles S. Taylor were elected from Nacogdoches.

The declaration was adopted March 2, 1836. Fifty-nine delegates elected from all the settled areas of Texas signed the declaration. During the convention, Taylor moved the adoption of a resolution designating the flag of the new republic to be a white field with a star in the middle and outside the star a letter between each point, spelling Texas. Though no flag was formally adopted for the republic at the convention, Taylor's design was used informally along with other handmade flags during the revolution.

As word of the massacres at the Alamo and Goliad spread, those left in the towns throughout much of East and South Texas feared that Santa Anna's army was moving toward them. The women and children fled eastward in the Runaway Scrape. Those fortunate enough to have horses or wagons rode. The others walked, under miserable conditions. Rain and cold prevailed, roads were muddy, and sickness spread among refugees weakened from exposure and lack of food and shelter. When people died, they were buried quickly, and the survivors moved on.

Anna Mary packed up her three living children (George had died before his first birthday) and fought the elements with her friend Polly Rusk and her children and many others hoping to reach Louisiana. All three Taylor girls—four-year-old Evariste,

Marie Rosine, three, and the infant Texana—died within days of each other and were buried in Natchitoches.

After the declaration was signed and preliminary selections for officers and military for the republic were made, the men at the convention either joined Sam Houston's forces to fight Santa Anna's army or dispersed to other areas of Texas to plan the next steps required to set up a government for the new republic. The battle was joined April 21, 1836, at San Jacinto, near present-day Houston. Santa Anna's army was defeated in a surprise attack by the Texans, which was timed to coincide with the Mexican troops' afternoon siestas.

Anna Mary and Charles later reunited in Nacogdoches to rebuild their family and bolster their young country. In December 1836, Charles was appointed the first chief justice of Nacogdoches County by President Sam Houston.

The Taylors had nine more children between 1837 and 1853, when the last, my great-grandmother Anna Mary Taylor, was born. After the tragedy of 1836, when they lost all their children, their indomitable spirit was rewarded. Each of the nine later children lived to adulthood.

By all accounts, including diaries and letters written in their lifetimes, Anna Mary and Charles had a happy marriage. He wrote in one of his letters after an extended trip, "I must confess home is very pleasant to me, and possesses charms and endearments I can find nowhere else." Their home had a large grove of trees in front and a substantial garden in the back, which was tended by Anna Mary. She was known for her love of trying new seeds to add to her mix, and her friends often brought new varieties to her to plant. Today a historical marker stands on the site of their home, on North Street in Nacogdoches.

The Sterne and Taylor families were very close; the Taylors named one of their sons Adolphus and a daughter Rosine; the Sternes had a son named Charles. The sisters took care of each other in times of need, especially sickness and pregnancies. This was chronicled in the diaries of Adolphus Sterne edited by noted East Texas historian the late Archie McDonald, a long-time professor at Stephen F. Austin State University. In one entry from 1850, Adolphus lamented that the seriously ill Anna Mary might not recover. She did recover, after five weeks, and even had another child, in 1853.

Many a night of dinner and dancing was noted in the diaries and letters of both Sterne and Taylor, at both of their houses. The hard work and constant struggle for funds was lightened with gatherings and celebrations. Writing to Robert Irion in October 1838, Taylor described the informal get-togethers, called "drop ins," where a few friends would meet, "a fiddle is sent for—the dance commences and is kept up for 3 or 4 hours—hilarity prevails, Judge Jeff [a Nacogdoches friend and fellow judge] by way of interlude, tells some of his amusing stories, a cold snack is provided, with plenty of the requisite to wash it down . . . the past week has been quite a Carnival."

Taylor had a scholarly side as well. Thanks to his formal education in England, he spoke and wrote excellent English and understood both Spanish and French. His extensive library included books ranging in subjects from law, history, and politics to geology, geography, and nature.

When a lawyer from Virginia wrote Charles in 1852 asking for information about Texas, he replied that the soil and climate were good and the people possessed the real spirit of hospitality. "Society upon the average is as good as a man can desire and better than he ought to expect in a comparatively new country."

Charles was elected chief justice of Nacogdoches County in 1860 and served in that position until his death, at the age of fifty-seven in 1865.

Anna Mary lived to see her youngest child and namesake reach the age of nineteen. She died in 1873 at the age of fifty-nine. The following year, her daughter Anna Mary married Robert Conrad Shindler, the son of Mary and the Reverend Robert Shindler.

Mary Shindler

Mary Bunce Palmer, born in 1810 in Beaufort, South Carolina, was the second of eight children of the Reverend Benjamin Palmer and his wife, the former Mary Bunce. Only four of the children survived infancy—Mary, her two sisters, Sarah and Jane, and a brother, Keith. Benjamin Palmer believed in educating girls as well as boys. He founded the first Sunday school in South Carolina and devoted considerable energy to improving church music, so it is not surprising that Mary's intellectual and artistic output eventually included a number of Christian hymns. Girls were rarely sent north to school at the time, but Mary studied for one year in Elizabethtown, New Jersey, and later she and her younger sister, Jane, attended Dr. Herrick's school in New Haven, Connecticut.

Mary started writing poems, stories, and essays when she was still a child. As a young woman, she found a kindred spirit in Charles Dana, a writer and editor whose cousins included Charles Anderson Dana, editor of the *New York Tribune*, and Richard Henry Dana Jr., author of *Two Years Before the Mast*. They married in 1835, moved to New York City, and enjoyed their first years of marriage, entertaining friends and family often. Their son, Charles Morgan Dana (Charlie), was born in May 1837. Mary wrote this poem expressing her joy.

THE MOTHER AND HER BABE
A mother sat with eye upturned,
Within her heart love's pure fire burned,
For by her side, bright as the day,
A smiling little cherub lay;
It was her darling little son,

Her sweet first-born, her only one.

. . .

I gaze in his confiding eyes,
And lo! Sweet tears in mine arise;
I kiss his rosy, velvet cheek,
And burn with thoughts I cannot speak;
My grateful heart overflows with joy,
That God has given me such a boy!

. . .

Five days after experiencing the pure joy of her son's birth, Mary suffered the first of a series of tragedies that were to mark her life. Her sister Jane, her closest sibling and dearest friend, died of tuberculosis. Less than a year later, her brother, Keith, a physician, died in Alabama.

Mary and Charles decided to venture west to pursue his dream of publishing a newspaper. They settled in Bloomington, Iowa, a new town on the Mississippi River. They had just arrived in the summer of 1839 when Mary was stunned by unexpected tragedy. Stagnant, contaminated water, caused by the low river level and lack of sanitation facilities, brought on an epidemic of cholera. First Mary caught the disease; then, as she recovered, little Charlie contracted cholera, and as the boy's condition worsened, Charles began to be affected.

On August 20, the baby Charlie died. Her husband was too ill to attend the funeral; a few sympathetic people prayed with Mary beside the child's grave. After a brief service, Mary returned to nurse her husband, but he died the next morning. Mary, bereft, wrote of her feelings, "Left entirely alone, thousands of miles from every relative I had on earth, there was no human arm on which I could lean." She sought to return to her parents' home in South Carolina as soon as possible, but it was October before she could get passage on a boat, which took weeks and made several stops en route to Charleston. After the long journey home, Mary found solace and purpose in writing. Her first book, a collection of religious poems titled *The Southern Harp*, was published in 1841; it sold twenty thousand copies. A more personal collection, *The Parted Family and Other Poems*, followed later in the year. Among the influential editors who encouraged Mary's literary ambitions were Sarah Josepha Hale, of *Godey's Lady's Book*, and Caroline Gilman, of *Rose-Bud*, who published some of her poems.

Mary's poetry was extremely well received, and the flood of her writing continued. She published *The Northern Harp* in 1842, in which she reflected on her past. One poem from the collection, "The Days of My Childhood," begins

I love to remember the days of my childhood,
Those days when my heart was a stranger to pain;
When I roved with delight through the vine-tangled wild-wood,
Ere sorrow had bound me so fast with its chain.
The bright morning sun every moment grew whiter,
My light youthful heart every moment grew lighter,
As gaily I frolick'd, a stranger to pain . . .

The success of these books gave Mary a measure of financial security.

When Mary met Robert Doyne Shindler, an Episcopal priest, in Charleston in 1846, she had apparently resigned herself to living out her life as a widow. But the scholarly, intellectually adventurous priest won her over, theologically and romantically, and they married in May 1848. The Shindlers settled in Upper Marlborough, Maryland, a suburb of Washington, D.C., where he assisted at church services but was not able to secure a church of his own. In 1851, Robert was appointed professor of ancient languages at Shelby College, in Shelbyville, Kentucky. Their only child, Robert Conrad, was born in 1852, when Mary was forty-two. The senior Robert left his professorship, and Mary tried to earn money from her writing. Late in the 1850s, the Shindlers started the Ripley Female Institute in Ripley,

Tennessee. The economic hard times brought on by the Civil War forced its closure after three years.

Throughout the war and afterward, work was scarce and even paper was in short supply. Mary continued to write, but she was unable to publish her books, and her poetry began to reflect even more prominently the themes of struggle and survival. She persevered, however, writing, looking for opportunities for herself and her husband, and keeping up their son Bobby's education. Mary ran into an old friend of Robert's and hers, Bishop Gregg, who had left South Carolina to become the Episcopal bishop of Texas. The bishop suggested that Robert go to Texas, where there was a job teaching school in San Augustine. After a year at the school, he left for Nacogdoches, where he served as rector of Christ Episcopal Church. His problems persisted, however; he stopped performing his ministerial duties, which in any case carried little or no salary (ministers were expected to do other work), and sank into depression. When Robert's father passed away and left his son out of his will, claiming that Robert's share of the family's wealth had been spent on his education, the disappointment dealt the final blow to his fragile equilibrium. One day in August 1874, Mary came home from town to find her husband dead. All indications were that he had taken his own life, and hers was again turned upside down.

Mary and her son (Bobby, now twenty-two, began to use his given name, Robert) decided to remain in Nacogdoches. Three months after his father's death, Robert married Anna Mary Taylor, the daughter of Charles and Anna Mary Taylor. According to family records, Anna Mary and Robert lived in Mary Shindler's home, where Mary and Anna Mary got along well. They gardened together and shared a bond of strong faith.

Mary traveled some and continued to write poetry and hymns. Robert became prominent in his local business, R. C. Shindler Dry Goods, and he and Anna Mary produced six children. Their third child, Anna Mary Shindler Sharp, was my grandmother.

Following a common practice of the period, Mary sometimes set her compositions to music by renowned composers such as Mozart and Rossini, as well as by English and Italian composers who are now largely forgotten. Her secular work increasingly advocated an active role for women in various public spheres, especially literature and the arts, among them suffrage and temperance.

Today Mary's hymns continue to be sung, and her poems have been included in anthologies of nineteenth-century American verse. A few of her best-loved compositions are "I'm a Pilgrim and a Stranger" (sometimes called "The Pilgrim's Song"), "Passing Under the Rod," and "Flee as a Bird."

"Flee as a Bird" is based on the Eleventh Psalm. In addition to its appearance in the collection *The Northern Harp*, this popular hymn was sold in large numbers as sheet music throughout the second half of the nineteenth century. In New Orleans, the melody of "Flee as a Bird" (identified simply as a "Spanish Melody" and described as sharing the characteristics of folk music) became the tune traditionally played at funerals as the hearse made its way from the church to the cemetery:

Flee as a bird to your mountain, thou who art weary of sin;
Go to the clear flowing fountain where you may wash and be clean.
Haste, then th'avenger is near thee; call, and the Savior will hear
  thee;
He on His bosom will bear thee; O thou who art weary of sin,
O thou who art weary of sin.
He will protect thee forever, wipe every falling tear;
He will forsake thee, O never, sheltered so tenderly there.
Haste, then, the hours are flying, spend not the moments in sighing,
Cease from your sorrow and crying: The Savior will wipe every tear,
The Savior will wipe every tear.

Mary died in Nacogdoches in 1883, one week before her seventy-third birthday. "Flee as a Bird" may not have been played en route to the cemetery, but at least one of her hymns was undoubtedly sung at her funeral service in Christ Episcopal Church. Mary had been a success at a time when few women were published in the literary world. She certainly added to the fabric of Texas woven by nineteenth-century women with tenacity, resilience, and an enduring spirit.

Martha Hall Sharp

Martha Ann Hall grew up in Tennessee, the daughter of William Hall, who succeeded Sam Houston as governor when Sam abruptly resigned in 1829 and left the state after his brief, disastrous marriage to Eliza Allen. Governor Hall had been serving as Speaker of the Tennessee State Senate and was elevated to serve out the term of Governor Houston. He did not stand for election to a full term as governor, but was elected to the U.S. Congress in 1831.

Martha was born in 1821 and grew up on the family farm, Locust Land, in Sumner County, near Castalian Springs, where her family was successful and prosperous. On May 25, 1841, she married Dr. Benjamin Franklin Sharp. He had just received his medical degree from Transylvania Medical College in Lexington, Kentucky. Between 1842 and 1848, Martha and Frank had five children: Phoebe, William Hall (Willie), Mary (Mollie), Frank, and Lafayette. They moved from Tennessee to San Augustine, Texas, in 1848.

Martha named her log home in San Augustine China Grove because of the chinaberry trees on the land. The home still stands on the original property and has been passed through the generations—the Historical Society of San Augustine now maintains it. My family still owns the share of the Sharp land that we inherited from my grandparents, Frank and Anna Mary Shindler Sharp. Our land is across the road from the two-room log house with the open-air space in the middle, called a "dog trot," that Martha Ann and Frank built.

It was from China Grove that she wrote a letter to her sister that demonstrates the spirit and resilience of these early pio-

neer women who came to Texas from genteel backgrounds and
adapted to stark new circumstances.

CHINA GROVE
May 1, 1849

Dear Lou,

I was on the eve of writing you a long letter when your
kind face came to mind. I need not tell you with what pleasure I found it, for you have been amongst strangers enough
to appreciate my feelings on the occasion. It is such a relief
to have anyone's sympathy, more especially a sister's. Out
in this new country, I see no one but strangers, but they are
the kindest people I have ever met with. The society is as
good as in any portion of Tennessee. There seems to be as
much refinement as you meet with at any place.

Lou, I was very lonely at first, but have never been dissatisfied. You know it must have been a pang to have left
all my dear family and friends, but hope has kept me from
being unhappy. It certainly is the place for us if we have
health. We certainly have very good prospects for living well. It surpasses any other place in the variety of its
productions. You can raise your own sugar, rice, figs and
pomegranates besides all other necessaries raised in Tennessee. I was very much pleased as well as astonished at
vegetation being so forward. Our earliest beans and peas,
radishes are gone and another planting almost ready for
use. Corn is tasseling. The Texans generally are poor
farmers so they raise cotton and then have corn enough
to do them. They take no pain to have any luxuries. You
and George must be sure and come out this Fall. You cannot help being pleased. There is not so much expected of
new beginners as in old countries. There is no such thing
as fine houses or furniture. They have very comfortable

houses, but cannot get the furniture. We are too far from navigation to get such things. By the time we make the money, they will navigate the Sabine. Then we can get all the little notions we fancy we need. If I had been in Ten., I would have thought the house we occupy would not do at all. We live in a very small house with two rooms and a passage. We have not even plank laid overhead, but with all these inconveniences, we are getting along finely. For the people do not require impossibilities of newcomers.

Martha died at the age of thirty-one, on October 4, 1852, in her father's home in Sumner County, Tennessee, where she had gone to visit her relatives. Her obituary notice stated she had contracted typhoid fever previously and it flared up, probably due to the rigors of her trip. She was said to have been very happy with her marriage and children, making their new home in Texas in her log cabin and garden. Written in the obituary found in a family Bible are these verses:

In the cold moist earth we laid her,
When the frost cast the leaf,
And we wept that one so lovely,
Should have a life so brief.

She was buried in Sumner County, Tennessee.

Martha Hall Sharp's grandson, Frank Sharp, was my grandfather; he married my grandmother, Anna Mary Shindler (Mary Shindler's granddaughter, Anna Mary Taylor's great-granddaughter).

Nacogdoches, Texas, today, is a town of about thirty-five thousand and has preserved much of its history. It is considered the oldest town in Texas. The Old Stone Fort was reconstructed on the campus of Stephen F. Austin University from the stones used in the original 1779 structure. It is now a small museum. The Adolphus Sterne home, where Sam Houston lived when he first entered Texas in 1832 and where he was baptized in a Catholic ceremony (under Mexican law, only Catholics could own land, so prior to 1836, many Texans made nominal conversions), has also been turned into a museum. China Grove and these two museums are just three of the historic sites in the Nacogdoches–San Augustine area that have been preserved in an effort to keep the tangible symbols of the region's past alive.

Part II

JANE LONG, MOTHER OF TEXAS

1820s–1830s

Jane Long

It was the Louisiana Purchase that brought Texas to America's doorstep. Claimed by both Spain and France, in 1762, at the end of the Seven Years' War, France ceded the Louisiana territory to Spain in an effort to prevent Britain from seizing it.

When President Thomas Jefferson learned in 1802 that Spain had secretly agreed to return Louisiana to France, he immediately instructed Robert R. Livingston, his minister to France, to obtain New Orleans and the territory east of the city (then part of West Florida) from the French. He also sent James Monroe to Paris as his special envoy in the negotiations. At the time, Jefferson was unaware that Spain had retained Florida, nor did he know that Napoleon had pledged not to transfer the Louisiana territory to a third party.

Napoleon, however, knew that without Florida, Louisiana was impossible to defend. More important, he was planning to go to war with England and needed funds to finance his campaign. For his part, Jefferson was prepared to form an alliance with the English and use the pretext of a European war to take control of New Orleans, situated at the mouth of the Mississippi River, which American settlers depended on for passenger travel and commercial trade. As President Jefferson wrote to Monroe:

All eyes, all hopes, are now fixed on you, for on the event of this mission depend the future destinies of the Republic. If we cannot by a purchase of the country, insure to

ourselves a course of perpetual peace and friendship with
all nations then, as war cannot be far distant it behooves
us to be immediately preparing for that course, without
however hastening it; and it may be necessary (on your
failure on the continent) to cross the channel.

A day before Monroe arrived in Paris, Napoleon's foreign
minister, Charles-Maurice de Talleyrand, informed Livingston
that France would not sell New Orleans alone but invited the
United States to make an offer for the entire Louisiana territory. Although the proposition far exceeded the envoys' authority, on April 30, less than three weeks after Monroe joined the
talks, the two men had agreed to pay $15 million for Louisi-
ana. The exact boundaries of the purchase were unclear, but
with the stroke of a pen, the United States had added roughly
827,000 square miles of land, doubling the size of the country.

The president wasn't certain that the Constitution permitted
the United States to enlarge its borders through purchase, but
encouraged by his cabinet and conscious that the alternative
meant war, he overcame his doubts in time for the Senate to
ratify the treaty before the end of October. On December 30,
1803, the Louisiana Purchase was officially absorbed into the
republic. To justify his actions, Jefferson wrote, "It is the case of
a guardian, investing the money of his ward in purchasing an
important adjacent territory; and saying to him when of age,
I did this for your good." When Spain objected that the purchase violated its treaty with France, the president dispatched
troops to protect the new border and hinted that Florida might
be next. As he wrote to Senator John Breckinridge (later Jefferson's attorney general), he was confident that through his strategy, to "push them strongly with one hand, holding out a price
in the other," the United States would "obtain the Floridas and
all in good time."

In addition to its southern border with East and West Florida, two colonies England ceded to Spain after the American

Revolution, the United States now bordered Spanish territory along a line that stretched from the Gulf of Mexico to present-day Wyoming. Many Americans, including Jefferson, believed that the southwestern boundary of Louisiana was the Rio Grande. Their claim was based on the ill-fated settlement near Matagorda Bay founded by René Robert Cavelier de La Salle, the French explorer who led four ships carrying three hundred colonists to Texas in 1685. La Salle was searching for the mouth of the Mississippi, which he had reached from the north three years earlier after descending the river by canoe. At that time, he christened the territory La Louisiane, in honor of Louis XIV, and claimed for France all the lands drained by the river. On his second voyage, La Salle planned to create a base from which France would harass the Spanish on land and sea, prevent the British from encroaching on the American West, and create a port that would support French trade with the Indians of the interior. Within three years, however, the settlement had disappeared, its demise hastened when La Salle proved himself as inept a leader as he was a navigator. Pierre Duhaut, a discontented member of La Salle's exploring party, killed him in March 1687. Toward the end of the following year, Karankawa Indians, who had initially made peace with the settlers after La Salle's death, massacred everyone remaining at the settlement except a handful of children, whom they adopted.

The Spanish insisted that the eastern border of Texas was the Arroyo Hondo, a meandering estuary (now called the Calcasieu River) halfway between the Sabine and Mississippi rivers. More than fifteen years would pass before this border dispute was resolved, with the Sabine River marking most of the eastern boundary of Texas. The reasons for the delay may have been that many Americans were convinced that, in the words of one Federalist newspaper, "it belongs of right to the United States to regulate the future destiny of North America." Jefferson himself anticipated that Americans would gradually spread out across the entire continent, until it was populated "with people speaking the same language, governed in similar forms, and by similar laws." While Jefferson adopted a patient stance with respect to expansion, he unambiguously looked forward to it. "Texas," he wrote to President Monroe in 1820, "will be the richest State of our Union."

Others, like the explorer John Hamilton Robinson, impatient with the glacial pace of diplomacy, insisted that "our citizens have a right to migrate whithersoever they choose—and it is beyond the power of the government to prevent them." Robinson was one of a number of would-be filibusterers (leaders of unauthorized attempts to foment revolution or declare independence in a foreign country) who led unsuccessful expeditions to Texas. His took place in 1814; earlier, he had accompanied Zebulon Pike's explorations of the West and Southwest, including Texas, in 1805–7. For years, traders and settlers had been crossing into Louisiana territory in small numbers, and a few even ventured beyond the west bank of the Mississippi River, where they made no secret of their lack of fealty to the European power nominally in control of the land at the time, whether Spain or France.

After the Louisiana Purchase was completed, there was increased activity along the border between Louisiana and Texas. The Spanish, eager to protect their claim to Texas, discouraged American intrusions across the Sabine River. Nevertheless, traders regularly crossed the border to maintain contacts, exchange goods, and explore opportunities for hunting. The Spanish protected their eastern border intermittently, whenever they felt threatened by French or American encroachment.

American attempts to penetrate Texas were complicated by internal struggles in Mexico. At the same time as Spain was trying to protect its claims to Texas and Mexico, it also faced a threat from Mexican insurgents eager to declare independence from their European overlord.

The Mother of Texas

Entering the world in this tumultuous period was Jane Herbert Wilkinson, who would be one of the first women to put her imprint on American claims to Texas. Born in Maryland in 1798, Jane never knew her father, Captain William Mackall Wilkinson, a member of a prominent Maryland military and political clan, who died before her first birthday. In 1811, Jane's mother, Anne Herbert Dent Wilkinson, moved to Mississippi, to be near her married daughters, Barbara Wilkinson Calvit and Anne Wilkinson Chesley. A year later, Mrs. Wilkinson was dead as well, and fourteen-year-old Jane moved in with the Calvits. In 1815, at the Calvits' plantation, Propinquity, Jane met James Long, who arrived in Natchez, Mississippi (see map, p. xix), after serving as a surgeon in General Andrew Jackson's New Orleans campaign. He earned praise from Jackson, who is said to have called Long "my brave young lion."

Jane, a "lovely southern girl with shining, dark ringletted hair, mischievous brown eyes, and magnolia-tinted satin smooth cheeks," was smitten from their first meeting, but she had to overcome her family's objections to her choice of James Long as her husband. Twenty-two and battle-tested, James was described by a contemporary as "daring" but also "wholly made up of impulses, who would do today a thing he would regret tomorrow, and perhaps a lifetime." Many years later, she told Mirabeau Lamar that she was packing to return to her boarding school when her maid told her "the handsomest man in the world" was attending to a wounded soldier who was recuperating at Propinquity. The meeting spelled the end of Jane's formal education. She was two months shy of her seventeenth birthday when she and James married in May 1815.

After the wedding and a two-month traveling honeymoon, James opened a medical practice in Port Gibson, Mississippi, but soon left medicine to try his hand as a plantation owner in Walnut Hills. Their daughter, Ann Herbert, was born there on November 26, 1816. The couple "spent the two happiest years of their lives" at Walnut Hills, but in 1817 James abandoned the life of a planter for nearby Vicksburg, where he became a merchant in partnership with W. W. Walker. It is not certain whether the Longs' frequent changes of residence and profession stemmed from restlessness or a desire to seize new opportunities, but in 1819 they found the cause that would fulfill James's dreams of heroic deeds and military glory, define their lives, and assure Jane a place in the pantheon of Texas heroes and heroines.

The 1819 Adams-Onís Treaty, which settled territorial and border disputes between the United States and Spain, was widely acclaimed as a political victory for President Monroe and a diplomatic coup by his secretary of state, John Quincy Adams. The agreement secured Florida from Spain, which also surrendered all claims to territory in the American Northwest. But the treaty's third article, whereby the United States abandoned its claims to Texas, infuriated many Americans, especially in the South. Newspapers called Texas "the richest and proudest plume in the brilliant cap of the illustrious Jefferson," who had claimed the region as United States territory but never seriously attempted to oust the Spanish, and lamented the fact that thanks to the treaty "more good land is given up on Red River than Florida is worth five times fold."

Almost as soon as the treaty was signed in February 1819, there was talk of organizing a filibustering expedition aimed at freeing Texas from Spain. In Natchez, James Long was at the center of efforts to raise money and volunteers. Command of the expedition was initially offered to General John Adair, a veteran of the Revolutionary War and the War of 1812 who was soon to become governor of Kentucky, and, some say, to James

Wilkinson, Jane Wilkinson Long's uncle, who was in Natchez at the time. Both older men—who, unlike James Long, had substantial battlefield experience—declined, and General Adair clearly disapproved of the expedition. He informed President Monroe that an expedition against "the Internal Provinces of Spain" [that is, Texas] was under way, and Secretary of State John Quincy Adams urged the president to condemn the "unlawful military expedition . . . against the Spanish province of Texas." When James Long, only twenty-six and short on military experience, was offered the position by investors interested in trade opportunities, he unhesitatingly accepted and "pledged his life and his entire fortune to the enterprise."

Sympathy for the Long expedition was by no means universal; the *Louisiana Gazette* editorialized, "[W]e are at a loss to conjecture how the general government has so long shut its eyes as to the impolicy of suffering such doings." Andrew Jackson, who had served with distinction in both regions—in the New Orleans campaign of the War of 1812 and the First Seminole War—warned Secretary of War John C. Calhoun that the expedition would be the cause of political conflict with Congress. Calhoun believed Florida was more valuable to the United States than Texas.

Jane, pregnant with her second child, fully shared her husband's enthusiasm and wanted to ride into Texas with the volunteers. She reluctantly agreed to wait until after the baby was born. She and her sister Anne Chesley fashioned a red-and-white-striped flag with a single white star on a red field, the first "Lone Star" flag of Texas, which James took with him when he left Natchez with seventy-five men in June 1819. By the time they joined the advance force in Nacogdoches on the twenty-first or twenty-second, the number of volunteers had swelled to three hundred. Meeting no opposition from the hundred or so residents of the village, James Long took just a day or two to set up headquarters in the Old Stone Fort, raise his flag over the building, and declare the independent "Republic of Texas."

Its declaration of independence, adapted from the 1776 American declaration, referred explicitly to the disappointment felt by "the citizens of Texas" (referring to the Americans who had arrived a few days prior) over the exclusion of Texas from "the territories of the United States" when its borders with "the Spanish possessions in America" were adjusted by the Adams-Onís treaty. Two months later, the *Texas Republican*, published in Nacogdoches (the first English-language newspaper printed in Texas), echoed the sentiments of the declaration. Of a proposed port on Galveston Bay, the paper wrote:

> We also hope through this channel to keep up a friendly commercial intercourse with all nations, particularly with the United States; a government to which we are all attached, and have long hoped that we would one day or other be governed by its laws; this hope having from recent evils vanished, we will now try to govern ourselves, and to have laws as nearly assimilated to them as possible.

Adding the presidency to his military title, Long established a rudimentary government, which declared a land grant policy to attract settlers, and proposed cooperation to the pirate Jean Lafitte, whose headquarters were on Galveston Bay and who controlled its port. Long was unaware that Lafitte and his brother Pierre were secret agents of the Spanish. About James's designs on the port of Galveston, Pierre Lafitte wrote to Juan Manuel Cagigal (sometimes spelled Cajigal), captain general of Cuba, "I foresee the most woeful consequences if they take possession, since it is evident that they are instruments of a Government that seeks means of territorial expansion and that is setting them at work as pioneers." The Lafittes obviously had their own reasons for casting suspicion on Long's aims, but they were also voicing the widely held belief that the United States was behind the venture.

Shortly after James left for Texas, Jane gave birth to their second daughter, whom she named Rebecca. Twelve days later, still in fragile condition, she set off on the first leg of her journey to join James in Nacogdoches. Together with Kian, her slave, and her two daughters, she headed to the port of Natchez to board a boat to Alexandria, Louisiana, now the home of her sister Barbara Calvit. Jane may have found a boat to take her small entourage as far as Alexandria, but in the end James Rowan, a friend who found them at the harborside, led the four overland to Alexandria and before leaving gave Jane enough cash for the trip to Nacogdoches and a letter of credit drawn on his Natchez business in the event that something unforeseen befell her.

It was another month before Jane was well enough to travel from Alexandria. Leaving her infant daughter, Rebecca, with her sister Barbara, she arranged for a carriage and horses and set off. This time she was accompanied by Randal Jones, a Nacogdoches trader who, with his brother James, planned to join the Long expedition. They passed through Natchitoches, Louisiana, where Jane's cousin, Captain Biddle Wilkinson, commanded the United States Army troops stationed in the town, before heading across the Sabine River and finally reaching Nacogdoches. Although the Long expedition was considered an illegal violation of Spanish sovereignty, Wilkinson apparently made no effort to prevent Jane's party from joining her husband in Texas. In general, however, civil and military authorities on the American side of the border attempted to turn back others who wanted to join the expedition.

As first lady of the newly declared republic, Jane enjoyed the best accommodations Nacogdoches afforded, one room in the Old Stone Fort. Her troubles, however—and those of General Long—were far from over. Lacking material support from the United States or the Lafittes, James stretched his men too thinly between the Red River and Galveston Bay, hoping that if they were dispersed they would be able to live off the land. He then departed for Galveston, with the intention of persuading the Lafitte brothers to support the fledgling republic. As soon as he left town, however, discipline among his ragtag volunteers in Nacogdoches collapsed. To make matters worse, word reached them that Colonel Ignacio Pérez was leading a trained Spanish army of seven hundred toward them, with orders to chase the interlopers out of Texas. Unable to regroup as a single force in Nacogdoches, some of Long's scattered, unprepared troops managed to retreat across the Sabine, but a few of those who remained behind were captured by Pérez's soldiers or killed by Indians who took advantage of the settlers' flight to attack. Pérez released most of his prisoners when American troops marshaled on the east bank of the Sabine demanded their return; he lacked supplies for feeding them and demanded only that they stay out of Spanish territory.

From her sister, Jane learned that her infant daughter, Rebecca, had died in June, shortly after Jane left for Texas. When James got to Galveston, many of his men awaited him at Point Bolivar on Galveston Bay. There he learned that his brother David had been killed by Indians while commanding volunteers on the Trinity River, but he was encouraged by the loyalty of the survivors. To revive the expedition, however, he needed money. He returned to Louisiana, hoping to find investors in New Orleans and Natchitoches, where he operated a trading post. These efforts were unsuccessful, but friends in Alexandria, Louisiana, and Natchez, Mississippi, came forward. Warren Hall, a veteran of several earlier expeditions to Texas, joined the effort in early 1820, and in February, the Longs, accompanied by supplies and men, set sail for Bolivar, across from Galveston.

When the Longs and their party reached Bolivar, they discovered that Jean Lafitte, whose assistance James still hoped for, was on the point of abandoning his longtime headquarters on Galveston Bay. Before departing, however, he invited the Longs to visit his ship, the *Pride*. For some reason, James did not accompany Jane to dinner with Lafitte, but she came away charmed by her host. Despite his reputation for a "manner as rough and boisterous as the winds and waves he dealt with," she found Lafitte to be "mild, placable and polite, but altogether unjocular and free from levity." He deflected Jane's efforts to get him to reveal anything about himself or his future plans, but Warren Hall later reported that Lafitte did give the expedition lumber and other supplies with which to improve the Point Bolivar encampment. There is also a powder horn carved in the shape of a fish and engraved with the words "El Perata" (the pirate) that Lafitte may have given to Jane. Years later, she presented it to Sam Houston, who awarded it to Robert Hall, one of the men who guarded Santa Anna after his capture at San Jacinto.

This visit to Texas by the Longs was brief. Jane and James returned to Louisiana in April or May 1820, leaving W. W. Walker in charge of the men who remained. The couple headed to New Orleans, where James was now able to raise money from several American investors. In return for their support, the investors demanded a role in shaping the expedition and asked that a Mexican, José Félix Trespalacios, be appointed commander in order to make the American presence acceptable to leaders of the Mexican revolutionary movement. Others who joined the group at the same time included Ben Milam, John Austin (a distant relative of Stephen F. Austin), and William H. Christy, who with Trespalacios had been planning to join the growing independence movement in Mexico. For most who signed on to the expedition, however, the pure political motive, to free Texas from its colonial overlord, was secondary to the desire for large grants of land—one league for each soldier and additional allotments for families. As Harris Gaylord Warren wrote in *The Sword Was Their Passport*, "The last filibustering expedition of the period was definitely a phase of the American expansion to the Pacific."

Jane believed that conditions at Bolivar were too primitive

to permit her to bring her daughter Ann, then four years old, to Texas. She planned to leave the girl with her sister Anne Chesley. At the last moment, however, after she had already left port, she decided that she couldn't bear to leave Ann behind and insisted on returning to her daughter. This delayed her departure, and she didn't join her husband in Bolivar until November or December. The rest of the party, except for Trespalacios, reached the fort at the beginning of June. There James struggled to maintain discipline over his men, who were eager for the excitement of fighting but reluctant to get their hands dirty clearing land and planting cotton, as the new investors—who had their eyes on profits—demanded. By the time Jane, Kian, and Ann arrived, however, order prevailed, and there were even several other women living at the fort, including the wives of two doctors, Allen and Edwards.

In September 1821, news reached Bolivar that the Mexican War of Independence was entering its final stages. Eager to claim a share of the credit for liberating Texas from Spain, Trespalacios and Milam hurried to Veracruz, Mexico, where they hoped to make contact with Agustín de Iturbide, a former royalist general who had joined forces with the rebel leader Vicente Guerrero. James himself led a number of men from Bolivar to La Bahia (now Goliad, Texas). They took control of the town but were soon opposed by Ignacio Pérez, the royalist officer who had driven the first Long expedition out of Texas two years earlier. When he attacked La Bahia, James was apparently unaware that Spain had recognized Mexican independence a month earlier and that his reasons for occupying the town, in the Mexicans' view, were suspect. Pérez professed reluctance to shed blood on either side and promised to treat the Americans humanely if they surrendered. When James hesitated, Pérez added that they were both insurgents and therefore allies, not adversaries, and finally the Americans capitulated. The leaders were taken immediately to San Antonio, and the rest were confined at La Bahia for several days before being transferred to San Antonio. Then all the Americans were marched under guard to Monterrey, Mexico, where they were held for eight months.

In March 1822, James and several of his officers were taken to Mexico City, where Trespalacios and Milam were also being held. Joel R. Poinsett, the American minister to Chile, was able to arrange the release of the Americans—James immediately and Milam in November. However, for Jane, months passed with no news of her husband.

When James left Bolivar for La Bahia in September 1821, between twenty-five and fifty men remained as a garrison for the fort. He promised to return in three weeks or a month. When the time elapsed without any word from him, Trespalacios (who had also been taken prisoner after landing in Mexico) and the troops who remained at Bolivar, fearing the worst, began to abandon the encampment. They took boats, supplies, and tools with them. Jane refused all entreaties to leave, but the continual departures soon left Bolivar without a means of defense and dangerously low on supplies. Finally, the doctors and their wives also decided they had no alternative but to leave. They urged Jane, who was expecting her third child in December, to join them and offered to take her to the home of one of her sisters (Barbara, now in Alexandria, Louisiana, or Anne, in Rodney, Mississippi). Jane, however, was adamant: "My husband left me here to wait for him and I shall stay until he returns," she said. A few days later, Jane, Kian, and Ann, now six years old, were left alone at the fort, with no supplies, only some arms and ammunition and a few fishhooks.

At night, the campfires of the Karankawa Indians on the mainland across Galveston Bay could be seen from Bolivar. To create the impression that the fort was still manned with troops, Jane raised a red flannel petticoat on the flagpole and fired their one small cannon from time to time. The ploy worked, and the Karankawas never threatened. But months passed and no one else came near the fort, either. When Jane went into labor on December 21, Kian was delirious from a fever, so she gave birth, unaided, to Mary James, who was popularly believed to be the first child born in Texas to English-speaking parents. The next morning Jane and Ann set out to hunt for food. All they found were some fish that had frozen near the shoreline; mother and daughter gathered them up and pickled them in a barrel of brine. Jane, Ann, and Kian subsisted on a diet of fish and oysters for nearly the entire winter, while Jane struggled to nurse her newborn.

Christmas 1821 must have been a gloomy affair for the forlorn, famished trio at Bolivar, despite the presence of Mary James. December 26, however, brought good news: Captain Rafael Gonzales arrived from Monterrey with a letter for Jane from James Long, written from his Mexican prison cell. She did not know when James would be able to return to her, but at least he was alive. Gonzales and his men left after two days, but early in 1822 Kian noticed occasional traffic on the bay: ships and boats, and one day, three men on foot not far from the fort. Fearing that Bolivar had been overrun by Indians, they steered clear until they caught sight of Jane, Ann, and Kian waving from the beach. A few of the men sailed over in a small boat; they were some of Stephen F. Austin's colonists, en route to settle their land in his first colony.

Jane's visitors, the only Americans she had seen in months, left food and supplies at the fort. The next day, John Smith and his family, acquaintances from Mississippi, passed on their way north and invited Jane to join them. When she insisted on remaining at Bolivar, John Smith left his fifteen-year-old daughter, Peggy, with the four survivors temporarily, until he could establish his own homestead on the San Jacinto and return with more supplies.

As word of Jane's ordeal spread among the settlers, many passersby stopped at the fort to share whatever news—or, more often, rumors—they had heard about James Long and his comrades. A sea captain reported reading in a New Orleans newspaper that Long would have to remain in Mexico for at least a year. The captain was en route to Matamoros and offered to take Jane with him and pay for her travel from there to Mexico City, where she could join her husband. Jane seriously considered going with him, until a second sailor turned up with what he claimed was more current news: James Long would be returning from Veracruz "any day." Still other travelers reported hearing that Long and his men were still imprisoned in Mexico, where they had been put to work in the silver mines.

Uncertain of whether any of these travelers' tales were true, Jane decided to stay where she was, so that James would know where to find her when he returned. But the long months of solitude and deprivation had taken their toll. A day or so later, John Smith's son James returned with the supplies his father had promised. He repeated his father's invitation to Jane to join his family, and at last Jane agreed to abandon Bolivar for the Smiths' rough camp on Cedar Bayou, not too far from her fort. She had spent more than a year at the fort, the final three or four months alone with Kian, Ann, and newborn Mary James, a period of indescribable isolation and hardship.

After a short stay with the Smiths, Jane moved her family into a small, crude home of her own near the San Jacinto River. Traffic on the river was plentiful, and Jane asked everyone who arrived for news of James Long. When Abil Terrill, a trader, brought some settlers to the vicinity, he told her that he was on his way to Matamoros, where he would do his best to find out what had happened to her husband and write to her. After he left, Jane moved again, to the Trinity River, and it was there that she received Terrill's letter in July 1822 with the sad news that James Long had been killed in Mexico City on April 8, ten days after he had arrived there from Monterrey. In the capital, he had hoped to convince General Agustín de Iturbide of his loyalty to the cause of Mexican independence. In the meantime, although he was not free to leave the city, he remained at liberty. As Terrill's letter reported:

General Long was well received in Mexico City, and had received several visits together with many invitations from our English Colonel, one of which he was about to return, when he was hailed by a sentinel and ordered to stop, at the same time, General Long put his hand to his side pocket, to draw a paper (his passport). The sentinel supposing it to be for the purpose of drawing his side fire arms to defend himself, at which time the sentinel fired at General Long: and the ball entered his side and passed through him; he expired in a few minutes.

At the time, Jane had no reason to suspect foul play, because Terrill went on to say that "[t]he Congress have it in contemplation, as soon as they get through the hurry of business as respects the government, to make a handsome appropriation for yours [*sic*] and children and support." He added that Long's funeral had been attended by a large crowd, including dignitaries, "that every respect was paid," and that he had been denied military honors only because he was not a Catholic. But Ben Milam and John Austin, who had been imprisoned with James, believed that he had been assassinated on Trespalacios's orders, and for a while Milam contemplated killing their former commander to avenge his friend's death.

Unaware that Trespalacios, who was appointed governor of Texas after Mexican independence, may have been responsible for her husband's murder, Jane wrote to him and was invited to San Antonio. Trespalacios went so far as to reply that he had not sent her money with his letter only because he feared that it might not reach her. In September, as soon as she could prepare for the journey, Jane left for San Antonio with her two daughters and Kian, accompanied by Randal and James Jones and two slaves, one the Calvits had sent to her with a mule and another belonging to the Jones brothers. Along the way, they stopped for several days to allow Mary James to recover from a high fever, and again in La Bahia (Goliad), where the citizenry insisted on giving a ball in honor of the wife of General James Long. Because she was in mourning, Jane at first refused to dance, but when the local priest insisted on dancing with her, she yielded.

After traveling for five weeks, Jane's party reached San Antonio. Almost immediately, she was taken to see Governor Trespalacios, who, in the words of one historian, "bestowed upon General Long's widow every courtesy except that for which she had come, remuneration for her husband's financial losses and death." Jane, her daughters, and Kian lived comfortably in the house of Don Erasmo Seguín, one of San Antonio's leading political and civic figures, but she made no progress with her petition. When the Jones brothers announced their desire to return home and complained that they would have to walk back to East Texas, Jane, because she hesitated to ask Trespalacios directly for money so soon, gave the men her own horse. Three months later, General Iturbide, who had appointed Trespalacios to the Texas governorship, was ousted, which meant that Trespalacios was also out of office. Although he invited Jane to go to Monterrey with him, she declined his offer, realizing that out of power he was even less likely to be able to help her. She decided that it would be best for her to return to one of her sisters, in Louisiana or Mississippi.

As often happened to Jane when all hope seemed lost, a friend turned up. In San Antonio, her rescuer was Leonard Peck, a trader from Philadelphia who had known James Long and Trespalacios. He was on his way to Monterrey, and insisted on paying the travel expenses to that city of the Trespalacios family. More important, he went to great lengths to make Jane's return to the United States possible before he left San Antonio. In exchange for five hundred dollars in cash, Jane gave Peck dresses and jewelry, which she had been given as gifts from her family, to sell in Mexico. For his part, the merchant also left five hundred dollars of his own with Jane, for safekeeping, until he should return from his trading mission. Before leaving the city,

Peck purchased bread, corn, and coffee for Jane, all of them scarce commodities. For his part, Trespalacios returned to Jane the weapons taken from James Long and his men when they were arrested in 1821, nearly two years earlier. Then Peck and the Mexicans headed to Monterrey, but as soon as they had traveled a short distance from San Antonio, Peck, the merchant trader, sent a messenger back with Jane's dresses and jewels.

Despite her disappointment at failing to receive either a pension or compensation from Trespalacios, Jane was gratified by the generosity and hospitality of San Antonio's citizens. When they discovered that Mary James had not been baptized, a number of them urged Jane to perform the ceremony before she left the city. She agreed. At the baptism, Mary James wore a long white christening robe lent by a local family, and on the way to the church, the guests, following local custom, handed one hundred dollars in silver to the poor and gave lavish gifts to the baby as well.

Jane remained in San Antonio for another ten months, heading back to Louisiana only in August 1823, when Leonard Peck, his business in Mexico concluded, passed through the city again on his way back to the United States. Peck was leading a pack of forty mules, carrying silver and other merchandise from Mexico. Jane had purchased a horse and mule with the proceeds from selling James Long's firearms, so she and Ann had their own animals to ride. Her brother-in-law, Alexander Calvit, rode out to meet the pack train before it reached Nacogdoches and escorted her back to his home in Louisiana, three years after she had left for Bolivar.

Jane stayed with the Calvits for six months and then went to Mississippi to visit her other sister, Anne. Shortly before she was to leave for Rodney, Mississippi, Ben Milam appeared, having returned from his long imprisonment in Mexico via Havana, Norfolk, and New Orleans. He had saved James's papers, correspondence, and clothing, which he presented to Jane, and then escorted her to Mississippi. It is said that James Long had a premonition of his early death and that Milam had promised to look after Jane and her children. Perhaps the Longs' most steadfast friend, he spent a week with her in Rodney, and he was in and out of Jane's life until his own death during the siege of Bexar in December 1835, where he died leading the attempt to drive an entrenched Mexican army out of San Antonio.

At the end of 1823, Jane Long had little to show for the four long years of struggle that she had shared with James. Her husband was dead, perhaps the victim of an assassination, and she had been rebuffed in her efforts to persuade the Mexican government to grant her a pension or compensate her for James's financial losses in Texas. She would later be told that she was ineligible for a military pension because James had declined Iturbide's offer of a generalship in the Mexican army. Worst of all, in June 1824, two-year-old Mary James, the child whose birth was to confer on Jane the title "Mother of Texas," died. Despite these tragic losses, Jane continued to thirst for a life in Texas, and by the end of the year she would be back, with the trusted Kian, her daughter Ann, and the Calvits.

In August 1824, Jane had been awarded grants of land in Fort Bend and Waller counties in the Austin colony. When she returned to Texas, however, she did not settle on either of her grants. After spending time as a guest of Jared and Mary Ann Groce, she lived in San Felipe de Austin from December 1825 until April 1830, when she took Ann, who was then fifteen, back to Mississippi to attend school. Meanwhile, however, Milam built a cabin for her on her Fort Bend property.

From all accounts, it seems that when Jane went to Natchez, Mississippi, with Ann in 1830, she had in mind finding her daughter a husband, not securing her an education. Indeed, in January 1831, less than a year after she enrolled in school, the sixteen-year-old married Edward Winston of Washington, Mississippi, and in April the enlarged family group landed in Matagorda, Texas. With a man in the family who could help manage a working plantation, Jane moved to her Fort Bend grant. The going must have been hard at first; in 1832 Jane moved to Brazoria, where she ran an inn, with Kian's help, for two years.

According to one source, Kian was briefly seized from Jane by a man to whom James Long had mortgaged her years before. Jane had the right to redeem Kian, but she lacked the funds with which to do so. Fortuitously, just when Jane most needed Kian's help in running her Brazoria inn, Leonard Peck resurfaced, supplied the necessary funds, and then vanished entirely from Jane's life.

Despite the stressful decade she had endured, in her thirties Jane still possessed much of her youthful beauty. J. C. Clopper, who had been charmed by her when they met several years earlier, described her as tall and beautiful, with sparkling eyes and an engaging manner, who spoke with "ease and fluency" about a wide variety of topics, whether with a beau, a fop, or a gallant, all of which she had in plentiful supply.

Jane knew many of the leading Texans of the time; they often stayed at her inn—in Brazoria or at the one she opened in Richmond in 1837. They took their meals there and sometimes adopted the place as an official or unofficial office or campaign headquarters. One of them was William Travis, a frequent guest who sometimes ate in Jane's dining room even when he was not staying at the inn, and whose diary is crowded with references to her. Travis represented her in her efforts to collect money owed to her (sometimes to work off his own debts to her for food and lodging), and one entry notes, perhaps with a hint of sorrow, that "Mrs. Long has sold out & quit." At the time, she placed a notice in the local paper, recommending the new owner, Mr. M. W. Smith, to her clientele.

Jane's visitors included prominent Mexican officials as well as Texans. In 1834, Colonel Juan N. Almonte stopped in Brazoria in the course of an inspection of Texas. It is said that the officer, who had studied in the United States and was fluent in English, was looking for signs of nascent revolutionary activity, and that while he made civilized conversation in the dining room he was secretly compiling dossiers on likely insurrectionists. Some historians believe that at the time of Almonte's visit, Jane's inn was already being used to stockpile guns and ammunition for the coming revolution, but this may be speculation.

At the inn Jane established in Richmond in 1837, David Burnet, Sam Houston, and Mirabeau B. Lamar, the first three presidents of the republic, spent a great deal of time and sometimes even lived there rather than in the executive mansion. Jane's relationship with Lamar was unquestionably the closest of the three. They may have met as early as 1835, shortly after Lamar arrived in Texas, and Jane encouraged his writing projects. Over time, these included collecting Stephen F. Austin's papers, after Austin's untimely death in 1836, and writing the biography of James Long, for which Lamar conducted lengthy interviews with his widow and studied Long's papers, without ever completing the hoped-for volume.

All three presidents were charmed by Jane, and there are rumors that Houston and Lamar both proposed marriage. Houston made a spirited denial of the rumor in one of his letters to Anna Raguet, but Lamar, whose first wife died in 1830, is known to have dedicated a poem to "Bonnie Jane." Years later he changed the name of the dedicatee to "Anne," thus fueling suspicions that Jane may have rejected his offer. Lamar also lent Jane money and informed his brother before the battle of San Jacinto that he might leave his will with her.

After the revolution, Jane, now thirty-nine, began spending more time on her grant in Fort Bend County, where she bought a slave and started growing cotton. For some years she prospered; she was able to pay off James Long's debts and also expand her operation. In 1840, Jane owned twelve slaves, two horses, and more than fifty head of cattle. She also had three lots in the town of Richmond, in addition to her plantation, and by 1850 her property was valued above twenty thousand dollars.

Ten years later, she owned nineteen slaves, and her working plantation covered some two thousand acres.

After the Civil War, however, her wealth dwindled, and she grew increasingly dependent on her daughter Ann. When Ann died in 1870, Jane lived with her grandchildren until her death in 1880. Her own property had shrunk in value to about two thousand dollars. But the reversal of fortunes never dimmed Jane's spirits. Sarah Jones Bruckmiller, the daughter of Jane's longtime friend Randal Jones, remembered her many years later as "a lovable old lady who got very angry when they used to say she had set her cap for Pa." Her grave, with its simple headstone, is in the Morton cemetery in Richmond.

Part III

THE TEXAS REVOLUTION

1830s–1850s

Susanna Dickinson
Dilue Rose
Anna Raguet
Mary "Polly" Rusk
Emily Austin Bryan Perry

Susanna Dickinson   *Anna Raguet*

The Austin family tree appears in the appendix.

Emily Austin Bryan Perry   *Mary "Polly" Rusk*

The men of Texas deserved much credit, but more was due the women. Armed men facing a foe could not but be brave; but the women, with their little children around them, without means of defense or power to resist, faced danger and death with unflinching courage.

-THOMAS JEFFERSON RUSK
Secretary of War,
Texas independence from Mexico, 1836

By 1835, the mood among settlers in Texas, Anglo and Tejano, had largely shifted toward favoring independence from Mexico. In September, when Stephen F. Austin returned after spending more than two years in Mexico, he added his influential voice to those in favor of severing ties with an increasingly despotic Mexican government. Austin had gone to Mexico City in July 1833 to petition the central government to repeal the 1830 law prohibiting further immigration from the United States to Texas, to grant separate statehood to the

region (it was then part of the state of Coahuila and Texas),
and to enlarge the power of local government. He succeeded
in restoring the right of immigration and gaining a measure
of home rule, but he left the capital in January 1834 convinced
that President Santa Anna would never allow Texas to become
a state in its own right. In Saltillo, on his way home, he was arrested, accused of inciting rebellion in Texas, and imprisoned
in Mexico City. He was never formally charged with a crime
and no trial was held, but he was confined for nearly a year
and for several months was imprisoned in what his nephew
Austin Bryan (son of Stephen's sister, Emily Austin Bryan
Perry) described as a dungeon "without seeing the light of the
sun." Released in December, Stephen was still not permitted to
leave the capital until July 1835, when a general amnesty was
declared. He returned to Texas via New Orleans, arriving on
September 2.

No sooner had Stephen Austin landed in what he called "this
my more than native country" than communities began to com-
pete for the privilege of celebrating his return. He headed for
Emily's home, Peach Point Plantation (see map, p. xx). Ben Fort
Smith sent this invitation to Stephen on September 4:

> The citizens of this town [Brazoria] and its vicinity desir-
> ous of, Expressing to you their approbation of your public
> services and their respect for your private virtues have se-
> lected us to invite you to partake with them, a dinner on
> Tuesday the 8 inst, at, Messrs Fitchett and Gill, [a tavern]
> in this town—
> We here avail ourselves of this opportunity to offer our
> hearty congratulations, on your safe return among us.

On September 8, six days after Stephen's return, Brazoria
was the site of the grand banquet and ball attended by "the
whole lower country," as Austin Bryan wrote to his friend

William Hunter. Emily Perry and many of the town's leading citizens planned the dinner for three o'clock in the afternoon, to be followed by the ball.

Stephen's close kin, the Austin and Perry families, turned out in full force among the overflowing crowd of several hundred. Writing to his sister Mary, Henry Austin, Stephen's cousin, took note of the crowd and their excitement: "There were 60 covers and despite the short notice the table was three times filled by men alone [it has been noted that women didn't attend the dinner because there were to be political speeches, and also, perhaps, because space was limited]. In the evening the long room was filled to a jam at least 60 or 80 ladies who danced the sun up and the Oyster Creek girls would not have quit then had not the room been wanted for breakfast—you never saw such enthusiasm."

Until Stephen's 1834 arrest and confinement in Mexico, he was optimistic that the rights of Texans under the Mexican Constitution of 1824 could be preserved through diplomatic means. By 1835, when he was allowed to return home, he was convinced that Santa Anna was determined to do away with the constitution and replace it with a centralized, dictatorial government with himself at its head. Before leaving Mexico, he had advised the president against invading Texas and warned that if Santa Anna sent an army to subdue the region, the Texans "would resist and repel it, and ought to do so." In Brazoria, he addressed a crowd of "more than a thousand Anglo-Americans [who] listened to him for nearly an hour with unbroken delight." In his usual temperate fashion, Stephen stopped short of calling for war, but he made it clear that he saw no alternative and called for a "general consultation" of delegates "composed of the best, and most calm, and intelligent, and firm men in the country" to decide the future course of Texas. Then he closed with a toast to "the constitutional rights and the security and peace of Texas," which were under threat from Santa Anna's autocratic policies.

A mere ten days later, Stephen was considerably more explicit in his opinion of what the future held in store for Texas. As chairman of the Committee of Safety, he wrote in his report of September 19, "War is our only resource. There is no other remedy but to defend our rights our country & our selves by force of arms. To do this we must be united: and in order to unite the delegates of the people must meet in General Consultation and organize a system of defence and give organization to the country so as to produce concert." The mood of the overwhelming majority of citizens almost certainly mirrored his own, as can be seen in the letter eighteen-year-old Austin Bryan wrote to William Hunter in Missouri on September 15: "If you feel like trying your spunk come down with your rifle as I think we will have fighting to do shortly. We go for fight or any thing else now Uncle has got home."

On September 17, barely a week after the banquet in Brazoria, General Martín Perfecto de Cos sailed from the Mexican border town of Matamoros at the head of a five-hundred-man army. It was almost as if Stephen's address had been the cue for the opening scene of the invasion of Texas. From San Antonio, where Cos's troops had reinforced the permanent Mexican garrison, one hundred Mexican cavalrymen were sent to nearby Gonzales, with orders to reclaim a cannon the residents had been given to defend against Indian raids. The town of Gonzales, within the Green DeWitt colony and on the east bank of the Guadalupe River, proved inaccessible to the Mexicans when they reached the opposite bank on September 29; the river had flooded, and the townspeople had moored all the boats on the eastern shore. Lieutenant Francisco Castañeda decided to wait for the waters to subside. Meanwhile, volunteers, including thirty mounted Indian fighters, poured into Gonzales until the Texans outnumbered their adversary.

***

Green DeWitt had died in May 1835, probably of cholera, but his widow, Sara Seely DeWitt, and daughter Naomi (her name is sometimes given as Evaline) remained in Gonzales. The two women are said to have fashioned a white flag out of Naomi's wedding dress, with a black cannon emblazoned in the center and the motto COME AND TAKE IT in black letters. Mounting the cannon on wheels, the Texans taunted the Mexican cavalry until October 1, then crossed the river and pursued them briefly. After suffering one or two casualties, the Mexicans withdrew. The battle of Gonzales was of no military significance, but it marked a point of no return for both sides that led inexorably to revolution the following year. The COME AND TAKE IT banner may also have seen service in the siege of Bexar, the opening campaign of the Texas Revolution.

Women did much more for the war effort than fashion flags, of course—as did many families. But flags were important symbols and morale boosters, and the women created a number of them. Sarah Dodson of Harrisburg designed a flag with red, white, and blue vertical bars and a lone five-pointed white star in the red field. To the Georgia Battalion of volunteers, Joanna Troutman of that state presented a white flag with a blue star in its center and the mottoes "Liberty or Death" and "Ubi libertas habitat ibi nostra patria est" ("Where Liberty Dwells, There is Our Home"). According to Guy M. Bryan, this flag was flown at Goliad. The Liberty flag presented to Sherman's Volunteers of Kentucky by the ladies of Newport depicted the figure of Liberty holding a sword over which a banner inscribed "Liberty or Death" is draped. It is said to have been the only battle flag the Texans had at San Jacinto.

Inspired by their nearly bloodless victory at Gonzales, a group of volunteers took control of the lightly defended presidio at Goliad on October 10, thereby cutting off General Cos's escape route to the Gulf of Mexico. Most of the fighters then joined the army under Stephen Austin's command, who was hoping to force Cos to withdraw from San Antonio. At Mission Concepcíon, San Patricio, and the nearby Nueces River, the volunteers, fighting from cover and armed with rifles that were effective at three times the range of Mexican muskets, won easy victories and in early November were poised to confront Cos's six-hundred-man army in San Antonio.

This series of battles was typical of military actions in Texas prior to the siege of the Alamo by Mexican president General Antonio López de Santa Anna in February 1836: little more than occasional skirmishes, often inconclusive, between small units of the opposing armies. For all their zeal and fearlessness, the undermanned, undisciplined Texas volunteers hardly resembled a professional army. More interested in fighting than learning the arts of war, they often simply ignored orders they didn't like. When Stephen Austin, then commander in chief, ordered the army to attack San Antonio in November 1835, the volunteers refused, agreeing to maintain the siege of the city only if they were allowed to elect their own commander. Austin, who had in any case been asked to return to the United States to solicit support for the independence efforts, was replaced by Edward Burleson, a veteran of the War of 1812 and an experienced Indian fighter.

Despite Burleson's considerable military experience (Austin had none), the new commander was no more successful than his predecessor at disciplining the troops and persuading them to follow orders. In late November 1835, when a Mexican column was spotted approaching San Antonio, Burleson sent one hundred cavalry to investigate. Soon rumors began spreading that the Mexicans were carrying a payroll for General Cos's troops, and the entire army raced off in pursuit of their share of the hoped-for treasure. The "payroll" turned out to be fodder that had been gathered for the Mexican cavalry's horses. This skirmish, which became known as the "Grass Fight," was of no military consequence, but it had a demoralizing effect on the

Texas soldiers. A week later, when Burleson ordered an attack on the city, most of the Texans refused. Faced with stubborn insubordination, Burleson opted to lift the siege rather than risk a mutiny. This pattern of Texan refusal to submit to the demands of military discipline was to plague every Texan commander, including Sam Houston. That said, Texans often willingly volunteered for the very missions they had refused to join when ordered to do so.

This time, after Burleson had backed off, Ben Milam, who sensed that inaction might doom the cause of independence, issued his famous challenge to the five hundred volunteers who remained. "Who will go with old Ben Milam into San Antonio?" he asked, and three hundred of the men answered his call. The Texans followed the forty-seven-year-old veteran of the War of 1812 into the city, and from December 5 to 9, they battled Cos's troops from house to house in the city's narrow streets. On the third day of fighting, Milam was killed by a sniper's bullet, but two days later General Cos surrendered to Burleson. He agreed to withdraw his troops across the Rio Grande and not to oppose the reestablishment of the federal Constitution of 1824— the liberal charter that Santa Anna had suspended when he assumed dictatorial powers in 1834.

In February 1836, when Santa Anna crossed the Rio Grande with an army of more than two thousand men, the Texas army consisted of about one hundred men at the Alamo and another five hundred in Goliad and San Patricio. A Mexican cavalry unit, five hundred strong, was headed to the Gulf coast at the same time. Santa Anna's first objective was to retake San Antonio, although it was of no strategic significance to either side. As a result, Commander in Chief Sam Houston sent Jim Bowie to San Antonio with orders to evacuate the city. However, Bowie decided that James Neill, who had strengthened the fortress-like mission with the cannon captured from General Cos, had made the Alamo impregnable. Bowie stayed to help defend it. Neill left to look after his family, who were ill, leaving William

B. Travis, who had brought a group of volunteers, in command in his absence. To placate popular sentiment, Travis and Bowie agreed to share command.

When the first Mexican troops reached San Antonio on February 23, Travis sent a courier to Gonzales with this appeal: "We want men and provisions. Send them to us. We have 150 men and are determined to defend the Alamo to the last." With reinforcements, the Texans might have been able to defend the fortresslike mission and convent buildings, whose walls, four feet thick in places, and emplacement of eighteen cannon, offered considerable protection. But without enough riflemen and cannoneers to defend the thirteen-hundred-foot perimeter (six men normally made up the crew of a single cannon), and with the Mexicans moving their artillery closer to the walls night after night, the question was only how long the Texans would manage to hold out. Fewer than forty men answered Travis's call for assistance before Santa Anna mounted his final assault on March 6.

One day before Santa Anna's attack on the Alamo, Henry Austin wrote to his brother-in-law James Perry, suggesting that he "send Emily and the younger children" to New Orleans, where he was about to go to help Stephen raise money and provisions for the new republic, and offering to secure passage for them on the ship *Comanche*, on which he would also be sailing. Although "I do not believe the enemy can ever penetrate into the heart of the Brazos timber," he wrote, "still I fear our hardest fighting will be on the Colorado or upper Brazos," and he worried that Emily's health might suffer because of the uncertainties if the fighting came near to Peach Point and the possibilities of attacks from hostile Indians or a slave revolt.

Once begun, the March 6 assault on the Alamo did not last long. The sparseness of defenders left too much of the perimeter exposed to deter the enemy. On the north side, a few Mexican troops managed to climb a wall and unlock a door through which hundreds of soldiers entered the yard of the compound.

Once inside, they turned the defenders' cannon against the convent and chapel walls, behind which the Texans had retreated, and fought hand to hand until only seven Texans—David Crockett may have been one of them—remained alive. Some Mexican officers objected to the murder of defenseless captives as being contrary to civilized rules of warfare, but Santa Anna's orders to execute all male prisoners prevailed.

Susanna Dickinson

*The few survivors of the Alamo included a number of women and
children and a handful of slaves. The women had taken refuge in
the compound after Santa Anna's troops reached San Antonio,
and the slaves' owners were among the men defending the Alamo.
All were set free by Santa Anna, in part, at least, to allow them
to spread the news of the fate of the defiant Texans and discourage
support for the revolution. The best-known survivors are Susanna
Dickinson and her daughter, Angelina, and William Travis's
slave, Joe, who was sent with Susanna Dickinson to report on the
outcome of the battle for the Alamo.*

Inside the Alamo on March 6, Susanna Dickinson and her
daughter, Angelina, hid in the sacristy. Susanna had settled
in Gonzales, Texas, with her husband, Almaron, in 1831, near
the San Marcos River in Green DeWitt's colony. Trained as an
artilleryman in the United States Army, Almaron volunteered
in the battle of Gonzales in October 1835 and then joined the
siege of Bexar (San Antonio). Because the safety of women and
children in Gonzales was being threatened by ruthless thieves
who knew that most of the men had left, Almaron insisted that
his wife and daughter join him in San Antonio. When the Mexican army marched into the city, most residents evacuated and
Almaron brought his family into the Alamo.

Susanna later reported that when Mexican troops entered
the compound, her husband momentarily left his post at one of
the cannon in the chapel to say goodbye to her and Angelina.
"Great God, Sue, the Mexicans are inside our walls! If they
spare you, save my child!" he told her. "Then, with a parting
kiss, he drew his sword and plunged into the strife, then rag-

ing in different portions of the fortifications." In the massacre that took the lives of all his comrades, Almaron was killed by a bayonet. Susanna did not see her husband's body after the battle, but from the townhouse to which she, Angelina, and other surviving women and children were taken, she was able to see the flaming pyres of the victims. Susanna believed that only the Texan victims were burned and that the Mexican dead were buried in the city cemetery, but according to other witnesses, all the Alamo dead were cremated within its walls except Gregorio Esparza, a Tejano whose brother Francisco, a Mexican soldier, obtained permission for a Christian burial. The lives of Gregorio's wife and two children were also spared.

Susanna told one interviewer that after the carnage subsided, a Mexican officer, Colonel (Juan) Almonte, approached her, asked whether she was Mrs. Dickinson, told her, "If you wish to save your life, follow me," and led her out of the Alamo. She did see the body of David Crockett, between the church and the barracks. Whether she saw Bowie's body or not is uncertain, but she reported that he had shot two of the Mexican soldiers who came to kill him in his bed before they ended his life with their sabers. She also noted in an account she gave of that day that a Texan soldier named Walker was shot and then stuck by the Mexican "horde" with their bayonets, and his body was lifted up "like a farmer does a bundle of fodder on a pitchfork." Blood was everywhere, and the soldiers desisted from their slaughter only after a Mexican officer ordered them to.

The next day, the survivors were taken to Santa Anna. Susanna and one-year-old Angelina, the only Anglo-Americans to survive the Alamo siege, apparently impressed the general, who wanted to take Angelina to Mexico City and have her educated there. If the offer was made, Susanna refused it. Santa Anna spared the lives of all the surviving women and children, but he may have acted more generously to Susanna because she had displayed her husband's Masonic apron to him, a ploy that the general himself is said to have tried after his own capture at San Jacinto. Freemasons often showed consideration to fellow members and their families even when they were enemies.

The general dispatched Susanna to Gonzales, with a letter of warning to Houston that threatened all Texans who opposed him with the same fate the Alamo's defenders had suffered. She traveled at least part of the way with Ben, a servant of Colonel Almonte, and William Travis's slave, Joe. When Houston's scouts Erastus "Deaf" Smith and Henry Karnes met the party, Smith took them to Gonzales. There, it is said, Susanna delivered Santa Anna's letter to General Sam Houston and poured out her story of the horrors she had witnessed. After this, Houston told his troops to break camp and ordered the town of Gonzales burned to the ground, so there would be nothing of use to the oncoming enemy. Susanna traveled with the family of Sarah and John Bruno, who had taken her in to rest during the journey from the Alamo to Gonzales. Until the dangers subsided, she and Angelina took refuge in Sarah's family's home on Nash Creek, near the present city of Houston.

The general flight to escape the march of the Mexican army had started as early as February, when women, children, and the elderly had begun to move eastward to get out of its path. The people of San Patricio and Refugio were among the first, after General José de Urrea approached those towns, but the war was brought home to many settlers only when the Alamo fell. The city of Gonzales was especially hard hit by the news of the slaughter that had been carried out there: thirty-two of the victims were volunteers from Gonzales who had answered Travis's appeal for aid. As one member of the community later wrote, "I remember most distinctively the shrieks of despair with which the soldiers' wives received the news of the death of their husbands. The piercing wails of woe that reached our camps from these bereaved women thrilled me and filled me with feelings I cannot express, nor ever forget. I now could understand that there is woe in warfare, as well as glory and labor."

But there was little time for grieving; the families of Gonzales immediately joined the other refugees in the Runaway Scrape, the mass exodus of women and children from all areas in the path of the Mexican army. Because able-bodied men were occupied in the war, all others were defenseless and sought refuge to the east—going toward Louisiana, by foot, horse, or wagon. The elements were harsh and many died from the rigors and hardships of the journey.

About several of the women who survived inside the Alamo, little is known. Anna Salazar Esparza, the wife of Gregorio Esparza, took refuge in the fortress with her husband, along with the daughter of her first marriage, and their three sons, Enrique, Manuel, and Francisco. Although Gregorio's brother Francisco was a member of the local Mexican militia, Gregorio sided with the Texans and served as a cannoneer during the battle.

Concepción Losoya, whose son José Toribio Losoya was a Tejano who lost his life at the siege, was one of the survivors, along with another son, Juan, and a daughter, Juana Francisca Melton. According to some accounts, José Losoya's wife and three children also survived inside the compound. Juana Francisca was married to Eliel Melton, the Alamo quartermaster. Enrique Esparza, who was about eight at the time of the siege (he later claimed to have been four years older), lived until 1917 and often spoke about the events. As late as 1907, he told an interviewer, "Neither age nor infirmity could make me forget [what happened at the Alamo], for the scene was one of such horror that it could never be forgotten by anyone who witnessed its incidents." Enrique reported seeing several survivors who were otherwise lost to history, including Victoriana de Salinas and her three young daughters, and an old woman, Petra Gonzales, whom Enrique called "Doña Petra." Some of the noncombatants, of course, perished in the battle. Joe, William Travis's slave, mentioned an unnamed black woman whose body lay between two of the cannons; Enrique recalled a boy about his age killed by musket fire as they stood side by side; and Susanna Dickinson reported that artilleryman Anthony Wolf's two sons, eleven and twelve years old, were bayoneted moments after their father.

Eyewitness accounts are often unreliable, so the fact that, in the aftermath of the chaotic siege, none of the known survivors said anything about having seen Andrea Castañón Villanueva during the battle may not mean that her claim of having nursed wounded fighters and being with Jim Bowie at the time of his death is untrue. Known as Madam Candelaria after her marriage to Candelario Villanueva, Andrea was a familiar personage in the city, a wife and mother of four who ministered to the needs of the sick and the poor. In San Antonio, she was said to have cared for twenty-two orphans and to have provided for destitute strangers. Her account of having been inside the Alamo during the siege, and to have been at Bowie's bedside in his final moments, however, is unsupported and has been questioned by some historians. Enrique Esparza did not report seeing her there, but he declined to contradict her claim. The Texas state legislature apparently believed her. In 1891, when Madam Candelaria was more than one hundred years old (she said she had been born in 1785), she was awarded a monthly pension of twelve dollars as an Alamo survivor and for her work with smallpox victims.

Not all of the women and children of the Alamo were as fortunate as Madam Candelaria. Susanna Dickinson, despite owning a league of land (4,428 acres) in Gonzales, was left without a means of support after the revolution. Her petition for a five-hundred-dollar grant from the government was rejected. At twenty-two, she was an illiterate widow with a one-year-old daughter. Over the next twenty years, she lived mostly in and around Houston, and was married four more times—to John Williams, who beat her and her daughter, Angelina, and whom she divorced within four months; to Francis Herring, who died five years later, in 1843; and to Peter Bellows, who sued her for divorce (on likely fabricated grounds of adultery and prostitution) in 1857. During this period she lived in near poverty. Dr. Rufus Burleson, former pastor of First Baptist Church in Houston and second president of Baylor University, baptized her at a revival in Lockhart in 1862. He said of her, "During all my pastorate in Houston, and especially during the cholera epidemic, she was a zealous co-laborer of mine in every good work." Then she met Joseph Hannig, a cabinetmaker and undertaker almost twenty years her junior, whom she married shortly after her divorce from Bellows. Susanna finally enjoyed an enduring marriage, which ended only with her death. According to Susanna's nephew E. A. Masur, the couple met in Lockhart, where she ran a boardinghouse. Hannig "really appreciated a good meal. When he sampled Susannah's [sic] cabbage, bacon, and cornbread, he just up and married her." They moved to Austin, where he prospered and they had a comfortable life. She returned to the Alamo only once, in 1881, accompanied by a reporter for the *San Antonio Express*, who wrote:

> She can give but little of the struggle, as she was in a little dark room in the rear of the building. . . . The old lady recognized almost every stone, however, and the arch overhead and the corners she said, with tears in her eyes, came back as vividly to memory as though her experience of yore had been but yesterday. She showed the reporter . . . the window through while she peeped to see the blood of noble men seeping into the ground, and the bodies of heroes lying cold in death. . . .

Susanna died on October 7, 1883. Her gravestone in Oakwood Cemetery reads:

> *We only know that thou hast gone*
> *And that the same relentless tide*
> *Which bore thee from us still glides*
> *And we who mourn thee with it glide.*

After Susanna's death, Hannig married Louisa Staacke, but when he died in 1890, he chose to be buried next to Susanna.

Angelina's life, however, did not end happily. Life was difficult for mother and daughter through most of the two decades that followed Texas independence. While Susanna struggled to eke out a subsistence as a boardinghouse proprietor, Angelina grew up with few prospects. In 1849, the Texas legislature debated a petition to grant Angelina three hundred dollars a year in recognition of Almaron Dickinson's military service. Among the representatives who supported the petition was Guy M. Bryan, Emily Austin Bryan Perry's son. After describing Angelina as "the Christian child of the Alamo—baptized in the blood of a Travis, a Bowie, a Crockett, and a Bonham," he urged the legislature to "give her what she asks, that she might be educated, and become a worthy child of the State!—that she may take that position in society to which she is entitled by the illustrious name of her martyred father." Although Bryan's plea was seconded by Representative James Wilson, who said "we cannot treat her with neglect without entailing lasting disgrace upon Texas," the legislature denied Angelina's petition because "many orphans were left in a more forlorn and dependent state than the one the bill is intended to relieve." It pointed to the more than five thousand acres of land—Almaron Dickinson's original DeWitt colony grant and another twenty-five hundred acres that Susanna and Angelina received in recognition of his military service—and argued that Angelina "does not appear to be in a distressed situation."

In 1851, Angelina married John Maynard Griffith, who had been one of Susanna's boarders, moved to his Montgomery County farm, and bore three children between 1853 and 1857. After the birth of the couple's third child, Joseph, Angelina apparently left her husband and moved to New Orleans, where in 1864 she was married a second time, to Oscar Holmes, with whom she had a daughter, Sallie. During Reconstruction, Angelina drifted back to Galveston, Texas, where according to the local newspapers she "embraced the life of a courtesan" and died in 1869 from a hemorrhage of the uterus. Guy Bryan later summed up Angelina's fate discreetly and tragically: "She failed to secure the education which she craved and later died in Galveston after a life of drifting, over which history has drawn a kindly veil."

The siege of the Alamo and the time Santa Anna took building up to the attack served the important purpose of giving General Houston time to organize the meager troops and arms available. The reports of the brutality of the massacre rallied Texans to the cause of independence. It also fostered sympathy for Texas in the United States. Before the siege ended, the convention at Washington-on-the-Brazos had declared independence, authorized the formation of an army, and appointed Houston commander in chief. Before leaving to gather and expand his army in Gonzales, Houston persuaded the other members not to go to the Alamo's defense, a gesture that could not have reversed the outcome, but to remain in session. The convention then drafted a constitution, modeled largely on the American Constitution, elected an interim government led by President David G. Burnet, Vice President Lorenzo de Zavala, and Secretary of War Thomas Rusk. On March 17, when news of the Mexican army's approach reached Washington-on-the-Brazos, the delegates adjourned and devoted their energies to protecting their families and defending their new republic.

Dilue Rose

"Then began the horrors of the 'Runaway Scrape,'" as Dilue Rose Harris later recalled in her "Reminiscences," based on her father's journal and her own childhood memories. When Dilue Rose's uncle, James Wells, left to join Houston's army, Dilue "spent the day melting lead in a pot, dipping it up with a spoon, and molding bullets," and her mother, Margaret, stayed up all night sewing "two striped hickory shirts and bags for provisions." The Rose family, who lived at Stafford's Point on the west bank of Buffalo Bayou, got ready to leave their home as soon as they heard General Houston's dispatch about the fall of the Alamo. They stuffed as many things as they could into a chest that Dr. Pleasant Rose hid in the bayou bottom, loaded clothes, bedding, and food onto the family's sleigh, and headed to the home of a neighbor who had offered to share his cart with them. Dilue's brother Granville drove the sleigh, while Dr. Rose, a veteran of the War of 1812, stayed behind to help another neighbor with his cattle before rejoining his wife and children.

Because a majority of the able-bodied men in Texas left their homes to join Houston's army in March and April 1836 (despite the fact that troop strength never exceeded two thousand, a total that included a large number of volunteers from the United States), responsibility throughout the Runaway Scrape fell largely on the women. One of these women was Stephen F. Austin's sister Emily Austin Bryan Perry, who with her family left their home at Peach Point when they learned of the Goliad massacre. They crossed the Brazos River in a wagon full of children and supplies, with Emily holding her baby, Cecilia, on the front seat. Their slaves traveled with them, probably on foot, as their wagon took its place in the long train of refugees. "As far as the eye could see," Emily's son Guy M. Bryan wrote, "extended backward and forward, was an indiscriminate mass of human beings . . . walking, riding on horseback, in carts, sleds, wagons, and every kind of transportation known to Texas."

Heavy traffic and frequent rain had turned miles of trails into muddy bogs, and witnesses spoke of "great confusion" and families in "deplorable condition." Angelina Peyton Eberly, at the time owner of the San Felipe Inn, noticed that horses and wagons were in short supply and that people were using "anything that could carry women and children," no matter its condition. She said "animals were loaded with bedding and provisions, until the person guiding them was hardly perceptible," and noted that people often jettisoned items in hopes of making better progress. Before joining the throngs herself, Angelina gave rice and hogs to the army rather than allow them to fall into the hands of the Mexican army.

At every water crossing there were inevitable delays, sometimes several days long. At the ford across Cedar Bayou, near the Trinity River, the Perrys found hundreds of people waiting behind a wagon drawn by two oxen that had gotten stuck in the marsh. The oxen had lain down in the water with their noses above the surface to allow them to breathe, and on a little rise nearby was a gaunt woman, her skirt hitched up to her knees and a leather whip in her hand, with her two young daughters at her side. Emily went over to the woman and speaking "tenderly but firmly" offered her own pair of oxen and the muscle power of her slaves to help get the wagon across the bayou. Emily's encouragement restored the woman's confidence, and she replied, "Thank you, ma'am, but they know my voice and would do more for me than anyone else." Then, snapping her whip, she called out to the oxen, "Up, Buck and Ball, and do your best!" The oxen responded, the wagon came free, and the line of travelers started moving again. For years afterward, whenever a great effort was needed in the Bryan-Perry family, the woman's cry, "Up, Buck and Ball, and do your best!" served as the call to arms. In 1856, when Guy Bryan was running for a seat in the state senate, he stopped at an isolated house in his district. A woman answered the door, explained that her husband wasn't home, and after a brief pause, she asked, "Mr. Bryan, do you remember two little girls and a stalled wagon in the Runaway Scrape? I am one of those little girls. My mother taught us that whenever we could do Mrs. Perry or one of her family a favor we must do it. You need not wait for my husband. He will vote for you." (Guy was elected.)

From Buffalo Bayou, the Perrys headed to a friend's plantation a few miles south of Lynch's Ferry on the San Jacinto River. With his family apparently safe, James Perry reported for military duty at Galveston Island, where he helped to provide for the many people who had taken refuge there. When Santa Anna's pursuit of the government and Houston put the people near the San Jacinto in peril, the Perrys joined James at Galveston Island and were on board a ship in the bay when the decisive battle took place.

After learning of the defeat at the Alamo, Sam Houston, from the city of Gonzales, ordered James Fannin to withdraw his troops from Goliad to Victoria, where they could help block a further eastward advance by Santa Anna's army toward the Anglo settlements. Fannin, a West Point dropout with little or no tactical expertise, delayed for five days before retreating, and even then moved so slowly that he and about three hundred men were overtaken by Mexican cavalry commanded by General José de Urrea at Coleto Creek, less than ten miles east of Goliad (the battle site is where the town of Fannin now stands; during the second half of the nineteenth century, the settlement was known both as Fanning's Defeat and Perdido). For one day, the Texans held off Urrea's troops, which had added infantry to bring their strength to about fifteen hundred. On the second day, with no water to clean and cool the Texans' cannons, Fannin, outnumbered by three or four to one, offered to surrender on condition that he and his men were to be treated as prisoners of war, allowed to treat their wounded, and receive parole to leave Texas for the United States. Unable to guarantee these terms, Urrea could promise only to recommend clemency to Santa Anna. A week after the surrender, on March 27, Colonel José Nicolás de la Portilla, acting on Santa Anna's orders, had all the prisoners (who thought that they were being put on work assignment or marched to prison in San Antonio) shot in what became known as the Goliad Massacre.

Vastly outnumbered by the Mexican army in Texas, Houston's troops were also no match for the enemy in training or weapons. Houston therefore pursued tactics aimed at avoiding a confrontation with Santa Anna until he was able to recruit more soldiers and train and equip them. As he wrote to James Collinsworth, chairman of the military affairs committee, "We could have met the enemy and avenged some of our wrongs but detached as we were, without supplies for the men in camp of either provisions, ammunition, or artillery and remote from succor, it would have been madness to hazard a contest. . . . By falling back, Texas can rally and defeat any force that can come against her." He was determined to bide his time and wait until the odds turned in the Texans' favor.

Houston burned Gonzales on March 13, then led his army on a retreat eastward toward the Colorado River, south of what is now Austin. Complaints from the men that they had come to fight, not run, didn't let up until the battle of San Jacinto on April 21. Complicating matters yet further, the route of the army's retreat often overlapped with that of the fleeing refugees. Along the way, Houston was sometimes forced to halt to assist the progress of the crowds of noncombatants. Of course, the farther east the Mexican army advanced, the more communities they overran, forcing the citizens to join the flight. Mary Rabb was one of those who was forced to join the exodus with her family. About the ordeal, Mary wrote, "Then we was all drove out of our houses with our little ones to suffer with cold and hungry and little Lorenzy not three months when we started died on the road . . . there was many births and deaths on that road while we was running from the Mexicans."

Somehow, Houston managed to maintain a semblance of order among both civilians and soldiers, despite the persistent problem of deserters, who often fled in a panic that "was contagious, and all who saw them breathed the poison and fled," as he wrote to Rusk. In that same letter, he congratulated Rusk on his appointment as secretary of war (with a touch of humor, he added, "I trust you will find in me a worthy subaltern") and confessed to the toll the Texans' perilous military situation had taken on his state of mind. "You know I am not easily depressed, but, before my God, since we parted, I have found the darkest hours of my past life! My excitement has been so great, that, for forty-eight hours, I have not eaten an ounce, nor have I slept." Nevertheless, he controlled his army with a firm hand, kept the provisional government of Texas informed of his movements, and safeguarded the welfare of the refugees, even when that required, as in one case near the Guadalupe River, sending a "guard thirty miles for a poor blind widow (and six children), whose husband was killed in the Alamo."

Through sheer force of will, he disciplined his army, and his confidence in his generalship was unassailable. "On my arrival on the Brazos, had I consulted the wishes of all, I should have been like the ass between two stacks of hay," he wrote to Rusk, referring to the famous logical dilemma of a donkey who starves to death because it cannot choose between two equidistant sources of food. But he complained that the decision of the government to relocate the provisional capital from Washington-on-the-Brazos to Harrisburg would have "a bad effect" on the troops' morale. "For Heaven's sake," he warned, "do not drop back again with the seat of government! Your removal to Harrisburg has done more to increase the panic in the country than anything else that has occurred in Texas, except the fall of the Alamo."

Crucially, Houston was unaffected by the shortage of well-trained fighting men and the drain of manpower through desertions, thanks to a continuing influx of new volunteers. When two captured Mexican spies reported that Santa Anna's troop strength was only three-quarters the size that had earlier been reported, he was pleased but not overly impressed. "Let the Mexican force be what it may, if the country will turn out, we can beat them. . . . The Mexicans cannot fight us upon anything like fair terms," he told Rusk. "I will get any advantage I can if I fight."

After Dilue Rose and her family contingent (five white families and some two dozen slaves from William Stafford's plantation) crossed Buffalo Bayou at Vince's Bridge, the ten miles or so through prairie and marsh to the San Jacinto crossing at Lynch's Ferry took an entire day. Dilue Rose estimated that five thousand people were already at the point, and there was a three-day wait for the ferry. One witness compared the crowd to "a camp meeting; it was covered with carts, wagons, horses, mules, tents, men, women and children, and all the baggage of a flying multitude," and Dilue Rose described the scene as "almost a riot."

Since the path the fleeing families followed brought them close to their fathers, brothers, and husbands who had volunteered for the Texas army, Dilue Rose thought it was only natural that some of those men joined their families as the twin migrations approached the Trinity River. "I know they have been blamed for this, but what else could they have done?" she asked, adding that the men planned "to see their families across the Sabine River, and then return and fight the Mexicans." The causes for concern went beyond the privations and disease that dogged the weary, ill-fed refugees at every step. They also feared attacks on the defenseless refugees by hostile Indians or rebellious slaves.

Despite some reports of slaves who took advantage of the chaos to escape, Dilue Rose's account attests to the fact that

they more often played a steadying role during a time when
many families were overwhelmed. In fact, when she wrote, "I
must say for the negroes that there was no insubordination
among them; they were loyal to their owners," she told only
part of the story. Some of the slaves' actions bespoke a selfless
devotion, and not only to their owners. The twenty to thirty
slaves who were traveling with the Rose family belonged to
Adam and Maria Stafford, who were away at the time. The person responsible for the Staffords' slaves, crowded onto a large
wagon drawn by five teams of oxen, horses, and mules, was one
of their number. Dilue knew him as Uncle Ned, and he was
most likely the slave foreman on the Stafford plantation itself.
When the Rose group's little caravan started on its way across
the prairie between the San Jacinto and Trinity rivers, the large
wagon and the four carts carrying all the white children got
bogged in the mud. Dilue's mother took all the children into
the cart she had been riding in and settled them down. All the
children quickly went to sleep, except one, Eli Dyer, who cried
until Uncle Ned carried him to his wagon, where the boy spent
the night sleeping in the old man's arms.

Once they had crossed to the east bank of the Trinity, the
Roses left the other members of their party behind and hurried toward the prairie, because one of Dilue's younger sisters was sick and suffering from convulsions. The other men
led the horses and oxen to the prairie so that they could feed;
the remaining travelers had to spend the night in the flooded
lowlands. To protect the white women and children overnight,
Uncle Ned shifted them to the large wagon, which had a cover,
transferred the black women and children to the open carts,
and kept watch on everyone, white and black, until daybreak.

When Dilue wrote, "Our hardships began at the Trinity," she
was thinking about her own gravely ill sister, of course, but also
about the nearly epidemic suffering that had spread through
the exhausted mass of refugees. "Measles, sore eyes, whooping
cough, and every other disease that man, woman, or child is

heir to, broke out among us." Along with the families of other seriously ill children, the Roses' group was among the first to cross the river, but still their progress was slow. The Trinity had flooded its banks; it took eight men to steer the ferryboat and several hours to make the crossing.

Back on land, one of their neighbors, the mother of Eli Dyer, lent the Roses her horse, which allowed both parents to ride, Pleasant Rose carrying their sick daughter in his arms and Margaret Rose riding the other horse while holding her infant girl with Dilue perched behind her. Besides the clothes they wore, they carried nothing else with them; bedding and extra clothing had been left behind. Luck was with them to the extent that they managed to get across a bridge over a slough that had flooded just before it collapsed under the weight of the ox-drawn cart behind them, drowning the oxen and stranding everyone who remained on the other side. The next morning the stranded travelers were floated across the slough on a raft that some of the men, including Dr. Rose, worked through the night to build. They had to assemble the raft in the water, using timber cut from the pine grove where the refugees were camped. Once safely across the slough, the people were carried on horseback to the prairie, the horses shuttling back and forth across the flooded lowlands. Retrieving clothing and bedding took another two days. There again, Uncle Ned made sure that the women and children were brought across first. Then he stayed behind with the carts and wagons until their contents had been unloaded and transported and all the vehicles brought to the prairie. The large Stafford wagon was the last to be moved, four days after the ordeal had begun.

Again and again as the refugees trudged eastward, people divided the little they had with complete strangers. When the Roses reached higher ground east of the Trinity River, a woman Dilue identified only as "Mrs. Foster" invited the newcomers to share their supper and bedding with them and provided mother and daughters with dry clothing. The women who offered meals and shelter did so spontaneously, out of their sense of common humanity and shared suffering. Although the interim government under President Burnet did set up one refugee camp on Buffalo Bayou and tried to supply the refugees with food, it had too few resources at its command to make much difference. Parents and children had to fend for themselves, and they mostly succeeded, despite the uncertainty, exhaustion, and danger. It was at the Trinity that Angelina Peyton Eberly was struck by the fact that the refugees often chose the "prettiest trees to camp under," and spent their evenings visiting, playing music, and dancing. On one occasion, she even witnessed a wedding.

On the east bank of the Trinity, the Roses camped a few miles from the town of Liberty. It was early April, according to Dilue's memoir, and the townsfolk, who had not been evacuated, came to the refugees' aid. Within a few days, however, Dilue's ailing sister died and was buried in the local cemetery. Afterward, the other families with whom the Roses had been traveling resumed their eastward journey, but the Roses decided to remain at Liberty. Margaret Rose was exhausted, physically and emotionally. "She had nursed an infant and the sick child until she was compelled to rest." They stayed put even after the news reached them that the government, pursued by Santa Anna, had fled to Galveston Island, and the residents of Liberty began to head east as well. Before leaving town, a local family named Martin invited the Roses to move into their house. That's where they were on the afternoon of April 21, when "all of a sudden we heard a sound like distant thunder." Dr. Rose, who had served in the War of 1812, recognized it as a cannonade that signaled that the Texan and Mexican armies were fighting. From the volume, Dr. Rose estimated that the armies were close to the Trinity River, and when the cannon reports stopped after a few minutes, he feared that the Texans had been defeated. The Roses fled Liberty immediately, in the cart Dr. Rose had bought from the man whose oxen had drowned, and on horseback, together with three other families who had been camping in the town. "We were as wretched as we could be; for we had been five weeks from home, and there was not much prospect of our ever returning. We had not heard a word from brother or the other boys that were driving the cattle. Mother was sick, and we had buried our dear little sister at Liberty."

The army's only artillery pieces were two cannon, a gift from supporters of Texan independence in Cincinnati, Ohio. The pair of six-pounders were christened the Twin Sisters in commemoration of the fact that they were presented to Texas officials by Elizabeth and Eleanor Rice, twin daughters of Dr. Charles Rice of Cincinnati, who accompanied them from New Orleans to Galveston Island. They arrived in Galveston in early April 1836 without limbers, the two-wheeled carriages on which cannon or other guns are mounted for mobility. As a result, they were difficult to transport and weren't delivered to the army, who were encamped west of the Brazos River, until April 11. Moving the cannon remained a problem, one that Houston thought he had solved when Pamelia Mann, a well-known innkeeper who was a friend and supporter of the general, agreed to lend the army a yoke of oxen. For several days, while it seemed that both the army and the train of refugees were heading in the same direction, toward Nacogdoches, Pamelia Mann's oxen dutifully hauled their valuable cargo.

But on April 17, Houston decided to begin stalking Santa Anna. At a fork in the road, he turned his army south, toward Harrisburg. From spies captured by his scouts or intercepted dispatches, Houston had learned that in his zeal to seize President Burnet and his cabinet, Santa Anna had personally led a relatively small force to Harrisburg and from there to New Washington before abandoning the chase, leaving the rest of the Mexican army west of the Brazos. Santa Anna's plan was to continue to Nacogdoches, in order to intercept Houston before he reached the Sabine and crossed over to safety in the United States. But Houston had seen his chance to engage the enemy while its forces were cut in two. He hurried his men toward Buffalo Bayou, marching them over fifty miles in just two and a half days. By acting swiftly, he would drive a wedge between the two halves of the Mexican army and be able to stake out a favorable position from which to confront Santa Anna at the San Jacinto River. Houston's strategy was sound, and it paid off.

According to Robert Hunter, a soldier whose diary is the source for several versions of the story, Houston had already covered ten miles when Pamelia Mann caught up with him. She was on horseback, with "a pair of holster pistols on her saddle pummel and a very large knife on her saddle." She accused Houston, who had famously confided his plans to no one, of lying to her about where his army was headed and demanded the return of her oxen. When Houston protested that he couldn't move the cannon without them, she replied, "I don't care a damn for your cannon, I want my oxen," and dismounting from her horse, cut the rawhide tug chain that bound the yoked oxen to the wagon, got back on her horse, and led the team away.

When Conrad Rohrer, Houston's wagonmaster, insisted on recovering the oxen, the general let him try his luck after warning him, "Rohrer, that woman will fight." As soon as Rohrer had ridden off, Houston, with the mud reaching the tops of his boots, led a group of men over to the wagon, freed it from the mud, and pushed it another six miles before stopping to camp for the night. When Rohrer returned, his shirt was badly torn, and some of the men joked that Mrs. Mann had turned it into "baby rags."

Outspoken, litigious, and sometimes profane, Pamelia Mann nevertheless ingratiated herself with the citizenry of San Felipe, Washington-on-the-Brazos, and Houston, where her Mansion House Hotel became a popular meeting place for officials of the republic, including President Sam Houston (who also attended the wedding of Pamelia's son Flournoy Hunt), and army officers. Her acceptance was surprising in view of the fact that between 1836 and her death in 1840, Pamelia Mann was said to have been involved in more lawsuits and prosecuted for more crimes than anyone in Texas. Charges ranged from counterfeiting, forgery, and larceny to assault and fornication (it was said that the Mansion House was a brothel as well as a hotel and the scene of frequent brawls). In 1839, she was convicted of forgery and sentenced to death, but President Mirabeau B. Lamar granted her a pardon. When she died of yellow fever a year later, her estate was valued at forty thousand dollars.

We will probably never know whether Pamelia Mann was the disreputable woman her court record makes her out to be or an independent, outspoken, tough businesswoman who, as she said about herself, could not be bought by money. One eulogist, the Methodist minister O. M. Addison, understood her as a creature of her time and place: "In the absence of law and order and the restraints of refined society," he wrote, Mrs. Mann was "a widow and forced, perhaps from injustice to others to step forward in her own defense, and meet lawless men on their own grounds; it was but natural that she should have developed the rude and free-spoken temper of times and people among whom she lived."

Nacogdoches, where nearly all the refugees were headed when Pamelia Mann and Sam Houston faced off over her oxen, was so far east that its citizens did not flee until shortly before the battle of San Jacinto. Even then, the townspeople were more alarmed about the possibility of Indian attacks on the elderly, women, and children than being overrun by the Mexican army. The small garrison, thirty men commanded by Hugh McLeod, a young West Point graduate, was unable to dispel the panic that swept through the residents. According to Kate Scurry Terrell, in her account of the Runaway Scrape, it was the men who were "wild with excitement and terror." The women, in contrast, told by McLeod to evacuate the town, remained calm as they "placed their children and such things

as were indispensable in the wagons, and started on their perilous march." One reason Kate Terrell gave was the presence of
Mary (Polly) Rusk, the wife of Secretary of War Thomas Rusk,
whom Terrell called "a true and fit 'helpmeet' . . . to the noblest
and most disinterested [selfless] patriot Texas ever knew." Men,
fleeing on horseback, rode full-speed past the women and children in wagons and on foot, trying to escape from pursuing Indians (who, as it happened, never appeared). Polly Rusk calmly
reassured her compatriots that "the army was between them
and the Mexicans, and the thirty men at Nacogdoches would
fill bloody graves before the Indians could reach them." To one
man who cried, "Hurry up or the Indians will scalp you!" as he
rushed past, Polly Rusk answered, "You will save *your* scalp if
your horse holds out."

As I mentioned earlier, my great-great-grandmother Anna
Mary Taylor also participated in the Runaway Scrape. Anna
Mary and her three young children fled from Nacogdoches,
east to Natchitoches, Louisiana, where all the children eventually died and were buried.

At Buffalo Bayou on April 19, Houston prepared his troops
for the battle ahead and reminded them of the score they had
come to settle:

> We view ourselves on the eve of battle. We are nerved for
> the contest, and must conquer or perish. It is vain to look
> for present aid: for it is not there. We must now act or
> abandon all hope! Rally to the standard, and be no longer
> the scoff of mercenary tongues! Be men, be free men, that
> your children may bless their father's name. . . . The army
> will cross, and we will meet the enemy. Some of us may
> be killed, and must be killed. But, soldiers, remember the
> Alamo! the Alamo! the Alamo!

According to the story, Rusk tried to speak to the men afterward but his voice failed him. He did manage to pen an appeal

for more volunteers, in which he wrote, "I look around and see that many, very many, whom I anticipated would be first in the field, are not here. Rise up at once, concentrate, and march to the field!—a vigorous effort and the country is safe!" Houston added a postscript that challenged Texas to "rally to the standard." Some new volunteers did trickle in before the decisive battle, but those who did were assigned to the camp guard. Houston's army in the field on April 21 was essentially the one he had led across the bayou two days earlier.

On the east side of Buffalo Bayou, Houston had his men encamp in the woods that bordered the water and positioned the "Twin Sisters" on the prairie facing San Jacinto Bay. When the Mexicans reached the area that afternoon they would be forced to take up a position that afforded less natural protection. After a brief, inconclusive exchange of artillery fire and an ill-advised cavalry attack on the Texans' part, in which Mirabeau Lamar led a sortie to extricate Thomas Rusk from possible capture, both sides retired to prepare for the next day's battle. Houston, impressed by Lamar's courage, promoted him to colonel in charge of the Texas cavalry.

On the morning of April 21, Houston waited until noon to hold a council of war with his six field officers and Secretary of War Rusk. After General Martín Perfecto de Cos crossed Vince's Bridge at Sims Bayou with five hundred additional Mexican troops, Erastus "Deaf" Smith set fire to the bridge, cutting off access to the battlefield for the other Mexican generals, Vicente Filisola and José de Urrea, and their armies. The question of whether even at this late hour Houston continued to delay until his officers forced his hand will probably never be settled, but as historian Randolph B. Campbell has written, "the fact is that the army did attack and Houston commanded it." Not only did Houston dictate the plan of attack, he led the Texans' charge to within twenty yards of the Mexican position, astride Saracen, the fine gray stallion he bought from Isom Parmer. Both horse and rider were among the first casualties of the battle; Houston's tibia was broken by a musket ball and Saracen was struck numerous times and finally collapsed. Unable to stand, Houston had to be put on another horse in order to return to the Texans' camp.

The Roses wrote that as they were searching for a way to cross the swollen Trinity that fateful day, they saw a rider approaching, waving his hat and shouting. When he was within earshot, they heard him crying, "Turn back! The Texas army has whipped the Mexican army and the Mexican army are prisoners! No danger! No danger! Turn back!" He carried with him a copy of Houston's statement describing the battle and informing the refugees that it was safe to return to their homes. The messenger, an Irishman named McDermot, had been at San Jacinto; he had crossed the Trinity River in a canoe, with his horse swimming alongside him, in order to bring word to families that had gotten caught up in the Runaway Scrape. There was also a group of young men camped nearby, volunteers from the United States who were on their way to join Houston's army. When they heard about the victory, they proposed firing a salute, but Dr. Rose told them to save their ammunition in case there were more battles to come. That was exactly what Houston himself was worried about at the time; Santa Anna had escaped from the battlefield, and if he had succeeded in reaching General Filisola and the eighteen hundred men under his command, the outcome of the war might have been different. In fact, when Houston saw Rusk, in the distance, at the head of a column of several hundred captured Mexican regulars to the rear of the battlefield, he momentarily mistook them for Filisola's troops, and cried, "All is lost; all is lost; my God, all is lost!" When the officers around Houston determined that it was Rusk leading the prisoners away from the continuing slaughter, one lieutenant joked, "Rusk has a very respectable army now."

There are any number of accounts of Santa Anna's escape from San Jacinto and his capture the next day, but the important differences between them have mainly to do with whether he revealed who he was immediately and demanded to be taken to Houston, or attempted to hide his identity. The most common belief is that when he was discovered, Santa Anna was hiding in the tall grass, dressed in just a shirt and pants. Brought in as a prisoner, his identity was discovered because the other Mexican captives said as he passed, "El General," "El Presidente!" Then the Texans knew they had captured the Mexican leader, and Santa Anna was brought to Houston. Unable to stand after having been shot during the battle's first moments, Houston lay under a large oak tree. Several officers gathered to help interpret for the two generals, among them Moses Austin Bryan, Stephen F. Austin's nephew, who spoke Spanish, and Lorenzo de Zavala Jr., son of the vice president. Colonel Juan Almonte, an American-educated Mexican officer, also joined the group, either at Houston's or Santa Anna's request.

Many versions of the exchange between the two leaders exist, and some purported quotes sound like lines that have been burnished over time. Santa Anna, upon surrendering, may not have addressed Houston in exactly these words, "The conqueror of the Napoleon of the West is born to no common destiny, and he can afford to be generous to the vanquished," nor can we be sure, as has been claimed, that Houston replied, "You should have remembered that, sir, at the Alamo." But George Bernard Erath, who was present, reported thinking that Santa Anna was "a great diplomatist," who gave ground only gradually, although in the end he agreed to everything Houston sought, in particular recognition of Texas independence and the withdrawal from the soil of the new republic of all the Mexican troops who had not been captured.

Secretary of War Thomas Rusk wrote the report of the battle of San Jacinto to President of Texas David G. Burnet:

The sun was sinking in the horizon as the battle commenced; but, at the close of the conflict, the sun of liberty and independence rose in Texas, never, it is to be hoped,

to be obscured by the clouds of despotism. . . . There was
a general cry which pervaded the ranks: "Remember the
Alamo!" "Remember La Bahia! (Goliad)" These words
electrified all. "Onward!" was the cry. The unerring aim
and irresistible energy of the Texas army could not be with-
stood. It was freemen fighting against the minions of tyr-
anny and the results proved the inequality of such a contest.

There were only nine Texans killed in the battle, while the
Mexicans lost 630 men.

Margaret (Peggy) McCormick owned the land on which the
battle of San Jacinto was fought. She and her husband, Arthur,
had come to Texas from Ireland in 1823 or 1824 and received
their league of land in August of that year. Arthur died, of
drowning, late in 1824; his widow and their two sons, Michael
and John, stayed on, raising cattle, which they sold to buyers
from Louisiana. When the McCormicks fled across the Trinity
as Santa Anna approached, their livestock was slaughtered for
food by Texans and Mexicans alike. After the battle, they found
their land littered with the more than six hundred bodies of the
Mexican casualties. The dead became counters in the battle of
wills between Houston, who wanted the Mexicans to bury their
comrades, and Santa Anna, who refused on the questionable
grounds that San Jacinto had not been a military encounter but
a massacre.

The illiterate but practical Mrs. McCormick surprised Houston when, two or three days after the battle, she demanded that
he remove the bodies from her property. Houston, who was renowned for his spontaneous eloquence, is said to have replied,
"Madam, your land will be famed in history as the classic spot
upon which the glorious victory of San Jacinto was gained! Here
was born, in the throes of revolution, and amid the strife of con-
tending legions, the infant of Texas independence! Here that
latest scourge of mankind, the arrogantly self-styled 'Napoleon
of the West,' met his fate!"

Peggy McCormick wasn't interested in posterity. Her reply was as pointed as it was brief: "To the devil with your 'glorious history'! Take off your stinking Mexicans." But for weeks afterward, no one buried the Mexican dead. When the Rose family visited the battlefield five days after the fighting, Dilue noted that "the dead Mexicans were lying around in every direction." When they left, "We had to pass among the dead Mexicans, and father pulled one out of the road, so we could get by without driving over the body, since we could not go around it." From their campsite on the prairie, the Roses "could hear the wolves howl and bark as they devoured the dead."

Unburied, the bodies lay exposed to the elements and were preyed upon by wolves, coyotes, and buzzards. Weeks later, their skeletons were finally buried by the locals, not out of a sense of propriety but because when their cows chewed on the bones, they "imparted such a sickening odor and taste to the beef and milk that neither could be used."

Despite her unsought notoriety as owner of the San Jacinto battlefield, Peggy McCormick's life should have been a success story. By 1850, she owned one of the largest cattle-raising operations in Harris County, quite an achievement for a self-made woman, widowed and with no education. Unbeknownst to her or her sons, however, local officials swindled her out of almost all her land, first by ordering a resurvey of her acreage that turned half her property into "unowned land" that ended up in the hands of the county surveyor, and then through an 1845 sheriff's auction that transferred ownership of her remaining land to the county clerk except for the fifty acres surrounding her home. Her son Michael discovered the sales only when he attempted to settle her estate after her death in 1854. Even her death itself, in a fire that consumed her house, was suspicious, and Michael McCormick's suit to recover his mother's property was denied.

With Santa Anna and his army now prisoners of war, the refugees no longer feared for their lives, but returning home was not without its own dangers. The Rose family set off the next morning, but it continued to rain and there were treacherous passages. On the west side of the Trinity River, travelers had to cross Trinity Bay by skirting a bayou where there were patches of quicksand and alligators. Dilue Rose reported that a few days before the battle of San Jacinto, one man crossing in the opposite direction had brought his family over safely but was caught by an alligator as he attempted to swim his horses across the bayou. Men who were nearby tried to shoot the alligator but were unable to save their neighbor. The Roses were fortunate; when they crossed, only Dilue's sunbonnet floated away in the current. Dr. Rose's horse also disappeared, but the family was in such a hurry to get home that he decided to return later to look for it.

When the returning refugees reached the burned-out bridge at Sims Bayou, many rested for a day or two to allow their animals to pasture. For them, the voyage home was bittersweet. They were relieved to be returning, of course, but signs of the destruction wrought by the war were visible everywhere. Entire towns and villages had been burned, by the advancing Mexican army or on Houston's orders as he retreated. "San Felipe had been burned, and dear old Harrisburg was in ashes," Dilue wrote. The loss of the few rudimentary elements of industry, such as the Harrisburg sawmill and the sugar and grist mills and cotton mill at the Stafford plantation near the Roses' home, was a demoralizing blow to the returnees. Only the store of corn at the plantation had not been destroyed, and as a result local residents were able to bake bread.

The Roses' small house in Stafford's Point had been ransacked. Dr. Rose's bookcase had been "broken open, his books, medicines, and other things scattered on the ground, and the hogs sleeping on them." Dilue, her sister, and a neighbor's children began tidying up. Among the things that were missing were the Sunday school books William B. Travis had sent the girls from San Felipe (he had befriended the Roses when he came to Stafford's Point for a trial in 1834), but they "did find broken toys that belonged to our dear little sister that died." Until that moment, Dilue said, the thrill of the victory at San Jacinto had put "our sad bereavement" (her sister's death) out of their minds. But at least the Rose family was home and starting to rebuild their lives. Dr. Rose immediately went out to plow his cornfield, and Dilue was sent to Stafford's Point, to bring her brother, Granville, home. When they got back, her mother was doing laundry. "I was shocked, for mother had always kept the Sabbath." But on Sunday, May 1, 1836, there was no time to lose in picking up the pieces.

Anna Raguet

The woman who was most on Houston's mind after the battle of San Jacinto was undoubtedly Anna Raguet, the seventeen-year-old daughter of his friend Henry Raguet, a businessman in Nacogdoches who had met Houston in New Orleans in 1833 and brought his family to Texas soon afterward. After meeting Anna, Houston, then forty, hired a lawyer to secure a divorce from Eliza Allen, from whom he had separated under mysterious circumstances in 1829. It is generally assumed that he entertained thoughts of marrying Anna as soon as he met her, despite the fact that she was only fourteen at the time. Although divorce was prohibited under Mexican law, it may be that Houston intended to secure a decree in Tennessee.

Anna, blue-eyed, blond-haired, and beautiful (like Eliza Allen, in fact), had grown up in Cincinnati, spoke French, Spanish, and German as well as English, and was a talented musician. By all accounts, she was the belle of Nacogdoches from the moment the Raguets settled there and was pursued by many men closer to her own age, but she seems to have enjoyed Houston's attentions and to have encouraged them, despite—or even because of—his notoriety. He posed as a bachelor, but after separating from Eliza Allen, he had spent two years living with the Cherokees, where he entered into a tribal marriage with Tiana Rogers, daughter of Chief Oolooteka. Houston had earlier lived with Oolooteka's band on Hiwassee Island, Tennessee, from 1809 to 1811. At that time the chief adopted Houston and gave him the Cherokee name Ka'lanu (Raven).

Houston's infatuation with the clever, beautiful young woman was probably all the justification he needed for dedicating his victory over the Mexican army to her, but the story is told that he promised to do so after Anna saved him from an assassination attempt on the night before he left Nacogdoches to take command of the Texas army in March 1836. At a dinner in his honor, in this account, Houston was seated with his back to an open doorway. Anna, sitting opposite the guest of honor, noticed a movement in the moonlit garden and rushed to catch the would-be assassin's wrist as he was about to plunge a knife into Houston's back.

Somewhat more plausible is the story that when Houston complained about not being able to wear his sword because he didn't have a sash for it, Anna jumped at the chance to stitch one together out of silk the Raguets had on hand, tied it about the general's waist, and, "in the custom of the day," cut off a lock of his hair as a keepsake.

In return, Houston promised to send the laurels of his military triumphs to the young woman.

Anna and her mother, Marcia Ann (Mercy) Raguet, are credited with designing and sewing a Lone Star flag for the new republic, which was hung from the second story of the Stone Fort before Houston departed the next morning. After the battle of San Jacinto, he made good on his promise, weaving a garland of leaves (some say of oak leaves, others of magnolia) that he sent to Anna with this brief note: "To Miss Anna Raguet, Nacogdoches, Texas: These are laurels I send you from the battle field of San Jacinto. Thine. Houston." Anna incorporated these motifs into the seal she later designed for the new republic, which included the lone star and branches of wild magnolia and oak.

Houston persisted in his attentions to Anna for several more years, although it is not clear whether she ever seriously considered him a suitable candidate for marriage. He undoubtedly saw her when he came to Nacogdoches and continued to write to her, often including reminders of the military honors he had dedicated to her and promising more in the future. In a new year's letter in 1837, Houston thanked Anna "for placing my armor when we parted," predicted more battles to come, and wrote, "I hope the spell will last, and if I am not mistaken you shall have more laurels. If I win them, you shall have them."

With the letter, he enclosed a poem, "March, Chieftain," on the same theme. It ends:

> Should I return from well-fought fields
> I'll bring again thy warrior's shield
> And at thy feet I'll proudly yield
> The laurels won for thee.

Nor did Houston hide his intentions. In another letter of January 1837, he told her, "I will not marry until I can once more go to Nacogdoches and see how my matters stand there! And if my tenants have erected me comfortable cabins, why then I may look out for a 'spare rib' to appropriate to myself."

The end of the courtship almost certainly came in 1837, when Houston, having received a Texas divorce from Eliza Allen, made his marriage hopes more explicit. Anna conceded that "aspiring demagogues cannot rob from the brow of the hero of San Jacinto laurels so justly earned. His fame is fixed," but she had no desire to become the hero's consort. Houston interpreted her rejection as proof that she believed the claims that he was not free to marry, and he defended himself with great indignation and a touch of self-pity:

> You (I assert it with great pleasure) and myself have been friends, and I so highly appreciate your worth as to believe that you would not assume to be the friend of anyone whom you did not believe possessed the most undoubted honor and sense of rectitude. Then had I addressed you or sought to win your love. . . . I must have acknowledged myself a "lily liver'd wretch"!!! I believed I was as free from all legal or moral hindrance to any union. . . . I was honest. I was devoted!!! . . . This much I have felt bound to say to

you on the score of old friendship and a desire to evince to you that I have merited (at least in part) the esteem with which you have honored me in bygone days.

Both Houston's feelings and those of Secretary of State Dr. Robert Irion were certainly well known in Nacogdoches. A letter to Irion from my great-great-grandfather, Judge Charles S. Taylor, dated July 17, 1837, was a report on a business issue; but the postscript written with a wry twist noted, " . . . A lady of your acquaintance [Anna Raguet] says she has no one to ride with her, and hopes you will return soon. Grievous, aint it?" Another, dated April 14, 1838, was a more social note, including the information that all their friends were well and "Miss Anna has not yet returned from the U.S. but is expected daily."

But Houston could not quite get the idea of marrying Anna out of his mind until he met Margaret Lea in May 1839. In July, he wrote to Robert Irion from Nashville, Tennessee, perhaps to encourage him in his own pursuit of Anna. Referring to her—more than once—as "a great woman," he wondered, rhetorically, "Who will marry her?" and admitted that "if she were out of the way, I would be better off in my feelings." Indeed, Irion did have his own hopes where Anna, now twenty, was concerned. When his first wife, Ann Vick, died of cholera in 1832, he left their daughter, Elizabeth, with his in-laws in Tennessee and sought a new start in Texas. As Houston's friend and secretary of state, he had gotten to know Anna well, in part because he often carried their letters back and forth. Despite the objections of Henry Raguet—perhaps because Irion was fifteen years Anna's senior—Anna and Robert married in March 1840. Sam and Margaret were married that May.

The Houstons and Irions remained close friends. Anna and Robert's first child, born in 1842, was named Sam Houston Irion.

Anna and Robert's marriage produced five children, but their relations were not always placid. Overindulgence in alcohol was not unusual in those turbulent times on the Texas frontier; it had affected Anna's earlier suitor, Sam Houston, and it caused a rift in her marriage to Robert. A series of personal letters written around Christmas 1852 revealed that they had separated. Robert beseeched Anna to forgive him and reconcile. He wrote that he was now sober and intended to remain so. They did reconcile and their fifth child, James Raguet Irion, was born in 1855.

Robert died in Nacogdoches in 1861; Anna survived him by twenty-two years. Their daughter, Harriet Durst Irion, married Charles and Anna Mary Taylor's son Lawrence in 1870 in Nacogdoches. (Anna and Harriet's ivory silk handmade wedding dresses have been preserved at the Old Stone Fort Museum on the campus of Stephen F. Austin State University in Nacogdoches.)

Mary "Polly" Rusk

What little is written about Mary Cleveland Rusk describes her as being very pretty and gentle. She came from a prominent military family in Georgia, where she met Thomas Rusk, who moved to Polly's hometown of Clarksville at the age of twenty-one to practice law. Her father, General John Cleveland, fought in the War of 1812 and also served in the Georgia legislature. After Polly and Thomas married in 1827, they remained in Clarksville for several years. At first, his law practice prospered, but after he was swindled in an investment, Thomas decided to start fresh and traveled on horseback to Texas. His first stop was Nacogdoches. There he met another lawyer, Sam Houston, who impressed and befriended him. There was unrest in this Mexican territory of Texas and Thomas quickly became a part of the revolution to separate from Mexico.

Thomas wrote to Polly from Nacogdoches in February 1835:

. . . I have been in this town about four weeks and have now seen enough of this country to make up my mind to remove to Texas and live. I prefer this part of the country for several reasons. It is not as rich land as some other part[s] but taking it all together it is better on account of health and good society than any part of the whole country. It will be as healthy here as on the Blue Ridge and the climate is much more mild and pleasant and the society here is much better than in Clarkesville.

There are in this town about three hundred Americans and two hundred Spaniards and the country affords all the conveniences and most of the luxuries of life and those who will be prudent and industrious here must become wealthy very soon. . . . I find the practice of law here will be pretty good business, there being few men in the country that are talented. Governor Houston lives in this place and has made over two thousand dollars in the last twelve months but he is very dissipated and in very bad health. The opening here I consider very good.

I have a speculation on foot here which if I succeed at it will make me a fortune and if I fail I shall lose nothing. I have become well acquainted with some of the most distinguished men in the country and they all profess great friendship and make many kind offers of their services to me and upon the whole I have taken a much better stand amongst them than I had any right to have expected so soon. I shall procure a tract of land in the neighborhood if I can. . . . I will try to have a year's provisions laid up for all of us by fall. . . .

You must write me to Natchitoches (Louisiana) from which place I can get your letter . . . a line from her on whom I think so often would relieve many a dull day and sleepless night . . . often do I think of that day on which we exchanged mutual pledges of our love. Often do I think of the little ones which indissolubly cement our feelings and our fate, and I pray God that the time will be short when we shall again meet each other's fond embrace, then and not until then, can I think of happiness and enjoyment. This world may have charms for others but to me it has none equal to the wife of my youth and my children . . . may heaven guide and protect you from harm and trouble and grant soon we may in love[']s fond embrace forget the past absence.

When away from thee my own loved one
And roving o'er life's shore
Fond memories of the past rush on
Of her whom I adore . . .

It was almost a year before his family was able to join him, and by that time the revolution against Mexico was in high gear. Thomas Rusk became a leader. He was elected a delegate to the convention at Washington-on-the-Brazos that declared Texas independence and was selected secretary of war for the Texan insurgents.

Though new to Texas, Polly became a beloved homemaker, known as someone who would help anyone in need during this perilous time. Her role in the Runaway Scrape as a calming influence on the nervous and scared women and children fleeing from Nacogdoches east toward Louisiana (and safety in the United States) was mentioned in writings of several participants.

Other stories relate her caring nature and generosity, bringing sick or troubled people into her home to nurse back to health. When General Hugh McLeod, the West Point graduate who helped the refugees in the Runaway Scrape, had a bout of fever in 1838, she nursed him in her home for nearly a month until he was able to regain his strength. McLeod wrote to Mirabeau B. Lamar that Mrs. Rusk had attended him with a mother's kindness.

Thomas Rusk wrote on several occasions of his guilt at leaving his beloved Polly for such long periods during the revolutionary period. He felt that she and the children were neglected in his absences. After the war, Thomas Rusk became one of the leaders in setting up the government of the new Republic of Texas. He was elected chief justice of the republic and later to its congress. When Texas became a state in 1845, he and Sam Houston were elected by the legislature to be the first U.S. senators from Texas. Nothing was ever mentioned to indicate that Polly complained. In fact, the opposite appeared to be the case. Although she raised their children with little help from her mostly absent husband, she supported his commitment to public service. She stayed home in Nacogdoches, rather than traveling with him to Austin or Washington, D.C. It appeared to both of them that providing a stable environment in which to raise the children was preferable, though personally harder for both of them.

On April 8, 1856, the family physician, Dr. Robert Irion, wrote to Senator Rusk that Polly was ill and suggested that he return home. Though her health had been deteriorating, she had not informed her husband, presumably not wanting to worry him. However, upon receiving Dr. Irion's letter and a telegraph from another friend, Senator Rusk made immediate plans to return to Nacogdoches.

On April 23, before Thomas could reach her, Polly Rusk died. According to contemporary accounts of her funeral, the church was crowded with mourners, and the minister recalled that she had borne the responsibilities of her home while her husband was gone. Rev. Yates is quoted in Mary Clarke's biography of Thomas Rusk as saying, "Who can forget her deeds of charity and goodness? She shone as a Christian mother, a good neighbor and friend."

When she died, at the age of forty-seven, Polly Rusk left five living children. The two youngest, Thomas David and Helena, ages fifteen and eleven, returned to Washington with their father, but Rusk, who was also suffering from a tumor in his neck, was inconsolable. Despite being elected president pro tempore of the U.S. Senate, he never regained his enthusiasm for his legislative calling.

A little over a year after his beloved Polly died, Thomas Rusk wrote the following letter to his children, dated July 9, 1857:

My Dear Children,

It is my design that these lines traced by the hand of a grief stricken father should not be read by you until I am cold and still in death. Since the death of your mother—now I do not doubt a Saint in heaven—a grief and melancholy has weighed me down which I have found it impossible to shake off. I have spoken but little of this matter for many reasons. If I am miserable myself I have never desired to make another human being so. I know also the uncharitable . . . of an unfriendly world and how very <u>few</u> there are who can really sympathize with distress that falls upon others. I have applied to business and as soon as an object was accomplished grief returned with more force. If I failed she was not here to sympathize with me. If I succeeded it was but a temporary gratification when she was gone from me forever. Finally I never expect to see any more peace and I feel myself totally unfitted to meet the troubles and trials of life. I must with patience suffer on my appointed time until the grave closes over and I look out upon this world no more.

On July 29, he wrote a letter ordering a tombstone for his wife's grave in Oak Grove Cemetery in Nacogdoches to be delivered to his friend James H. Starr with the following inscription:

Mary Rusk
Born August 1809
Died April 26, 1856

———

"Blessed are the pure in heart
for they shall see God"

That afternoon Thomas Rusk took his life with his own gun at his home in Nacogdoches. He was buried next to his beloved wife.

Emily Austin Bryan Perry

Prominent among the women who fought the elements and endured the trials of the Runaway Scrape was Stephen F. Austin's sister. Like many of the women who migrated to the new frontier of Texas from a privileged background in another state, Emily Margaret Austin learned resilience as well as deep love for Texas.

She was born June 22, 1795, in Austinville (named by her father), Virginia, to Maria Brown and Moses Austin. The family moved to Missouri, where Moses built a substantial home for them, but Emily spent her early school years at Mrs. Beck's Boarding School in Lexington, Kentucky.

Emily's education prepared her for an upper-class marriage, but her father's financial reverses affected both her and her brother Stephen's prospects. Stephen was forced to leave Transylvania University in Kentucky in 1810, and Emily began a relationship with a local merchant, James Bryan, five years her senior. Her mother did not approve of the budding courtship and took Emily on a trip east to look for further schooling for her and her younger brother, Brown. During their extended stay in Philadelphia with Maria's sister, Emily was introduced to art museums, libraries, and the bustling society of the biggest city she had ever encountered. After that pleasant sojourn, they moved on to New Haven, Connecticut, where Emily spent time with her cousins Henry and Mary Austin, the children of Moses's brother Elisha. They were thirteen and eleven years older than Emily, but they became very close and remained prominent in her life and in the history of Texas as well. Maria enrolled Emily in the Hermitage Academy in New York and Brown in an Episcopal school in Connecticut. Emily's education emphasized the arts, literature, and music; she became an accomplished pianist. According to her biographer, Light Townsend Cummins, after this early experience she never lived in a house without a piano.

Once again, financial reverses interfered and Moses was unable to pay for the continued schooling for the children. Moses sent James Bryan to escort his family back to Missouri in the fall of 1812. Maria dropped her opposition to James's pursuit of Emily and they were married on August 13, 1813, at Durham Hall, the home Moses Austin had built in 1798.

Emily's relatively stable life of comfort began to change in 1814, when her first child, Stephen Austin Bryan, was born and died within a month. Then more serious financial reverses afflicted the whole family—her father, brother, and husband, who had many joint business projects.

Over the next few years, Moses, Stephen, and James Bryan tried to recoup their business losses in Missouri in various ventures, and the two brothers-in-law also tried their luck in real estate in Arkansas.

In 1820, Moses went to Spanish Texas to acquire land and build a settlement in the vast untapped territory. He returned to Missouri exhausted, weak, and with a high fever. He told Maria, Emily, and James that Stephen should take his place in Texas, where he saw great promise, until Moses was able to return. That was never to be. He died June 10, 1821.

The family was destitute. Stephen, who was in New Orleans when his father died, never returned to Missouri; instead, he headed straight to Texas. His brother Brown, who had been in school on the east coast for seven years, no longer had the funds to continue his education. The family scraped money together to bring him home to Missouri, and from there Brown joined Stephen in Texas, where he was embarking on his colony adventure.

Emily now cared for her husband, three children, and her

ailing mother in their home, with no money. James's venture in Arkansas had been a failure and he tried to settle the debts, but he struggled.

In the summer of 1822, Emily had her fifth baby, Mary Elizabeth. But a fever was spreading through the town and James caught it. Days after Mary Elizabeth came into the world, James Bryan succumbed to the fever on July 16, 1822.

With four children, Emily's desperate financial straits tested her mettle. She sold her parents' home, took in a boarder, taught neighborhood children in the house, and put her family to work taking in sewing and making handicrafts to sell.

Stephen wanted Emily and the children to join him in Texas. She wanted to go but instead married James F. Perry, a Missouri merchant, on September 23, 1824, and put off moving to Texas. She was a different woman now; the obstacles she had faced made her more independent and self-reliant. That trait stayed with her the rest of her life . . . and her life in Texas was going to further test her acquired strength.

Emily had a son, Stephen Samuel, on June 24, 1825, followed by three other children in Missouri, but only two, Stephen and Eliza Perry, lived past childhood. All told, Emily bore eleven children, six of whom survived, three Bryans (Joel, Austin, Guy) and three Perrys (Stephen, Eliza, Henry). She continued to wear two wedding rings, one from each marriage, and James Perry treated all the children as his own.

The tie between Emily and her brothers was always close, and her yearning to move to Texas, along with Stephen's continued encouragement, finally persuaded James Perry as well.

Timing became more critical in the late 1820s for two reasons. Stephen procured land for the Perrys, but they needed to be in Texas to claim and protect it; and slavery was prohibited by a new Mexican constitution, which permitted slaves already within its borders to continue as indentured servants, but only if they entered Texas by 1830.

When their brother Brown died suddenly in Texas, leaving

one baby son, Stephen F. Austin Jr., Stephen was insistent that Emily and the Perry family come to Texas, writing that the prospects in the new country were on the rise, but the colony would fill up and rights to own slaves would end soon.

On June 7, 1831, James and Emily, with the Bryan and Perry children; a niece, Lavinia Perry; and nine slaves began the move to Texas. Emily also brought household goods that were hard to obtain in Texas, and defying the advice of her brother Stephen not to bring heavy furniture, insisted on taking her piano and a bed frame. The arduous journey took three months.

Their first impression of the small South Texas town, San Felipe, was similar to the experience of many new settlers—women from comfortable backgrounds moving to the primitive conditions of an undeveloped territory. Though San Felipe would not be their permanent home, Emily could not travel farther and stayed there for the birth of the baby, while James and his sons and slaves began to build a house on the property that would be their plantation. The first house the Perrys built was closer to the Gulf of Mexico, but at Stephen's urging, they eventually moved to a more populated area and settled into their permanent home at Peach Point Plantation, near present-day Freeport, Texas.

In the summer of 1833, a cholera epidemic hit the area. Many neighbors died; both Emily and James contracted the fever, but they recovered. Eleven-year-old Mary Elizabeth Bryan, however, did not survive the fever. She died in August.

Though the Perry and Austin families now owned large tracts of land, money was always scarce, and the ravages of the revolution would continue for the years leading up to and through the War of Independence in 1836, including the Runaway Scrape.

Texas had won its independence. Only months after the victory, on December 27, 1836, Emily's brother Stephen, secretary of state of the Republic of Texas, fell ill and died at the age of forty-three. James Perry and Austin Bryan were at his bedside.

When James returned home to Peach Point with the sad news,

Emily prepared to bury Stephen in the same cemetery where her daughter Mary Elizabeth lay. A large throng attended the service, including President Sam Houston, who pronounced the concluding prayer.

Emily and Stephen's nephew, Stephen F. Austin Jr. (the young son of Stephen's deceased brother, Brown), were his heirs, and James Perry was named executor of Stephen's will. However, just six weeks after Stephen's death, his eight-year-old namesake passed away as well, leaving Emily the sole heir.

Emily and James jointly administered Stephen's estate. From these earliest days, Texas was a community property state, meaning a wife owned one-half of a married couple's assets. It was also accepted that a woman's inheritance was her separate property and she had the right to control it. It seems that her independence was accepted by James, as their marriage had always been one of sharing and mutual respect.

Emily became a successful businesswoman, through her vast landholdings, and investments made possible from her joint holdings with her brother's estate. She was a founder of the San Luis Development Company. Emily raised money for and invested in Texas's first railroad, the Brazos & Galveston Railroad, of which she became the largest shareholder. The Brazos & Galveston spawned a transportation hub in the city of Bryan, Texas, named for her son Joel, who helped develop the railroad.

Peach Point and the other Perry landholdings produced both cattle and sugar in the 1840s and '50s. Emily's sons helped run the operations, but she was integral to all business decisions. Peach Point was the gathering place for the Bryan and Perry children and grandchildren. Perhaps the grandest occasion at Peach Point was the 1848 visit of Rutherford B. Hayes, her son Guy's friend from their college days at Kenyon in Ohio. Hayes had hosted Guy at his uncle's home when they were classmates at Kenyon, and Guy was pleased to reciprocate.

The future president wrote in his diary that Peach Point was "delightfully situated in the edge of timber looking out upon a plain on the south extending five or eight miles to the gulf." He described Emily as an excellent motherly sort of woman, whose happiness consists of making others happy. He was impressed with the abundance and variety of the food served at meals, the gaiety of the dances, and the enjoyment of hunting.

Emily became ill in 1850 and sought treatment in Philadelphia the following year. Her daughter Eliza, who had chronic medical problems, accompanied her. The doctors in Pennsylvania believed they could help Eliza, but Emily's illness was too advanced. She returned to Peach Point in July and died peacefully on August 15, 1851. She was buried next to her brother Stephen and daughter Mary Elizabeth Bryan. (In 1910, Stephen's body was moved to a prominent location in the Texas State Cemetery in Austin.) At her death, she was thought to be the wealthiest woman in Texas.

Guy Bryan had a distinguished public service career; he was elected to the Texas House and Senate, served in the Confederate army, and represented Texas in the U.S. Congress. The Austin, Bryan, and Perry descendants continue to play prominent roles in Texas, in business, ranching, education, and historic preservation.

One day, when I was campaigning for the Senate in 1993, I attended a reception at the home of my friends Hally and Thurman Clements, in Victoria. When I admired the silver service on the dining room sideboard, Hally responded, "Oh, thank you; it belonged to Stephen F. Austin." She had never mentioned that he was her great-grand-uncle! In fact, her grandfather was Guy Bryan . . . and her great-grandmother was Emily Austin Bryan Perry.

Part IV

INDIAN CAPTIVES

1830s–1860s

Rachel Parker Plummer
Cynthia Ann Parker

Cynthia Ann and Topsannah

The Parker family tree appears in the appendix.

Early in 1836, Sarah Creath Hibbins returned to Texas from a long visit to her family in Illinois. With her were her two sons and her brother, George Creath. Sarah's older child was the son of her first marriage, to John McSherry, who was killed by Indians in 1829. Her second husband, John, joined them at the Brazos River in February, and they continued toward their home in DeWitt County. Only fifteen miles from home, they were attacked by a small Comanche raiding party, who killed the two men and took Sarah and her children captive.

The prisoners were closely guarded by their captors at all times, as they stealthily made their way toward unsettled territory. When Sarah's infant cried on their second night, one of the Comanches crushed his skull against a tree in full view of his mother and brother. After they had taken Sarah and her surviving son, who was seven years old, across the Colorado River, the Indians' vigilance relaxed and Sarah began searching for a means of escape. One night, while everyone else was asleep, she stole away from camp, temporarily abandoning her son but hoping to find friends who would return and rescue the boy. For twenty-four hours, she searched for signs of settlement, until finally she stumbled on a herd of cattle and followed them home. By a stroke of luck, Captain John J. Tumlinson Jr. and a group of Texas Rangers were nearby, and they set off immediately in an effort to save the Hibbins boy. With a guide who knew the territory and with Sarah's directions to orient their search, they soon found the Indians' trail. They had not gone far; instead of beating a swift retreat after Sarah's escape, they had apparently spent the previous day trying to find her.

At Walnut Creek, near Austin, the Comanches were surprised by the company of Rangers. They didn't even have time to mount their horses before their pursuers gave chase, on horseback and on foot, and killed four of them. The rest of the band escaped, and two Rangers were wounded. The Comanches had fled into thick undergrowth without attempting to reach their horses; the Rangers found Sarah's son wrapped in a buffalo robe and tied to a pack mule. When the boy was reunited with his mother, Tumlinson wrote that the scene "beggars description. A mother meeting with her child released from Indian captivity, rescued, as it were, from the very jaws of death! Not an eye was dry. She called us brothers, and every other endearing name, and would have fallen on her knees to worship us. She hugged the child—her only remaining treasure—to her bosom as if fearful that she would again lose him."

Tumlinson's phrase "her only remaining treasure" serves as a grim reminder of the constant dangers surrounding settlers in Texas through much of the nineteenth century. By the time she was thirty, Sarah would be widowed three times and survive further "Indian troubles" before finally settling into a peaceful life with her fourth husband, Phillip Howard, in the 1840s.

Originally northern Shoshone Indians who lived in Idaho, Wyoming, and northeastern Utah, Comanches began migrating south in large numbers in the seventeenth century, when horses became available in the Southwest. Brought to the Americas by Spanish conquistadors, the horse made it possible for nomadic tribes like the Comanches to track the bison, central to their diets and their culture, more easily and over a much wider area. Introduced to Native Americans by Pueblo Indians, who traded the horses left behind by the Spanish when they withdrew from New Mexico toward the end of the seventeenth century, the horse drew many tribes south. Now, instead of traveling on foot and using dogs to haul their tipis and other supplies, tribes like the Comanches evolved a way of life that exploited horses for transport, hunting, and waging war.

The shift to a pastoral economy meant that Comanches were almost constantly on the move in search of grazing for their large horse herds. Instead of following the seasonal migration of the bison, they learned to balance the pursuit of their main protein source with a concern for pasturage for their horses. At their peak population of between thirty and forty thousand in the early nineteenth century, the Comanches split into more than one hundred settlements, or rancherías, each with up-wards of a thousand horses, mules, and donkeys. Settlements, comprising one or more extended families and led by a single headman, had to move as often as twice a week in search of new supplies of fodder and water. To satisfy their needs without com-peting with one another for pasturage, the rancherías ranged over a vast territory that stretched from southern Colorado in the north almost to San Antonio, and much of the area came to be known as Comanchería. Except for the winter months, when they remained relatively sedentary in encampments along river valleys, the Comanche rancherías were continually in motion.

Thanks to the horse, bison hunting, once an arduous, pro-tracted process conducted on foot, was transformed into a relatively effortless operation. Caring for the horse herds, how-ever, filled the vacuum. The job of horse herding was generally given to boys, who were kept busy pasturing and watering the animals, keeping them fit, and guarding them at night. Dur-ing the winter, when the ranchería sometimes contended with snow and cold temperatures, the herders often had to seek out grazing land, clear snow from pasturage, or collect cottonwood bark when grass was not available. Men did not take part in the mundane chores of herding, but they occupied themselves in breeding horses, caring for the prized animals they reserved for warfare and hunting, and capturing and breaking the wild horses that abounded in the territory. When tending the herd was too much for the boys, women helped out. Already responsible for nearly every aspect of daily life, from caring for children, curing and cooking meat, and dressing hides, to making and repairing tents and clothing, halters and saddles, they were also called on to assist with the herds when necessary.

The chief and senior members of each ranchería directed the work of the community, assigning boys to look after specific animals and deciding when and where to search for new campgrounds and fresh grazing areas. However, they spent most of their time planning and carrying out raids—for livestock and captives—and breeding horses. By the end of the eighteenth century, Comanches had become such skillful horse and mule breeders that the animals they raised were adjudged hardier and more agile than the larger Spanish and Mexican breeds. One nineteenth-century visitor to Comanchería was struck by the contrast between the Comanches' reputation for ruthlessness and their concern for their horses. The Comanche, he wrote, "chooses his ponies well, and shows more good sense in breeding than one would give him credit for."

For more than a century, Comanches, as well as Apaches and Kiowas, among other tribes, plundered ranches, farms, and homesteads over a wide area of the American Southwest and northern Mexico. The objectives of their raids were primarily livestock, but the raiders also seized human captives. These included Anglos, African-Americans, Mexicans, and even members of other Indian tribes. As the Comanche economy grew, thanks to the mobility and efficiency that horses made possible, the manpower required to support their pastoral way of life, to produce food and clothing, and secure hides for trading, increased as well. The captives were one solution to this labor shortage. Many were simply enslaved, but others, especially children, were adopted into tribal families, frequently to replace members who had died, and some adoptees became the "extra wives" of wealthy Comanche warriors and chiefs. Women had always been responsible for feeding and clothing their families, butchering and curing meat, tanning hides, and even making weapons, but as the practice of polygyny (men taking multiple wives) expanded, the women's burdens increased and their status fell further.

Captives also proved valuable in negotiations between the Comanches and settlers, who were always eager to ransom their captured compatriots. An exchange of captives often eased peace negotiations with American or Mexican representatives. However, this practical consideration did not discourage Comanches from torturing and killing many of their captives, actions they sometimes justified as "compensation" for members of their community who had been killed or as demonstrating their power over their adversaries. Not many slaves escaped, but even those who were not ransomed might not remain slaves permanently. Comanche slavery was a fluid institution wherein captives were often able to achieve freedom or at least to marry and enjoy many of the privileges of full membership in the community. The Indians may also have welcomed Anglo and Hispanic outsiders because they had greater resistance to diseases of European origin, especially smallpox and cholera, that periodically swept through Comanchería during the first half of the nineteenth century.

Among those who were captured when young, some became so acculturated to their new lives that even after they had been ransomed they sometimes ran away in order to return to their rancherías. Others insisted on remaining in their new environment, like one Mexican boy of twelve who told Josiah Gregg, the early-nineteenth-century trader, explorer, and naturalist, that he had become too uncivilized to live with Christians. For others, the reasons were more ambiguous. Gregg quoted the story of a woman from Matamoros whose family was prepared to pay one thousand dollars for her ransom. She explained that the Indians "had disfigured her by tattooing; that she was married and perhaps *enceinte* [pregnant]; and that she would be more unhappy by returning to her father under these circumstances than by remaining where she was."

Horses and iron weapons, especially guns, were introduced to the New World by the Spaniards, but the Comanches devised novel ways of employing them in warfare that enabled them to subdue their neighbors and, well into the nineteenth century, repulse all attempts by Europeans to colonize the territory of Comanchería and drive them out. Their new mobility also opened up a trading realm that enriched them and gave them access to new sources of food to supplement their traditional bison-based diet. With their trading partners, they also formed alliances and often played one group off against the other, as they did the French and Americans in the east and the Spanish in the west. Comanche dominance did not breed complacency; there were always up-and-coming young warriors desirous of gaining a place among the tribal elite through the only means available: conquest, capture, and the ability to inspire others to follow their example.

Just as the Comanches adapted to an equestrian way of life, they also came to embrace trading. They were even willing to barter with their enemies, directly or through intermediaries, as they discovered how valuable agricultural produce and weaponry could be to them. However, the possession of land signified to Comanches free access rather than outright ownership. Because they were a nomadic society, the rights to hunt, encamp, and graze on the lands they controlled were ownership enough; but when their prerogatives were threatened, whether by Apaches who were shifting to permanent agricultural settlements, by Spanish efforts to implant colonies and missions, or, later, by American planters, homesteaders, and ranchers in Texas, they often went to war.

Even then, their aims were generally not to drive the intruders out. For roughly one hundred years, from the mid-eighteenth through the mid-nineteenth centuries, they treated the regions of the Southwest and Mexico that lay within or abutted Comanchería as what one historian has called "a carefully managed livestock repository." Rather than drive settlers out of an area they periodically looted, the Comanches usually preferred to allow most livestock raiders to remain and rebuild their herds, ensuring that the region would continue to supply them with cattle, horses, and human captives, whom they enslaved, ransomed, or occasionally adopted. Because of these raids, however, survivors often did abandon their homesteads.

The Raid on Fort Parker

*Of the thousands of Texas settlers taken captive by Indians, none
had a greater impact on the history and mythology of the region
than the handful captured at Fort Parker on May 19, 1836. Located in present-day Limestone County (near Waco), the fort was
built in 1835 by James and Silas Parker; James's son-in-law,
Luther Thomas Martin (L. T. M.) Plummer; and some of their
neighbors in Sterling Robertson's colony. It was designed to protect the families and their livestock from Indian predators. Almost
all of the Parker-Plummer land, three grants totaling almost fourteen thousand acres, lay outside the walls of the fort, but four acres
were enclosed by a twelve-foot-high palisade, the tops of the stakes
sharpened to points, with blockhouses on two of the corners. Inside
the walls were six small log cabins, which housed members of the
extended Parker family and, on occasion, when danger threatened,
neighboring families as well. There were two entrances: a large
double gate and a small one that led to a nearby spring. On May
18, at least thirty-one members of the Parker clan spent the night
inside the fort. There may have been other settlers there as well,
but if there were they left early the next morning and were not
caught up in the raid that occurred that day.*

There are conflicting accounts about whether the Parkers
had been warned that Indians were planning an attack,
but on the morning of May 19, most of the adult men went out
as usual to work their fields. Remaining behind were a handful of men and the large number of women and children who
made up the extended household. When a horde of Indians on
horseback came into view some distance away, James Parker's
eighteen-year-old daughter, Sarah Nixon, led a small group out
to the fields to warn her father and the other men. By this time,

one or two of the Parker men at the fort were attempting to negotiate with the warriors, in order to give the women and children a chance to flee. James Parker led the women and children with him to safety; his daughter Rachel Parker Plummer's husband, L. T. M., headed toward neighboring farms to round up help; and Sarah Nixon's husband, Lorenzo, rushed back to the fort to try to save as many people as possible.

Rachel Plummer later estimated the number of Comanche raiders alone at between six and seven hundred; that was almost certainly an exaggeration, but the odds against the settlers were doubtless overwhelming. Furthermore, the Parkers owned only a small number of livestock, so raiding was not likely to have been a motive for the attack, although the Indians did steal some horses when they rode away from the fort. Its purpose was almost certainly to terrorize the Parkers and discourage others from encroaching on territory the Comanches and their allies considered theirs for purposes of hunting, grazing, and encampment. It may even be that by building their fort the Parkers were asserting their intentions to take up permanent residence in terms the Comanches could not ignore. It is remarkable, then, that only five of the Parker clan and their neighbors were killed—the patriarch, "Elder" John Parker, was among the dead—and five others captured: Rachel Plummer, then seventeen, and her infant son, James Pratt Plummer; John Parker's stepdaughter, Elizabeth Kellogg; and two of Silas Parker's children, Cynthia Ann, who was about nine, and five-year-old John Richard. Sarah, Elder John Parker's wife, known as "Granny," had been forced to witness the brutal torture of her husband, before being raped, scalped, and left for dead herself.

Many of those who had eluded capture or death took cover along the banks of the Navasota River, which flowed near the fort. The raiding party did not linger long; they destroyed much of what was in the cabins, shot some of the livestock, and rode off with their handful of captives. After the Indians had withdrawn, four of the men made their way back to the fort, where they found Granny Parker still alive, dressed her wounds, and carried her back to the river, where they rejoined the other survivors. A second group, six adults and twelve children led by James Parker, including his pregnant wife, Patsy, also escaped but were separated from the others. The next morning both groups set off toward safety, one heading to Fort Houston and the second, the James Parker party, for the homestead of Lawrence Tinnin, some ninety miles away. Parker's party, afraid to go back to the fort for horses or supplies, was on foot, but the others retrieved horses and some food. The Parker group, near starvation after walking for five days with nothing to eat but two skunks and two terrapins divided among eighteen people, finally sent James Parker ahead to Tinnin's settlement. He returned the next day with two settlers and five horses, on which they carried the exhausted refugees to the settlement. A day later, L. T. M. Plummer, having found no trace of his wife Rachel and their son, reached Tinnin's settlement as well.

Rachel Parker Plummer

Rachel Plummer, who later wrote that her "flesh was never clear of wounds from the lash, and bruises from clubs," shared the fate of nearly all women captives. In addition to being beaten and often burned, women with long hair often had it cut short, the young and the old were gang-raped, and mothers were forced to watch their children being tortured. Rachel recalled how her captors brought her one-year-old "James Pratt [Plummer] so near me that I could hear him cry. He would call for mother; and often was his voice weakened by the blows they would give him. I could hear the blows, I could hear his cries; but oh, alas, could offer him no relief." When captives were within hearing distance of one another, they weren't allowed to converse. Once, when Rachel's aunt, Elizabeth Kellogg, called to her and Rachel answered, their captors stomped on them; and if children cried, they too were beaten.

In the nineteenth century, captive women who published memoirs rarely if ever described in print the degradation and sexual abuse they had suffered. Rachel alluded to it indirectly when she wrote that "to narrate their barbarous treatment would only add to my present distress, for it is with feelings of the deepest mortification that I think of it. . . . while I record this painful part of my narrative, I can almost feel the same heart-rending pains of body and mind that I then endured, my very soul becomes sick at the dreadful thought." In the first few days following her abduction, however, Rachel was probably too busy trying to bear up in the face of constant threats and abuse and apprehensiveness about her fate and that of her son, her aunt, and her cousins to spend time in reflection. After traveling for several days, during which the captives were allowed only a little water, the Indians divided their five captives among

several groups, who then headed in different directions. Elizabeth Kellogg was taken by a Kichai contingent that had joined
with the Comanches for the raid and Cynthia and her brother
John Parker by a band of Comanches. When James Pratt was
brought to his mother, Rachel believed that she was going to be
allowed to keep him with her, but as soon as they saw that she
was no longer nursing him, he was handed over to a different
Comanche group. "I looked after him as he was borne from me,
and I sobbed aloud. This was the last I ever heard of my little
Pratt." Although James Pratt was eventually ransomed, in 1842,
Rachel would die without knowing that her son was still alive.

James Parker, now the head of the Parker clan, was determined to rescue his relatives. Although he had no idea where
the nomadic Comanches might have taken them, he traveled
to San Augustine in deep East Texas (near Nacogdoches) to
ask Sam Houston for men who could join him in searching.
Houston, who preferred diplomacy rather than force to reach
accommodations with the neighboring tribes, declined to help.
While James searched for a means of persuading Houston to
change his mind, his half-sister Elizabeth Kellogg appeared in
Nacogdoches one day in August 1836, having been ransomed
from the Kichais by Delawares, a peaceful tribe. In exchange
for Elizabeth, they asked for one hundred fifty dollars. When
James Parker protested that he didn't have the money, Sam
Houston paid it for him, and Elizabeth was soon reunited with
the other surviving members of the family. In 1837, Houston
did authorize James Parker to raise a company of men to take
action against Indians in the region, but he rescinded the au-
thorization a month later.

Rachel, meanwhile, became the slave of "an old man," someone who was most likely not one of the Fort Parker raiders, wandering with the band to which she was now attached across the
High Plains of Colorado. In her memoir, she referred to two
"mistresses," one old and one young; these were probably the
old man's two wives. Already pregnant with her second child

when she was captured, Rachel struggled to keep up as the Comanches traveled north and west into the foothills of the Rocky Mountains. In October 1836, friendless, ill-fed, ill-clothed, and constantly laboring over the buffalo hides she was assigned to dress, she gave birth to a son, whom she named Luther T. M., after his father. For six weeks, the Comanches permitted Rachel to nurse her child, but then they took the infant from her and choked, tossed, and dragged him until he was dead. In her memoir, she recalled that "one of them took it up by one leg and brought it to me, and threw it in my lap. But, in praise to the savages, I must say they gave me time to dig a small hole in the earth and deposit it away. I was truly glad when I found it was entirely over its sufferings. I rejoice now to reflect, that its soul is now in the sweet mansions of eternal day—may I be prepared to meet my little infants there. I would have rejoiced to have had the pleasure of laying my little James Pratt with it."

In March 1837, Rachel's band joined dozens and perhaps hundreds of others in a massive tribal gathering in the Colorado Rockies. Their purpose: to coordinate a series of attacks in Texas and Mexico. "It was the greatest assemblage of people I ever saw," Rachel later wrote. "The council was held on a high eminence, descending every way;—the encampments were just as close as they could stand to one another, but how far they extended I know not, for I could not discern the outer edge of the encampment with my naked eye." According to some historians, the conclave was held at the instigation of Mexican interests, who wanted the Indians' help to defeat the newly independent Republic of Texas and drive the Anglo settlers out. Rachel, who by now understood Comanche, tried to glean as much as she could about the war plans, in hopes of learning something that might help her to escape. Any invasion of Texas, however, would not occur until 1838 or even later, and Rachel's optimism soon drained away.

It had been nearly a year since her abduction. Rachel was not certain that any of her family had survived the attack on

Fort Parker, and she eventually succumbed to deep depression. She contemplated suicide but wasn't able to take her own life with the small knife she had acquired. One day, however, when her young mistress gave her an order, she decided to refuse, expecting the Indians to beat her to death. When only the young woman attacked her, Rachel surprised herself by fighting back, beating the woman with a piece of bone until she surrendered. The woman was bleeding, but the Indians did not go to her aid, nor did they discipline Rachel for brutalizing one of their own. Rachel helped her young mistress recover—washing her wounds and giving her water to drink—while the others acted as if nothing unusual had occurred.

Except for the old mistress, that is. Although one of the chiefs told Rachel, "You are brave to fight—good to fallen enemy— you are directed by the Great Spirit. . . . She began with you, and you had the right to kill her. Your noble spirit forbid you," the older woman was not appeased. She had Rachel gather straw, but when Rachel realized that her mistress planned to burn her alive, she defended herself a second time. After being singed by burning straw, she held the old mistress to the fire as well and continued to scuffle when the old woman came at her with a wooden club. Once more Rachel came out on top, and again no one punished her or helped her adversary. Not even the young mistress offered to join Rachel in dressing the older woman's wounds or carry her back to the tent they all shared.

The next morning, the three women were called to stand trial in the presence of twelve of the tribal chiefs. There was no disagreement about what had happened, but when the women were invited to address the court, Rachel unburdened herself of her sorrows. "I told the court that they had mistreated me— they had not taken me honorably; that they had used the white flag to deceive us [the raiders at Fort Parker had approached bearing a flag of truce], and by which they had killed my friends—that I had been faithful, and served them from fear of death, and that I would now rather die than be treated as I had been. I said that the Great Spirit would reward them for their treachery and their abuse of me."

When Rachel was ordered to replace a tent pole that had broken during her fight with the old mistress, she insisted that the young mistress help her to do so, and the chiefs agreed. Her display of courage seemed also to raise her status within the group. "I took my own part, and fared much the better by it." She remained a slave, however, a thousand miles from home, where her father was obsessively searching for her but with no idea where she was. Ironically, perhaps, her rescue resulted from the fact that Anglo and Mexican captives had long been among the valuable commodities traded by the Comanches and their allies throughout Comanchería, along with buffalo hides, furs, horses, and mules, in exchange for guns, ammunition, tools, whiskey, and other manufactured goods. In 1837, several New Mexican comancheros, traders who specialized in commerce with the Indians, arrived in Colorado to barter with Rachel's band either at their encampment or at one of the trading centers where the comancheros and Comanches periodically gathered to do business. An American couple, William and Mary Donoho, traders who owned the only hotel in Santa Fe, New Mexico, had commissioned the comancheros to ransom any Anglo captives they located. The "old man" quickly accepted their generous offer for Rachel.

The comancheros brought Rachel back to Santa Fe, where she met her benefactors, the Donohos, and two Englishwomen the couple had also recently ransomed, Sarah Ann Horn and a Mrs. Harris. These two women and their sons had been abducted near the Nueces River by Comanches only a month or so before the raid on Fort Parker. John Horn, Sarah Ann's husband, was one of several men killed during that raid, and Mrs. Harris's husband and son and another man were murdered not long afterward. As often happened to families who survived their capture, mother and sons were separated soon afterward. Whether that was done because they had been claimed by different raiders or in order to destroy the captives' sense of family connection is difficult to say.

Sarah Ann Horn did benefit from one bit of good fortune that increased her chances of surviving and shielded her from the sexual abuse that was the fate of many women captives. Since captives, perhaps especially women, were also important sources of labor, Sarah Ann was providentially adopted by a widow who put her to work dressing hides but also protected her from the repeated rapes or forced prostitution that were the fates of many captured women. Although she was, in fact, a slave, Sarah Ann's treatment at the hands of her mistress was, as she later wrote, "an exception to the general character of these merciless beings, and greatly did she contribute, by her acts of kindness and soothing manner, to reconcile me to my fate."

Through the Donohos' intervention, the two Englishwomen were ransomed several months after their capture, Sarah Ann at a trading post near what is now Las Vegas, New Mexico. Efforts to locate and ransom the two Horn boys were unsuccessful. When intermediaries attempted to learn about them, they were told that one of them had died and the other the Comanches refused to sell. In August 1837, when the unpopular Mexican governor of the New Mexico territory, Albino Pérez, was killed by local rebels who objected to his injustices and attempts to impose new taxes ordered by President Santa Anna, the Donohos decided that it was time to leave Santa Fe. Loading a train of wagons with as many of their possessions as possible, their three children—the younger two are believed to be the first Anglo-Americans born in Santa Fe—as well as Rachel, Sarah Ann, and Mrs. Harris, headed to Independence, Missouri.

Rachel was free, and she was well taken care of in the home of Mary Donoho's mother, Lucy Dodson, but she was desperate to be reunited with her family. Although she wasn't certain where her relatives were and how many of them were still alive, "[m]y anxiety grew so high that I could not sleep." A January

1838 ad placed in a Houston newspaper announced that Rachel was in Independence, and not long afterward, Lorenzo Nixon, Rachel's brother-in-law, arrived at the Dodson home. James Parker, exhausted from his own futile travels in search of Rachel, had sent Nixon to Missouri in his place. William Donoho rode back to Texas with the pair, a distance of more than one thousand miles, much of it sparsely settled and unsafe. Rachel was finally reunited with her family, who had searched for her since the horrendous capture more than a year earlier. "I am now once more in the company of dear father and mother and other friends," she wrote, "and moreover have the great pleasure of embracing my beloved husband. But oh! dreadful reflection, where is [*sic*] my little children?" Rachel was home, but home was not the haven she had left. The memories of her ordeal never ceased to torment her, and, as her father observed, even after months of care at the hands of the generous Donohos, "[s]he was in very bad health."

In January 1839, Rachel gave birth to a third son, whom she and L. T. M. named Wilson P. Plummer. She had never recovered from the ordeal of her yearlong mistreatment at the hands of her captors, nor from the trauma of separation from her son James Pratt and being forced to witness the brutal murder of her second son, Luther T. M. She was sick when she delivered her third son and died on March 19. Two days later, Wilson P. was dead as well. It would be another three years before James Pratt was returned to his family.

The return of captives became a focus of a new commander of Oklahoma's Fort Gibson, then the largest garrison in the United States. In 1842, Zachary Taylor convened a conference with the large number of tribes in the region of the fort and many of them responded. In August, Kickapoo Indians delivered James Pratt Plummer to the fort; they had paid the Comanches who held the boy four hundred dollars for his release. A month later, his cousin, John Richard Parker, was handed over by a member of the Delawares. Abducted when he was

just over a year old, James Pratt did not speak any English, and
the soldiers at Fort Gibson began tutoring him. But the lessons
ended when John Richard arrived. "The two boys 'found much
pleasure in each other's society as both spoke Comanche and it
was difficult to induce either to attempt the English language.'"

This time James Parker was well enough to make the trip to
Indian Territory to reclaim his grandson and nephew. At first,
James Pratt tried to run away from his grandfather, but finally,
with help from some of the soldiers who spoke Comanche, the
men succeeded in persuading the boy to go home with James.
The soldiers explained to James Pratt that the elder Parker was
his grandfather. Later, James Parker wrote of this first meeting
with James Pratt. His recollection was, "The boy asked me if he
had a mother. I told him he had not, as she had died. He then
asked if he had a father. I told him he had, and if he would go
with me he should see him. He then consented to accompany
me."

James Parker remembered coming home to Cincinnati,
Texas, with the two boys as "[j]oyous indeed." Perhaps it was
at first, but before long strains were visible, especially between
James and his son-in-law, L. T. M. Plummer, father of James
Pratt. Parker feuded with L. T. M. over custody of James Pratt;
he apparently complained that the boy's father had not repaid
the ransom money to the elder Parker, but the monetary issue
may have been only a pretext. Not long after Rachel died, L. T. M.
had remarried, and he and his second wife, Lizzie Lauderdale,
had two children by the time of James Pratt's return. Perhaps
Parker, obsessed as he was with restoring the family that had
been decimated in the 1836 raid, objected to the marriage, or
perhaps he wanted to keep his family as close to him as possible. It has been suggested by some that he may also have been
motivated by a wish to gain ownership of Rachel's half of the
Plummers' Robertson's Colony land grant.

Unable to persuade his father-in-law to relent, Plummer
wrote to Sam Houston, then president of the Republic of Texas,

early in 1843, asking him to intercede. In April, Houston replied, "In a case of this kind, the attempt to swindle a distressed father on account of his long lost child is in every way deserving of the severest reprehension. Though I had some reason to suspect the professions of Mr. Parker, yet, until this case was presented, I had not supposed him capable of practicing such scandalous fraud upon his kindred and connexions. . . . His pretensions about his liability for two hundred dollars, etc., are utterly groundless. You will, therefore, take your child home. Mr. Parker has not the shadow of right to detain him, and by so doing is not only laying himself under the imputation of extreme brutality, but is subjecting himself to the penalties of the law."

Whether Houston's letter succeeded in breaking the deadlock over custody of James Pratt is not known. The boy may have remained with his grandfather for a while, but there is no record of his having returned to live with his father. By 1850 he was living with an uncle, John Harrold, third husband of James's daughter Sarah. James Pratt Plummer lived long enough to marry twice, have four children, and serve in the Civil War. He died of pneumonia at a Confederate army camp in Little Rock, Arkansas. He was twenty-seven years old.

Cynthia Ann Parker

Captured in the same raid as her cousin Rachel Plummer, Cynthia Ann Parker met a very different fate. In the immediate aftermath of the raid, she may have been mistreated, as captives commonly were, but perhaps not as harshly. Cynthia was nine at the time, and her brother, John Richard Parker, was five, ages that made them good candidates for adoption by their captors. In Comanche culture, adoption of captives did not guarantee equal status, since Comanches generally drew a distinction between people "born of Comanche parents" and others who merely "live as Comanche." Cynthia Ann may have been selected for future marriage to Peta Nocona, the chief who was one of the leaders of the Fort Parker raid, and thus spared the worst forms of abuse and degradation. That she was not merely a "secondary wife" who was in reality little more than a household servant is suggested by the fact that her son Quanah rose to become the last great chief of the Comanche nation.

In 1846, two Indian commissioners, P. M. Butler and M. G. Lewis, reported that the siblings had been located among a group of Yamparika Comanches, and that attempts to ransom them had been made. According to the report, Cynthia Ann would hide when anyone attempted to ransom her, but the tribal chiefs seemed amenable to releasing her if the price was right. "A large amount of goods and four or five hundred dollars were offered" for the sister and brother, and the chief of the Yamparikas may have promised to "take measures to have her delivered up to the authorities of the United States upon the next 'fall of the leaves.'"

Only two months earlier, however, the *Clarksville Northern Standard* reported that Leonard Williams, an army officer and

Indian agent, had offered twelve mules and two mule loads of merchandise for Cynthia Ann, but that the Comanches had refused the offer, saying "they will rather die than give her up." The article went on to claim that some of the Comanches plotted to murder Williams and the other members of his party but were prevented from doing so by their chief, Pahauca. The two accounts, which most likely refer to the same encounter, cast doubt on whether at the time—ten years after her capture—she was a reluctant member of the Comanche nation. Only one of the stories mentions Cynthia Ann's brother. One year later, Robert Neighbors, the Texas commissioner of Indian affairs, stated that "the Comanches have yet in their possession one White prisoner," Cynthia Ann. Perhaps John Richard had left the band by then; years later, Cynthia Ann seemed to know little or nothing about her brother's fate, at one time saying that he had died of smallpox while still a child. She was unaware that in 1842 he had been returned to his family.

Relations with many of the Comanche bands, including Cynthia Ann's Yamparikas, were at a low ebb by the mid-1840s. Earlier attempts by both sides to negotiate peaceful releases of captives had ended in misunderstanding and bloodshed. In 1840, for example, sixty-five Comanche chiefs and warriors entered San Antonio for talks with Texas officials aimed at negotiating peace between the Comanches and the people of Texas. One of the Texan demands had been the release of all captives held by the Comanches, but the Indians, led by the prominent Penateka chief Muguara (Muk-wah-rah), had brought only a handful of their prisoners with them. One of them was sixteen-year-old Matilda Lockhart, who had been tortured, abused, and mutilated during her two-year-long captivity. Matilda told the commissioners that the Comanches were still holding more than a dozen other captives they had not brought with them. The Texans suspected that the Comanches planned to negotiate for each captive separately, in order to receive larger ransom payments; they did not believe

Muguara's claim that because Comanche bands enjoyed considerable autonomy, he had not been able to persuade all of them to give up their captives.

With peace talks at an impasse, the commissioners ordered the arrest of the thirty-three chiefs; they were to be held hostage until all captives remaining in Comanche possession were released. Fighting broke out, and many of the Indians were killed by Texas soldiers and citizens. The surviving chiefs were imprisoned, pending the return of the rest of the captives. From the Comanche perspective, the arrest of chiefs who were engaged in treaty negotiations was a breach of diplomatic protocol. Most of the imprisoned chiefs soon escaped, but the affair ended all prospects of a peaceful accommodation between Comanches and Texans.

In response, Chief Buffalo Hump led a large group of warriors in an extended raid of Victoria and Linnville in August 1840. About two dozen area settlers were killed, and the raiders slaughtered a large number of cattle as well in what was the last large-scale Comanche raid on the Texas coast. They also carried off a number of captives, perhaps as many as three thousand horses, and a variety of goods looted from the warehouses in the port of Linnville. The army of volunteers and Texas Rangers who pursued them described the warriors as wearing stolen cloth coats, shoes, and hats. "They spread the calico over their horses, and tied hundreds of yards of ribbon to their horses' manes and to their tails." At the battle of Plum Creek, the Comanches were routed, but during the battle the Indians killed some of the captives taken in Victoria and Linnville before retreating westward. Among the equipment the Indians abandoned were items of Mexican origin, suggesting that Mexico may have supplied the Comanches in hopes that they would strike the first blow of an invasion leading to a Mexican reconquest of Texas.

Randolph Marcy, a West Point graduate and explorer, led

a seventy-man expedition across the Great Plains in search of the source of the Red River. Along the way, Marcy and his team made numerous discoveries, including several dozen new species of mammals and reptiles. He also reported an encounter with John Richard Parker, whose mother had sent him to try to persuade Cynthia Ann to rejoin her family. By then a woman of twenty-five with two children, Cynthia refused, "saying that her husband, children, and all that she held most dear, were with the Indians, and there she should remain." Within a few years, however, with the zone of settlement expanding and the bison population shrinking, the days of the Indians' traditional autonomous, nomadic way of life were numbered.

Increasingly, Comanche raids became less horse-gathering tactics and more desperate attempts to drive the encroaching settlements out of Comanchería. The presence of the U.S. Army and the Texas Rangers in the borderlands also made things more difficult for the Indians. The American Civil War would grant the Comanches and their allies a brief reprieve, but the endgame in the long war of attrition being waged against them had already begun. In the words of John Salmon "Rip" Ford, soldier, politician, and journalist who was appointed commander of the Texas Rangers in 1858, "The intention was, from the beginning, to carry the war into the hunting grounds of the Comanches and their confederate tribes, to let their families hear the crack of Texas rifles and feel the disagreeable effects of hostile operations in their own camps. No one advocated any but a civilized mode of warfare. As far as the braves were concerned—the savages who had visited our frontier and slaughtered our people, regardless of age and sex—with them it was war to the knife."

Other Texas Rangers were destined to play important roles in the struggle to make Texas safe for its settlers. In 1859, Governor Sam Houston ordered twenty-two-year-old Lawrence Sullivan "Sul" Ross to recruit and lead a company of Rangers. A recent graduate of Wesleyan University in Alabama, Ross had distinguished himself while fighting Comanches at the battle of Wichita Village during his 1858 summer vacation from college. Despite the opposition of people who suspected him of harboring sympathy for the Indians, Ross was determined. A letter he wrote long afterward expressed his resolve: "I determined to make a desperate attempt to curb the insolence of these implacable hereditary enemies of Texas who were greatly emboldened by the small force left to confront them. . . . I planned to accomplish this by following them into their fastnesses and carry the war into their own homes where this tribe, the most inveterate raiders on the border, retired with their captives and booty to their wild haunts amid the hills and valleys of the beautiful Canadian and Pease rivers."

Toward the end of 1860, Ross set out at the head of a combined company of Rangers, volunteers, and U.S. soldiers that numbered about 140. As they made their way along the Pease River in present-day Hardeman County on the Texas-Oklahoma border, Captain J. J. "Jack" Cureton, who commanded the volunteers, struggled to imbue military discipline in his untrained troops, whose numbers had grown with the addition of about thirty late arrivals. After six days on the trail, Ross discovered a Comanche encampment getting ready to depart. Ordering the soldiers to block the Indians' escape route, Ross and the Rangers charged. There are differing accounts of the brief battle itself, but they all agree that most of the occupants of the camp were women and children and that many of them were killed. The chief and a small number of warriors returned in an attempt to allow the women to escape; most of them were killed as well.

According to Charles Goodnight, a ranger who was not directly involved in the assault, Ross and his men "shot the Indians as they came to them," and the "six or eight" women trapped by Cureton's soldiers were all killed. "They were so heavily loaded with meat, tent poles and camp equipage that their horses could not run. We supposed they had about a thousand pounds of buffalo meat in various stages of curing."

Ross and another ranger, Tom Kelliheir, pursued what they thought were the chief and two warriors trying to escape on a pair of horses, one of them a handsome gray. Ross drew near to the chief, who was riding double, fired his army Colt, and struck the second rider, who fell off the horse along with the chief. When the Rangers got close enough to the iron-gray horse to shoot its rider, they saw that it was a woman carrying a young child. According to some versions of the story, she called out, "Americano! Americano!" Ross left her in Kelliheir's charge and went after the chief, who wounded the ranger's horse with an arrow and let fly others intended for his pursuer. According to Ross, "He would have killed me but for a random shot from my pistol, which broke his right arm at the elbow, completely disabling him. . . . I shot the chief twice through the body, whereupon he deliberately walked to a small tree, the only one in sight, and leaning against it began to sing a wild, weird song."

The wounded chief was Peta Nocona. The woman on the iron-gray horse was Cynthia Ann Parker, whom Nocona had captured in the raid on Fort Parker twenty-four years earlier and who was now the mother of three of his children. At this point, however, the Texans did not know who she was, only that she was a blue-eyed, Anglo-American who apparently neither spoke nor understood English. It is possible that her blond hair was now dark, as Comanches were known to mix charcoal and buffalo tallow to darken the hair of hostages, and pictures of Cynthia Ann during this time showed dark hair and light eyes. According to one account, Nocona, who probably knew that his wounds were fatal, was holding on to the tree and chanting a death song, making his peace with his god. The song and Nocona's stoic indifference profoundly impressed Ross. "There was a plaintive melody in it which, under the circumstances, filled my heart with sorrow. He was a gigantic Indian, as graceful and handsome a warrior as ever rode to deadly lists; he fought with superb bravery and skill."

Ross asked Anton (or Antonio) Martínez, a former Comanche captive who was Ross's interpreter in the campaign, whether he could speak to Nocona. "Tell him if he will surrender he will not be shot any more." Nocona answered, "You tell the white captain that when I am dead I will surrender but not before, and not to him." He released his hold on the tree, picked up a spear attached to a lariat, and hurled it at Ross. Then he resumed his chanting as if he were alone.

Ross said, "This is the bravest man I ever saw. I can't shoot him any more. . . . I could only look upon him with pity and admiration, for deplorable as was his situation with no possible chance of escape, his army utterly destroyed, his wife and child captives in his sight, he was undaunted by the fate that awaited him and preferred death to life." Martínez, however, who said that he had witnessed the murder of his mother by Nocona and who had been a captive of the Comanches, felt less charitable and asked permission to dispatch the wounded chief. Afterward, Ross collected Nocona's weapons and headdress as gifts for Governor Houston.

While the soldiers and Rangers collected buffalo hides, blankets, and other mementoes and objects of value that lay strewn around the campsite, Cynthia Ann asked to be allowed to return to the spot where the body of Nocona and the other woman—a Mexican girl who may have been another of Nocona's wives—lay. She paid her respects and recited prayers, and then repeated these gestures as she walked among the dead at the campsite. Some of the men thought that she should be allowed to rejoin the Comanches, but Ross countered that it was imperative to find out who she was for the sake of the many families in Texas who were searching for their captured children and family members. When the Rangers made camp, he interrogated the woman, who did not recall her name or where she was from. But she recounted enough details of her abduction from a fort and of the other captives taken during the raid that Ross was sure that she was Cynthia Ann Parker. That evening, when one of the men reminisced about the Fort Parker raid and mentioned that one of the captured children was named Cynthia Ann Parker, she broke in, "Me Cynthia Ann." At the time of this exchange, Ross wasn't present, and for some reason the men did not tell him that Cynthia Ann had acknowledged who she was. Ross was convinced, however, and sent a message to Cynthia Ann's uncle, Isaac Parker, who met her at Camp Cooper. When Parker asked the interpreter to inquire whether she remembered her name, Cynthia Ann Parker, she stood up before the question could be translated, struck her chest, and said, as she had at the Pease River, "Me Cynthia Ann."

Cynthia Ann made continual attempts to escape from Ross and his men in order to return to her two sons. Although American soldiers and Rangers often turned a blind eye when captured Indian women attempted to escape, Ross was firm about making sure that this most famous of "white squaws" was reunited with her Anglo relatives. At Camp Cooper, some of the army wives made an effort to "civilize" Cynthia Ann by bathing her and dressing her in American clothing, but she immediately raced back to her tent, shedding her dress as she ran, and later reappeared in the buckskin garments she had become accustomed to. Later, Cynthia Ann got used to wearing dresses again, but she was never completely comfortable in the environment that had become alien to her.

On the trip from Camp Cooper to Isaac Parker's home near the Trinity River, Cynthia Ann and her daughter Prairie Flower were often treated like celebrities. In Fort Worth, mother and daughter were photographed at a photographer's studio, and a schoolgirl later recalled that school was suspended so that the children could join the crowds who lined up for a glimpse of the two of them at Turner & Daggett, the local general store.

Medora Robinson Turner remembered the cruel spectacle of Cynthia Ann, "bound with rope" and wearing a "torn calico dress." Although the portrait shows an unsmiling woman holding her infant daughter in her arms as she stares intently at the camera, contemporary accounts described Cynthia Ann as crying and speaking in Comanche the entire time she was on display. When the schoolchildren asked their principal what the former captive was saying, they were told that she was asking to be allowed to return home.

Isaac Parker took Cynthia Ann and Prairie Flower to his home outside Birdville, where he lived in an isolated log cabin near the Trinity River. However harsh life had been among the Comanches, she had been the wife of a chief, part of a society of women, and the mother of two young sons. Back with the Parker clan, she was unhappy, unable to communicate in English (or unwilling to), and she often tried to escape. The family kept Cynthia Ann under close watch, and in January 1861, just a month after her return, Isaac Parker took Cynthia Ann to Austin, where he petitioned the legislature for support for his niece and her daughter. At the capital, the legislature generously granted Cynthia Ann a pension of $100 a year for five years and a league of land. It's not certain where the land grant was supposed to be or whether Cynthia Ann ever received it, but the following year, she left Birdville to join her brother, Silas Parker Jr., and his wife, Ann, in Van Zandt County. Eventually, Cynthia Ann and Prairie Flower moved a short distance away to the home of her younger sister Orlena and Orlena's husband J. R. O'Quinn. Other Parker relatives lived in the area as well, and Cynthia Ann finally settled into a cabin of her own that the O'Quinns built for her. There she seemed to reconcile herself to her life, resumed speaking English, and thus was able to share memories of her past with family members. She helped with chores like spinning, sewing, and tanning hides, in which she especially excelled.

Widowed and unaware of the fate of her sons, Cynthia Ann

continued to practice some Comanche customs—sometimes to her family's horror, especially in the case of mourning rituals. When a relative died, she chanted mourning songs intelligible only to herself and cut herself with a knife, a "primitive" act that seemed out of place in her new surroundings. It isn't clear whether she ever knew what had happened to John Richard Parker, the brother who was captured with her.

In fact, the historical record is blurred where John Richard's life is concerned. Although his ransom in 1842 is documented, there are divergent accounts of what happened later. He may have served in the Civil War as a civilian guide for the Texas Mounted Rifles. It has also been claimed that he was unable to readjust to life among the Anglos and went back to live with the Comanches. There he may have contracted smallpox (as Cynthia Ann had heard) and been left to die by the other members of his ranchería, who often uprooted their settlements when smallpox struck because they had no way of treating the deadly disease. According to one story, however, John Richard didn't die. A young Mexican woman, Dona Juanita, herself perhaps a Comanche captive, nursed him back to health, and they married and settled in Mexico, where John Richard owned a ranch until his death.

There was talk of helping Cynthia Ann return to the Comanches once the Civil War was over, but while the war continued that was impossible. Tom Champion, a relative who wrote about Cynthia Ann, admitted that she suffered from spells of melancholy, but he believed that these grew less frequent with the passage of time. A neighbor, however, reported seeing her crying while holding Prairie Flower. The little girl herself was said to have been an outgoing child who thrived in her new surroundings and excelled at the local school. But whatever comfort the girl gave her mother was short-lived; Prairie Flower died of pneumonia in 1864. Cynthia Ann lived another six years after her daughter's death. The claim that in her grief over Prairie Flower she had starved herself to death is probably baseless, but losing her only remaining link to her former life must have affected Cynthia Ann deeply. Champion, who seems to have gotten close to her, later wrote:

> I don't think she ever knew but that her sons were killed and to hear her tell of the happy days of the Indian dances and see the excitement and pure joy which shown [sic] on her face, the memory of it, I am convinced that the white people did more harm by keeping her away from them than the Indians did by taking her at first.

In present day Limestone County, the state of Texas operates a park of more than fourteen hundred acres, Fort Parker State Park, where the original private Fort Parker was built and raided by the Comanche Indians who took Rachel and her cousin Cynthia Ann in 1836. The town of Groesbeck has preserved the site of the original fort near the state park.

There is also a state park, Copper Breaks State Park, in present-day Hardeman County, on the Texas border with Oklahoma, near the Comanche grounds where Sul Ross's Rangers discovered Cynthia Ann and killed her husband, Chief Peta Nocona. The county seat of Hardeman County is the town of Quanah, named for the chief who was Cynthia Ann Parker's son. There is also a county named for Isaac Parker, Cynthia Ann's uncle. The Trinity River runs through Parker County, which includes a small part of the city of Fort Worth.

Part V

MARGARET LEA HOUSTON, PART 1

1830s–1840s

The Courtship of Sam and Margaret
Marriage
Republic of Texas

Margaret, age twenty-one or twenty-two

The Houston and Lea family trees appear in the appendix.

Oh my love, if you could only look
into my heart this moment,
I know you would never leave me again.

-MARGARET TO SAM HOUSTON, MAY 16, 1846

When the ship carrying the hero of San Jacinto docked at New Orleans on May 22, 1836, according to a family story, seventeen-year-old Margaret Lea was in the crowd that thronged the waterfront to greet Sam Houston and listen to his brief impromptu speech. Margaret happened to be in New Orleans on a school trip, and she is said to have told one of her classmates, "I have a strange feeling that one day I will meet this man." It would be several years before her presentiment was borne out, when Houston was in Alabama to promote investment in land on the Gulf coast of Texas. He had met Margaret's brother Martin and her brother-in-law William Bledsoe in Mobile. Martin invited Houston to Spring Hill, his home outside Mobile, thinking that Nancy Lea, his widowed mother, who was visiting from Marion, Alabama, might want to invest in Texas land. Margaret was three years older than her sister Antoinette, who had married Bledsoe at seventeen, and when Houston was introduced to the two sisters at Spring Hill, he mistakenly took the elder sister for the wife. Indicating Margaret, he said to another guest, "If she were not already married,

I believe I would give that charming lady a chance to say no."
Houston's pulse undoubtedly quickened when he heard the man
reply, "But that's not Mrs. Bledsoe, that's the older unmarried
sister. So you are free to give her that chance, General."

That first evening, Margaret entertained the gathering by
singing and accompanying herself on the piano. One person who
was present described her as "tall and slender with a queenly
bearing." At five feet, seven inches, Margaret was well above
average height for the time, with dark blue eyes and light brown
hair parted in the middle and held by combs. Both parents were
strict Protestants; Temple Lea was a "zealous Baptist" and lay
preacher, and Nancy Moffette Lea's ancestors were Huguenots
who left France for South Carolina to escape religious persecu-
tion. There was a marked gap in ages between the Leas' three
eldest children, Martin, Varilla, and Henry, born between 1799
and 1804, and Vernal, Margaret, and Antoinette, who were
born between 1816 and 1822. After Temple Lea's death in 1834,
his widow and her two teenage daughters moved into Henry
Lea's home in Marion. In 1839, Margaret enrolled as one of the
first students at Judson Female Institute (now Judson College).
Henry, a businessman and member of the state legislature, was
one of the founders of the Baptist school.

Throughout his life, Houston was a commanding presence,
six feet, three inches tall, with a muscular frame and a courtly
bearing. Washington Irving, who met Houston in Texas in 1832,
described him in his notebook as "tall, large, well formed," a
"fascinating man . . . given to grandiloquence." His presence
was mesmerizing, and it is easy to imagine the impression he
made on Margaret in 1836. Even in old age, he continued to
awe nearly everyone who met him. When he delivered a speech
in 1863, one member of the audience described him as:

> . . . six feet and three inches high, straight as an arrow,
> with deep set and penetrating eyes, looking out from un-
> der heavy and thundering eyebrows, a high open forehead,

with something of the infinite intellectual shadowed there, crowned with thin white locks . . . and a voice of the deep basso tone, which shook and commanded the soul of the hearer. Adding to all this is a powerful manner, made up of deliberation, self-possession and restrained modesty of action, leaving the hearer impressed with the feeling that more of his power was hidden than revealed.

Judging from all reports, the romance of Sam Houston and Margaret Lea burst into full flower the moment they met in May 1839. Within a few days of the party, Margaret had composed a poem, "To a Withered Pink," whose lines speak of the "holy spell" that lingered in the dried petals of the flower (probably a carnation) Houston picked for her as they walked in the garden at Spring Hill. In June, he proposed and she accepted, but it would be months before they were able to overcome her family's objections to the match, and fully a year before they married. Houston's stature as a general and statesman were beyond dispute, but he was twenty-six years older than his sheltered, devout fiancée, and his past was riddled with scandal: heavy drinking; free use of profanity; years of living with the Cherokee Indians, during which he made a tribal marriage with Tiana Rogers, the chief's daughter; and—perhaps most damaging—the sudden, unexplained rupture of his marriage to Eliza Allen, which led him to resign as governor of Tennessee and leave the state.

The couple's profuse, passionate correspondence, which continued almost to the end of Sam Houston's life, began as soon as he left Mobile to visit Andrew Jackson in Tennessee. Margaret's reply, which followed several anxious letters of Houston's caused by the slow pace of mail delivery, revealed that her letter "is the first I have addressed to any gentleman." Houston was not the first suitor to pursue the serious, even severe young woman, but she had apparently never entered into a correspondence with any of the others or otherwise encouraged their interest in her. With Houston, in contrast, exchanging letters served as a means of calming her "constant dread of severing some link in this beautiful chain." She compared her heart to a "caged bird" that was at last spreading its wings.

In August, Sam returned for a second visit with Margaret and her family, this time in Marion, where he spent several weeks as a guest at Henry Lea's home. As an engagement gift, he brought Margaret a cameo brooch with his profile that he had commissioned especially for her, and he tried to cajole the Leas into accepting his and Margaret's plans to marry. According to family lore, Houston took to his bed with a cold during this visit, whereupon Nancy stationed two servants as sentries to prevent him from leaving his room (or perhaps to ensure that Margaret would not be tempted to enter it). Then, to her captive audience, she read passages from the Bible, presumably chosen to disabuse Houston of his desire to marry her daughter. For herself, Nancy Lea found Houston charming and was weighing the twin possibilities of purchasing land in Texas and moving there, but she did not give her approval to the marriage plans.

The real battle of wills Houston faced, however, was not over *whether* he and Margaret would marry—on this point her mind was made up—but *where*. About that Margaret and Nancy Lea were of one mind: it would be in Marion or nowhere. Houston continually tried to persuade Margaret to move to Texas first and get married there, but Margaret refused. While he was still in Nashville, he attempted to escape the formality of paying a visit to Margaret's family in Marion, presumably to obtain their blessing, by insisting that urgent political matters demanded his immediate return to Texas. After reading his claim, Margaret called Sam's bluff. She wrote, "Far be it from me to raise my voice against that of your country! No—if she requires your presence, go without delay! I would scorn to call him friend— who would desert his country at such a time. Go—and when her cries of oppression are hushed, we will welcome you again to my native state. Let the time of your return depend entirely on the state of your country."

Later, Houston attempted to talk Margaret into joining her mother and the Bledsoes when they sailed to Galveston in November. This time she replied somewhat astringently to his suggestion: "I will not refuse to deliberate upon it, but I imagine that my second decision will not differ from the first. I will promise however to think of it." Hoping, perhaps, that she had changed her mind, Houston made certain to meet the ship when it docked. The story has it that when Nancy disembarked, she imperiously declared, "General Houston, my daughter is in Alabama. She goes forth in the world to marry no man. The one who receives her hand will receive it in my home and not elsewhere." Back in Marion, Margaret studied Spanish and read up on Texas geography to prepare for her eventual move, and she wrote passionate letters to her fiancé, but she stayed put.

After all his stratagems to avoid putting in an appearance at the Lea family seat in Marion had failed—including a suggestion to meet at the nearby resort of Blount Springs (Margaret dismissed that ploy by writing, "Marion is but a trifling journey from that place, and we will expect you to perform it")—Houston capitulated. He traveled from Texas to Alabama alone and reached Marion on May 7, 1840. He had asked his good friend, physician, and most trusted confidant, Ashbel Smith, to join him and act as best man at the wedding. Smith, however, "had no funds and I knew the Old Chief had none" (in fact Houston had to borrow money to pay for his own passage). The wedding was to take place on the ninth, in the reception hall of her brother Henry and Serena Lea's Virginia Colonial mansion. Five years younger than Martin Lea, the prosperous Henry had assumed the role of paterfamilias after Temple Lea's death. In what may have been a desperate attempt to sabotage the wedding, he and Serena informed Sam that before the ceremony could begin, he must explain to the family why his first marriage had failed. Houston, who for eleven years had consistently refused to speak about the end of his marriage to Eliza Allen, declined. Instead he asked that Margaret be told that "it would be a mockery for me to seek to take leave of her, but please bear this message to her, that amidst all this desolation, my love for her is the holiest thing that was ever in my poor broken heart." To Henry, he reportedly said that if the family insisted on an explanation they might as well "pay the fiddlers" and send them away.

Margaret, who felt that Sam had satisfied the demands of etiquette and propriety by coming to Marion for the wedding, had another idea for the fiddlers. She signaled to them to start playing, and the Reverend Peter Crawford of the Siloam Baptist Church began the marriage service, effectively mooting her brother's ploy. In fact, Houston may already have discussed the end of his first marriage with Margaret. Four months after their wedding, in a letter, he counseled, "Let it be kept a profound secret—be always guarded. You are 'Houston's wife' and many would joy to dash our cup of bliss. My joy is in your life!"

Skeptics about the prospects of the marriage quickly reversed their dire predictions. In one curious—and perhaps prophetic—revision of the traditional marriage vows, Rev. Crawford did not ask Margaret to promise to obey her husband (she later teased Houston that since she hadn't promised obedience, he couldn't accuse her of rebellion). If anything, it was Houston who increasingly conformed to her hopes and expectations. It may have been more than mere hyperbole, then, when Major Townes toasted Margaret as the "Conqueress of the Conqueror." Just two months after the wedding, Ashbel Smith, after admitting that "I had dreadful misgivings as to the propriety of his taking this step," wrote to Barnard Bee, "I have been most agreeably disappointed. His health and ways are infinitely mended. Will it last? I always hope for the best." At about the same time, another of Sam's close friends (and sometime secretary of war), George Hockley, noted "that if permanent reformation *can* be effected his estimable wife will succeed in doing so." Even Henry Lea, who had done his best to obstruct if not prevent his sister from marrying Houston, eventually wrote an affectionate note to his brother-in-law, though it was nearly two years in coming. When Margaret heard the news, she admitted that it made her like Henry "a little better."

Houston was almost certainly as pleasantly surprised by Margaret's reforming effect on him as his friends were. In August 1840, when Margaret was at Antoinette and William Bledsoe's home in Grand Cane, Texas (see map, p.xxii), and he was busy with his law practice in San Augustine, he wrote of how fortunate he was to "find in a wife a perfect companion and one who would be capable by her wisdom and prudence to sustain me." As remarkable as their sense of mutual harmony was the fact that Sam and Margaret maintained it despite frequent and prolonged separations. He craved company and was restless, rarely remaining in one place for long, and she inclined to solitude, was often unwell, and was a poor traveler. Despite his professed desire for a quiet life in the country, Houston constantly felt the attraction of the political arena and to the end of his life could never stay away from it for long. In fact, when he wrote the line just quoted, Margaret was convalescing at Grand Cane after falling ill while she and Sam were on the way from Cedar Point to San Augustine. They were still newlyweds and wanted to be together, so when Houston prepared to return to his law practice in San Augustine—and to campaign for a seat in the Texas Congress—Margaret proposed going with him, but the 150-mile voyage may have been too much for her. Ashbel Smith diagnosed Margaret as suffering from exhaustion and advised her to rest up at the Bledsoes'. Dr. Smith wrote about the episode that "General Houston was a model of domestic propriety and kindness." But he did leave, and almost immediately wrote a letter to her that balanced his dismay at their separation—"I am more lonely each day"—with his acceptance of it—"But for a while I must be reconciled and pray for your health, safety, and happiness."

When Houston returned to the routine of frequent public addresses that kept him busy even when he did not hold or seek public office, Margaret often spent her time at Cedar Point, which she proposed renaming "Ben Lomond," after the mountain on the shore of Scotland's Loch Lomond mentioned by Sir Walter Scott in "The Lady of the Lake." The romantic name failed to catch on, but there, not far from Galveston Bay, she could be away from her sometimes overbearing mother, but not completely isolated. Houston's close friends Ashbel Smith and George Hockley, who lived nearby, kept an eye on her. "I cannot be happy but where you are!" Houston wrote, but they were to spend much of the twenty-three years of their marriage apart. One reason for their frequent separations was that Margaret's health was delicate; she was asthmatic and suffered from other respiratory ailments that were aggravated by the climate—in places like Austin, for example, where Houston served as president, congressman, or governor from shortly after their marriage until the end of 1844 and again from 1859 to 1861. There were other reasons Houston discouraged Margaret from joining him in the capital: he had no house for them to live in (though despite his chronic shortage of money, he probably could have remedied that); there were reports that Indians had scalped hunters and abducted women in raids near Austin; and Mexican troops were present in the contested area between the Nueces River and the Rio Grande. Austin, just sixty miles from San Antonio, was vulnerable; by remaining near the coast, Houston reasoned, Margaret could always cross into the United States if war threatened.

Even in drier climates, such as that of Houston City, where Sam and Margaret spent the last two months of 1840, Margaret was not content to remain long. According to one biographer, despite its "agreeable society," Margaret soon came to resent the parties that left her too little time to read and the visitors who intruded on her periods of reflection and necessitated that the house be kept in readiness for company. She received many invitations in Houston, but she accepted very few. Doubtless, she also found the city disconcerting. Although at the time, Houston's population numbered less than two thousand, its boomtown atmosphere—with its theaters, saloons, balls, and brothels—was inescapable. "This busy world with its boisterous scenes of mirth and its wily snares is no home for me," Margaret wrote to her husband. She much preferred sleepy Galveston. In December, when Sam left for the legislative session in Austin, Margaret immediately took a boat back to her mother's in Galveston. There she was content, writing to Sam that on the "holy Sabbath" Nancy had gone to church and "left me to commune with my heart and to think of you. Oh how delightful is solitude when absent from the idol of your soul!"

Of course, Margaret always preferred her husband's company to solitude. But there was more than affection behind her desire to be near Houston: she believed that he was more likely to succeed in curbing his bad habits—especially his drinking—when they were together. Houston had not forsworn alcohol, as much as Margaret would have liked him to; he had promised only to drink less. It would not take long for Margaret to learn to trust Houston implicitly and to appreciate his almost fanatical aversion to giving his word unless he was certain that he would be able to keep it. But some years were to pass before he succeeded in weaning himself off alcohol completely by drinking bitters flavored with orange peel (he even asked friends to save their peels for him). Meanwhile, when rumors that Houston had been drinking reached Margaret, she shared her disquiet with her husband, and he eagerly wrote to quash the false reports. Almost as soon as he had gone to Austin, the rumors started, and Houston felt obliged to counter them. "My love I do sincerely hope that you will hear no more slanders of me," he wrote in September. "It is the malice of the world to abuse me, and really were it not that they reach my beloved Margaret, I would not care one picayune—but that you should be distressed is inexpressible wretchedness to me. . . . [I]f you hear the truth you shall never hear of my being on a spree."

Anxious to reassure Margaret even when no rumors were circulating, Sam explained that he wrote often so that she wouldn't suspect that he was too drunk to write to her, and in another letter he boasted of attending a wedding reception where he'd drunk nothing but coffee. He also boasted that "[m]y health is restored and my colour is returning," but in the next breath stressed that he was motivated more by the desire to make her happy through his abstinence than to improve his health. By mid-January 1841, their mutual trust had grown to the point that Houston seemed almost to tease Margaret about her strictness, addressing her as "my dearly beloved Maggy— whose only dread is that I may abandon myself at some time to intemperance."

Margaret genuinely idolized Sam Houston and told him that to her he "combined all the ideas of human greatness and excellence that had haunted the visions of my youth." Her adulation, however, did not blind her to the imperfections that imperiled his soul. And if drinking was Houston's cardinal vice, swearing was apparently a close second. After Sam wrote in December 1840 that he was trying to break his habit of profaning, she replied that it gave her more pleasure to read about his struggle to rid himself of that "dreadful practice" than anything else in his letter. "Oh continue those efforts! I entreat you Love, by all the sacred happiness we have enjoyed together." Margaret's marriage was not only a romantic journey but a spiritual quest to save her husband's soul. Houston's friend A. W. Terrell paid tribute to Margaret for exercising a "wonderful influence on his habits of drinking and using profane language."

Margaret's plans were not confined to her desires to reform Houston's character. She also hoped that he would put his political ambitions aside and dedicate himself to life with her just as she had dedicated herself to him. Again and again, he insisted, as in this letter from February 1841, that her happiness mattered "more to me than all the Geegaws of ambition, or the pageantry of Royalty," and he offered her veto power over his decisions about political matters. In the end, Margaret never stood in the way of his ambitions, and he continued to run for office. In September 1841 he was elected president of the Republic of Texas by an overwhelming majority over his archrival, David G. Burnet. In the course of that campaign, Margaret probably discovered that Houston often bristled at political advice that was at odds with his own inclinations, even when it came from people close to him. During the campaign, Houston published a series of articles critical of the outgoing president, Mirabeau B. Lamar, and his opponent, Burnet. His allies feared that the articles might hurt Houston's chances and sent Ashbel Smith to Cedar Point to persuade him to stop the attacks. Margaret agreed that Sam should alter his tactics and base his campaign on the ideological differences between the candidates. Houston responded indignantly, "Mr. Smith, the interests of history and of *Truth* are of far more importance than General Lamar's support of Sam Houston can ever be."

After that experience, it is safe to assume that Margaret trod carefully where political tactics were concerned. She often praised Houston's talents for politics and statesmanship and his devotion to the work of governing, but she also made no secret of her true feelings about the life she would like them to lead. She did not accompany him to Austin for the inauguration, and on the night before he was sworn in as president, she wrote from Houston, "Oh how willingly would I resign all the honours of our station and retire into some obscure forest if I could have you, my beloved, always with me." Acutely conscious that her desires would seem unrealistic, she insisted, "It is no romantic picture for, oh my love, the vain plaudits of the crown can not repay us for the severe trials and disappointments which we are compelled to endure, the painful parting, the agonizing fears and the long, long dreary hours of absence."

The postelection tour, which Margaret did join, included a stop in Nacogdoches, where the Houstons were the guests of Adolphus and Eva Sterne, old friends who had acted as god-

parents when Sam made his token conversion to Roman Ca-
tholicism in 1833 (a prerequisite to owning property in Mexican
Texas). Sterne, who was close to Anna Raguet's family, praised
Margaret's skill as a musician and thought she was well matched
to Houston, though he wrote in his diary that he didn't consider
her a great beauty. In this assessment, he was most likely com-
paring unostentatious Margaret to Anna Raguet, the flamboy-
ant and flirtatious daughter of his Nacogdoches friends Henry
and Mercy Raguet. Anna had rejected Houston as a suitor in
1837 and married his friend and former secretary of state, Robert Irion, in 1840.

At another party during this visit to Nacogdoches, Margaret
met the Irions for the first time. Anna was pregnant with her
first child, but in contrast to staid Marion, Alabama, in Texas
visibly pregnant women often went out in public. Although it has
been suggested that the Houstons and Irions were not friends,
Sam and Margaret spent three days at the Irions' farm on the
Angelina River at the end of their Nacogdoches visit. There
were undeniable differences between the outgoing Anna and the
more reticent Margaret. But the Irions named their first child
after Sam Houston, and Margaret embroidered a baby blanket
for the boy shortly after he was born. Before leaving Nacogdoches, Houston gave the town lot he owned to the Sternes' infant
daughter Eugenia, symbolically closing the chapter of his life
when he dreamed of settling down there with Anna Raguet.

From the capital, Houston wrote to Margaret that among the
crowds of celebrants at his inaugural ball, he alone was lonely
and unhappy—because she was absent. Had she been in Austin, he asserted, she would have been as popular as he was. In
fact, Margaret seemed always to have been a social success on
the rare occasions when she appeared in public. After the September election, when Margaret accompanied her husband on
his victory tour, the San Augustine paper observed that she had

"won a popularity, by her kind and Ladylike manner, greater if possible than that which clings to her patriotic husband."

Houston, however, despite his frequent claims that he would be happier at home with Margaret, revealed himself as a quintessentially political being. "In promoting the interests of my country," he said, "I feel that I am promoting my own individual happiness. All that I have, either in reputation or in property, is in Texas. . . . [T]his is my home, my nation, the home of my friends. . . . When my country calls, I have ever deemed it my duty and my privilege to peril my life upon the issue of her glory."

In that November 25 address, Houston asserted that when men acted heroically, it was women who had inspired them. Although he had proved himself in politics and on the battlefield long before he met Margaret, Houston likely had her in mind when he said, "A nation that possesses patriotic women, must ever boast of her gallant sons, brave defenders and successful generals." After the inauguration, he reported that friends in Austin who had known him in his dissolute days praised her for having restored his fortunes, "and that's a most famous work, for it was more than all the world besides could do." He agreed, of course, and thanked her for being "the kind and ministering angel" who had transformed him into a devoted husband and made his political successes possible. Madge Thornall Roberts, the Houstons' great-great-granddaughter, in her dual biography of the couple, argues that Houston "was torn between two loves—Texas and Margaret." Few question his sincerity when he wrote, after being called on to declare himself a candidate for the presidency, "I have flung away ambition. I wish to retire to quiet and rural life where I can live and love my dear, dear Margaret." Yet there was also a side to him that relished the "common world" he claimed to despise, and he never seriously considered renouncing it. Margaret, however, never ceased hoping for a quiet rural life with her husband. She imagined the two of them at Cedar Point or another of their secluded homes, where "[y]ou shall assist me in planting my flowers and training my vines and we will wander through those sweet groves and be as happy as the spirits of some enchanted isle."

Reports that Mexico, which had never formally recognized Texas independence, was contemplating a major invasion of the country reignited a debate about whether the capital should relocate. Margaret and Sam both favored Houston, which its founders, the brothers Augustus and John Allen, designed with the intention of establishing the capital there at their own expense. That plan, endorsed by the Texas Congress in 1836, came to a halt in 1839, when President Mirabeau B. Lamar chose Austin instead. In Houston, Capitol Avenue still led to a vacant lot where the legislature was to have stood, and the "President's House" was so small and rudimentary that when the Houstons had no house of their own in town, Margaret preferred being a guest in the more comfortable homes of their friends John and Eugenia Andrews and Francis and Adele Lubbock. As usual, she camouflaged her preferences by expressing them as a concern for her husband's entitlement—"if you are to serve the people for nothing, I think you ought at least to have the privilege of performing the labour in safety and in some civilized spot"—and diplomatically retreated by deferring to him: "If you are satisfied it will be all right with me, for your happiness is mine."

Not long after Houston's term as president began, the rumors of a Mexican invasion of Texas took on a concrete form. The previous September, Antonio López de Santa Anna had again seized power in Mexico, and he may have been bent on settling his old score with the general who had humiliated him in 1836 and wrested control of Texas away from him. Houston wrote Margaret that the republic's former colonial ruler was now more capable of mounting an invasion than it had been at any time since the revolution. On hearing reports that the United States had agreed to send an army into Mexico whenever Houston gave them the signal, Margaret told her husband, "I hope you will not oppose it, but I know your course will be right."

Houston's reply had in it an unwonted hint of tartness, noting that she had written "that you will rely upon my opinion, *or say so*" (emphasis added). Perhaps he was mildly surprised that Margaret had been so outspoken about a political question. He assured her that he hadn't requested the United States to send troops through Texas or to invade Mexico and had not heard that anyone else had done so. War fever was high in Texas, however, both within the population and among members of its Congress. Volunteers were already organizing, and in June the Congress passed a bill calling for war against Mexico and tried to pressure Houston into signing it. Shrewdly, Houston elected not to confront the issue head-on and refrained from speaking against going to war. Instead he warned that an untrained volunteer army would be incapable of achieving victory. Remembering how unwilling Texans had been six years earlier when it came to the hard work of training and the rigors of military discipline, he stressed that six months would be required to transform recruits into soldiers and at least another half year to fight a war. To clinch his argument, he stressed that because the Texas economy was too poor to feed and maintain an army, the troops might deteriorate into a discontented, insubordinate force, "more dangerous to the security of citizens and the liberties of a country than all the external enemies that could invade its rights."

Houston was adamantly opposed to waging a war or going into battle unless the conditions were favorable, just as he had avoided a military encounter with Santa Anna's army during the Texas Revolution until circumstances presaged victory. But he did nothing to dispel the rumors that were fanning the martial flames. One probable reason was that he hoped the widespread fears would help persuade the public to favor moving the capital from Austin to someplace more secure, ideally a location where Margaret could join him. "I will never occupy any situation that will require me to remain apart from you!" he wrote. "Separation from you is the most painful of all my endurance. If spared to embrace you my dearest, I will not leave you again until you bid me go! . . . and say 'your country demands your services in the field! Go and defend her.' This event I hope will never occur." Meanwhile, though Houston maintained a discreet silence about where he would like to establish the capital, he hoped the Congress would select a spot that suited him or authorize him to make the choice.

The second reason was that the threat was real enough, even if Mexico had no intention of mounting a full-scale invasion of Texas and wished only to make a show of force to highlight its claim of sovereignty over the region. Early in March, a Mexican army crossed into Texas and in short order occupied Goliad, Refugio, and Victoria, followed by San Antonio, which General Rafael Vásquez entered on March 5. With too few men to defend the town, the Texans, under Jack Hays, retreated. Ten days later, a Texas militia force led by Edward Burleson converged on San Antonio, only to discover that the Mexican troops had already departed. Burleson opted not to pursue the enemy, and his militia soon disbanded.

Despite the Mexican withdrawal, unease reigned, especially in West Texas. Outwardly, Sam Houston projected an aura of calm. Mindful that the danger was real, however, he also considered emergency measures—for example, calling a special legislative session in June where he requested Congress to authorize the removal of government records from Austin to a safer place.

Houston considered the risk of war real enough that he wanted to dispatch Margaret to the safety of her relatives in Alabama until all danger was past. He was especially concerned that a repetition of the 1836 Runaway Scrape would be disastrous for someone whose health was as delicate as Margaret's. She shared his apprehension but refused to consider abandoning Texas. To counter her husband's urgings, she quoted lines from *The Siege of Antwerp*, a romantic play of 1838 by William Kennedy, whose protagonists, Frederick and Cassilda Giambelli, are trapped in the siege of the play's title. Frederick declares, "I care not for the issues of the war!" and pledges to his love, "Should darkness settle on our destinies, Like twin stars falling in the thick of night, We'll quit our spheres together." Margaret, fantasizing that Houston's attitude in a military crisis might be equally passive, asked, "Dearest, is that not something like our own love?"

Margaret had met Kennedy, a British journalist and author, in Houston. Kennedy's 1841 *The Rise, Progress, and Prospects of the Republic of Texas* was her favorite history of the republic, and she considered him the ideal person to write her husband's biography. She arranged for him to meet Houston to discuss the idea, and the president quickly endorsed it. He gave Kennedy some materials about San Jacinto that he hadn't shown to any other writer and called him "a gentleman of very correct moral feelings, and clearly intellectual!"

Houston may have indulged Margaret's search for the ideal biographer—and he may have agreed with her choice of Kennedy—but he was determined to have her out of harm's way in the United States as long as war with Mexico threatened. He appointed Margaret's brother Martin Lea as Texas agent for the United States and had him escort Margaret back to Marion in May 1842. One of Margaret's twentieth-century biographers believed that Houston thought the Alabama climate would help Margaret, who had been suffering from asthma and the aftereffects of a bout with malaria. Ironically, her asthma flared up in Marion as well, and the local doctor, Nathaniel Fletcher, said that for someone with pulmonary problems, this was the worst possible season to be in that region. Margaret told her husband the same thing: "To be candid, my Love, I hardly think this climate agrees with me so well as that of Houston." She returned to Texas in July.

Although Houston had sounded Margaret out about whether

he should consider taking command of the Texas army himself if there was war with Mexico, she worried more about whether his antiwar stance put his life in jeopardy with his own people. There were rumors of assassination plots, and some cabinet members were thinking about resigning. Even some of Houston's friends visited him only under cover of darkness. The president was "calm and cheerful" (as he generally was in crises); he assured Margaret that he wasn't going to hide and insisted that they live their normal lives. In *Sam Houston and His Republic*, a campaign biography published in 1846, Charles Lester wrote of this period that "the gay voice of his wife, mingling with the tones of the harp and the piano, which she had carried with her to the wilderness, was heard coming forth from the open windows of Houston's dwelling."

Houston's politically unpopular position against war with Mexico was ultimately vindicated. He waited until the day before Congress adjourned to veto the war bill. No attempt was made to override the veto; Texans had realized that the president had saved them from a costly mistake, and as James Morgan wrote to Ashbel Smith, calm had returned "and 'Old Sam' is more popular than ever I believe." Although he was secure in the rightness of his position, Houston's spirits were undoubtedly buoyed when Andrew Jackson wrote to him on August 17, 1842, "What? to engage in offensive war without a regular army and ample means in money to sustain it, to me appears the height of folly. . . . By your veto you have saved your country, and yourself from disgrace."

There was no sign of Mexican plans to invade Texas, but in the spirit of caution, the capital was temporarily moved to Washington-on-the-Brazos, where Margaret, who was pregnant, was able to join her husband. Either because the chronically cash-poor Houstons could not pay the rent for the rooms that had been selected for them or because the house that was being built for them wasn't yet habitable, they initially stayed in the home of John and Eliza Lockhart—like Margaret, originally from Alabama, although the two families had not been acquainted there. To give the presidential couple a measure of privacy, a door was cut in an exterior wall of their room, so that Sam and Margaret could come and go without having to pass through the other rooms. Their hosts' son, John Washington Lockhart, who was eighteen at the time, wrote that Margaret was "tall and of fine figure, handsome and intelligent, . . . well educated and a good writer of verse. She would have graced the household of any man, be he president or prince."

The younger John Lockhart, who became a physician in Chappell Hill, Texas, after graduating from Louisville Medical College, published observations of Texas and its inhabitants until his death in 1900. Between 1842 and 1845, while the capital was in Washington-on-the-Brazos and the president and his first lady were constantly together, Lockhart had an opportunity to see close-up how profoundly Margaret had transformed Houston. In his judgment, Margaret, "by her great good sense and excellent management, had gained complete control over the general, and it is to her we owe as great a debt of gratitude as to the general himself, for it was owing to her wonderful influence over him that Texas received the benefaction of his great mind. After he married her he quit all of his old habits and dissipation and became a new man."

When the capital moved to Washington-on-the-Brazos in September 1842, the relocation was intended to be temporary, but no one could predict how long it would be before conditions would permit a resumption of business as usual in Austin. In addition, there were still those—Houston among them—who would have preferred to relocate the capital permanently. However, after an abortive attempt to remove the government records from the archives in Austin brought the issue to a head, the matter was settled in favor of Austin, and the capital was reestablished there in 1844.

Eighteen forty-three was to be a roller-coaster year for Margaret. She was due to give birth to her first child in May, and by January her condition was beginning to show. Modest to a fault, Margaret had kept the news secret for as long as possible; except for her husband and her mother, it is not certain that she told anyone. The pregnancy was also difficult, and she was sometimes unwell. During one such period, she left Washington-on-the-Brazos to spend time closer to her family, staying at the home of Vernal and Mary Lea on the Trinity River, not far from the Grand Cane residence of William and Antoinette Bledsoe. While Margaret was there, Nancy Lea visited from Galveston as well. At about this time, the family received the news that Margaret's brother Martin had died in Alabama in March, probably a suicide, although they were never to be certain.

Margaret returned to the capital when she and Sam were able to move into a rented cottage of their own, which further assured their privacy. While waiting to give birth, she rarely went out, except for occasional buggy rides with Eliza, her servant, who was inseparable from Margaret and virtually a member of the family. Houston's mixture of elation and nervousness about the arrival of their firstborn almost certainly mirrored Margaret's. He had been hoping for children ever since their marriage almost three years earlier. In 1841, he appended a wistful postscript to a letter to Robert Irion, "No Name-sake," when he discovered that what he and Margaret had believed were signs of pregnancy turned out be a false alarm. Now, he confessed to his friend, "I feel gratified, of course, but the idea of assuming the dignity of a 'daddy' rather throws me aback."

A son, Sam Houston Jr., was born on May 25, and the arrival soon afterward of the proud but autocratic grandmother probably did little to bring calm to the household. Nancy Lea, in addition to supplying what she considered proper foods for the family, brought a cow as well, so that Margaret could stop nursing. When Houston objected that he was responsible for feeding his family, family legend has it that Nancy replied that he could starve if he wished, but she would not permit her grandchild to suffer that fate. She was said to remind him often, "You may have conquered Santa Anna, but you will never conquer me!" They ultimately compromised: Nancy would lay in provisions as she saw fit, and Houston would reimburse her.

The Houston household mushroomed after the birth of Sam Jr. Besides Nancy Lea, Margaret's eighteen-year-old niece, Sarah Ann "Sallie" Royston, came from Marion, and after Mary Lea died, Virginia Thorn, a troubled child Vernal and Mary had adopted, also moved into the Houstons' Washington home. Fortunately, motherhood seemed to make Margaret more sociable. Earlier, she was sometimes said to be uncomfortable when Indians came to call on Houston, who had many Native American friends, especially among the Cherokees. But in October, she wrote of a visit from the family of the old chief Coleta, who "have been camping near us several days. . . . He took Sam in his arms, and his dim eyes sparkled with delight. Oh how I wish I could speak their language! . . . It pains my heart to know . . . they are passing away, and soon the lone forests they inhabit will know them no more."

Despite the gloom that accompanied their occasional separations, the Houstons' mood brightened throughout the year, due, no doubt, to the presence of Sam Jr., but also to the fact that much of the time when Margaret and Houston were apart, she now usually stayed with her relatives in Grand Cane and was rarely left alone to brood on gloomy thoughts. In addition, Houston detected "the glow of happiness" on the faces of many Texans, which he attributed to the fact that the country was at peace and growing more prosperous, conditions that he traced to his policies. Such public affirmation of his providential leadership, however, could not compare to what he described to Margaret as "the pleasure which greeted me at home, when I returned care worn from my office, embraced you, and took a look at Sam." Margaret must have felt especially gratified when Houston went on to claim that he aspired to be remembered as a virtuous and pious man rather than a military hero and statesman. Not long afterward, Margaret mentioned Houston's "astonishing" change to Nancy Lea, writing that she was sure "it is the work of God and that his heart is under the influence of the Holy Spirit. His walk is certainly that of a pure Christian."

In 1844, Houston's last year as president, the couple, anticipating a return to private life, searched for a new family home. Much of the time, Margaret and Sam Jr. remained at Grand Cane. Houston, on his travels in East Texas to discuss treaty terms with the Indians, found a plantation fourteen miles outside Huntsville. He bought the property and drew up plans for a house—a larger version of the cabin at Cedar Point—the construction of which he entrusted to Joshua, a gifted craftsman whom Margaret had inherited as a slave from her father. The house, he decided, would be called Raven Hill—probably alluding to the name (the Raven) he had been given by the Cherokees.

By May 25, 1844, Houston had returned to Grand Cane, in time to celebrate Sam Jr.'s first birthday with Margaret and the extended family. Throughout that summer, he was able to spend time there only sporadically. Stumping for Anson Jones, his choice as successor in the September election against Edward Burleson (who had in fact been Houston's vice president), consumed much of the ensuing months, but he also continued treaty negotiations with the Indians and spent some time in the Redlands, in northeastern Texas, calming riots over land speculation. Ill and exhausted after the election, he rode his mule, Bruin, back to Grand Cane and spent a week in bed.

Margaret herself was anything but idle that summer. The Baptist community in the vicinity of Grand Cane was growing, and Margaret, along with Nancy Lea and other friends and relatives, embarked on discussions that led to the founding of the Concord Baptist Church in the town. She wrote excitedly to Houston about these developments, and he later assisted in the building of the church edifice itself, although his thoughts were probably more on Huntsville and the new house he envisioned there than on the nascent Baptist congregation in Grand Cane.

Anson Jones was inaugurated in Washington-on-the-Brazos on December 9, and Houston immediately left the capital for Grand Cane. At the winter solstice, he wrote to the new president of his joy at being home, and added, "I found my mind falling back into a channel, where the current flows in domestic peace and quiet, without one care about the affairs of Government, and only intent upon domestic happiness and prosperity." That same day, Margaret presented him with "To My Husband," a poem celebrating his release from the burdens of safeguarding the republic. Now, the last verse declared, "Thy task is done. The holy shade / Of Calm retirement waits thee now, / The lamp of hope relit hath shed / Its sweet refulgence o'er thy brow." More than one reader has seen Margaret's composition as little more than fond hope. As Madge Thornall Roberts observed, when he stepped down from his second term as president, Houston's "long service to Texas" was only beginning.

In January 1845, with the annexation of Texas on everyone's mind, an ailing Andrew Jackson wrote to Houston, "I tell you in sincerity & friendship, if you will achieve this annexation your name & fame will be enrolled amongst the greatest chieftains of the age." A formal proposal of annexation was made by the United States Congress in February. Houston had been president of Texas when the first overtures regarding American statehood were made in 1837; that effort and a subsequent one went nowhere. Now he explained to Jackson that he had kept silent on the question only because he feared that a third rejection would deal a death blow to Texas's prospects for merger.

Not even Andrew Jackson Donelson, Jackson's nephew and the American chargé d'affaires in Texas, was able to penetrate Houston's wall of silence until April. It's possible that not even Margaret was privy to his thoughts on the matter until he wrote to her on April 1, "All wish to know how I look upon or in what fashion of thought I entertain about the matter and my reply is 'I do not know what action has taken place or what may be necessary to be done. Therefore I can give no satisfactory opinion in the case.'" He may, of course, have privately shared his opinion with Margaret earlier, but on crucial questions, Houston often kept his cards close to his colorful vest. And for him this was a crucial question; on it hung his political future and, possibly, his ambitions for national office once Texas was part of the United States.

In order to sound Houston out on annexation, Donelson went to see him in person. On April 9, shortly after Donelson left, Houston laid his cards on the table. "I am in favor of annexation, if it can take place on terms mutually beneficial to both countries." Significantly, he also insisted, "I have, on all occasions . . . withheld no means in my power towards its completion." He was evidently satisfied that the tide of public opinion had now turned in favor of annexation, and that the arrangement would be in the best interest of Texas. He was thus ready to endorse the idea, and to this end, he wrote letters to the papers and spoke out on the issue. In an address in Houston in May, he declared, "I can truly rejoice with you, my fellow citizens, . . . that our annexation to the mother country is assured. . . . I consider the benefit to be derived . . . great beyond the power of language to describe." A convention held in Austin approved the agreement on July 4, 1845, and took up the business of writing a new state constitution. On December 29 Texas became the twenty-eighth state of the Union.

As he wrapped up his affairs in Washington-on-the-Brazos after Jones's inauguration, Houston wrote Andrew Jackson of his plans to visit him in Tennessee in the spring. Late in May, Houston, Margaret, and Sam Jr. sailed to New Orleans, where he addressed an "immense crowd" on the annexation of Texas. There the news reached them that Jackson was gravely ill, and they immediately booked passage to Nashville, but their ship ran aground on the Mississippi and was not freed for two days. As a result of the delay, they reached the Hermitage a few hours after Jackson died. With his two-year-old son in his arms, Houston entered the room where his friend's body lay and said to Sam Jr., "My son, try to remember that you have looked upon the face of this great man."

The Houstons stayed with Andrew Jackson Donelson and his family, whose house was adjacent to the Hermitage. It was Houston who wrote to President James Knox Polk to inform him of Jackson's death, expressing his regret that he had not reached his friend in time to offer "some comfort in the closing scene of his eventful life." Houston served as a pallbearer at Jackson's funeral, and the Houstons stayed with the Donelsons for some days before leaving to visit other friends and relatives in the state, including Eliza Moore, Houston's sister. They then continued south to Alabama. Margaret and Sam Jr. enjoyed a long visit with her relatives. Houston, after a speaking tour of the South, headed back to Texas in September, but he persuaded Margaret to remain in Alabama until an outbreak of yellow fever had subsided.

On his return, Houston learned that Margaret's brother-in-law William Bledsoe had died. Before he had a chance to inform Margaret, she read Bledsoe's obituary in a Mobile newspaper. Learning of the death in this secondhand fashion intensified her sense of distance from her husband and her home. She "long[ed] for our time of departure to come" and worried that Houston has still not consented to be baptized. "[H]ow intensely I feel for your eternal welfare!" she wrote. "Oh that the Lord would enlighten your darkness!"

Margaret finally landed in Galveston on November 10. Sam was waiting at the dock. He had considered sailing to New Orleans to accompany her on the return but was afraid he might arrive only after she had already left. After visiting with the Lea relatives, especially the recently widowed Antoinette and Margaret's brother Vernal, who had remarried, to Catherine Davis, the Houstons installed themselves in their new house at Raven Hill. The rooms were on either side of an open passage, with galleries running the length of the building. A separate building housed the kitchen, as a precaution against fire, and there were also cabins for the slaves. Keeping Margaret's love of fruits and flowers in mind, Houston had asked Joshua to plant fruit trees—figs, plums, and quinces—and berries, as well as shrubs and flowers. Margaret was pleased with Raven Hill, where she imagined settling into a quiet life as the wife of a Huntsville lawyer, who would return home each evening to his adoring wife and children. But Houston, and the soon-to-be state of Texas, had other plans.

Part VI

MARGARET LEA HOUSTON, PART 2

1840s–1860s

Statehood
Secession
Civil War

Margaret in middle age

No wonder my father loved you so.

-NETTIE TO MARGARET HOUSTON, 1865

The annexation of Texas was a boon to Texans and to Sam Houston's political career, but for Margaret it meant more years of frequent, prolonged separation from her husband. Aware that Margaret hoped he would remain a private citizen, on December 8, 1845, Sam nonetheless declared his interest in a seat in the United States Senate. There was no doubt that Houston and fellow candidate Thomas Rusk would be elected. Margaret was undoubtedly disappointed, but she could not have been surprised that this intensely political creature had again chosen love of country over his avowedly passionate love for her. Their parting was anything but easy, however, and at first Margaret considered going to Washington, D.C., with her husband. But after discovering that she was pregnant with their second child, she agreed to wait until after Houston's sister Eliza Moore arrived from Tennessee.

Settled in at Raven Hill, Margaret was pleased when their

nephew Houston Moore turned up ahead of the rest of his family and stayed to help her run the farm even after his parents settled nearby. She wrote Sam of how unhappy it made her to contemplate the growing distance between them as he made his way north, and she spoke of their home in idyllic terms: "All is peace and quiet on Raven Hill," she wrote. "The balmy breeze murmurs so sweetly among the lofty pines and the spring flowers look up so cheerfully that I sometimes almost forget my grief and fancy that you are at my side."

Eliza Moore's arrival relieved Margaret's feelings of isolation. The Moores rented a farm not far from Raven Hill, and Eliza quickly talked her sister-in-law out of trying to join Houston in Washington. He had already encouraged Margaret to join him if she thought she could travel without jeopardizing her pregnancy, and a few weeks later, she wrote about how tempted she had been to let her emotions prevail over her reason, until Eliza persuaded her that "with me, feeling had so much to do in the matter that it would really be unwise to decide for myself."

Margaret wasn't the only Lea family member to feel the pull of her heart's desires that April. Margaret's sister, Antoinette, barely six months after the death of her husband, William Bledsoe, married Charles Power, an English merchant in Galveston. The wedding took place on a ship in the Galveston harbor, with no one from the family present. At first, even Sam was scandalized, writing to Margaret, "So soon to marry and from home too, distresses me." At the same time, he urged her to treat Antoinette and her new husband kindly if they visited. Soon afterward, Power wrote to Houston, and the letter evidently made a favorable impression on his brother-in-law. Sam sent it on to Margaret and added an exculpatory postscript to his own letter: "Dear, I have just thought of it! We married to please ourselves, and Antoinette and Mr. Power have only done the same thing!"

Although Houston referred to the marriage as "apparently hasty," Antoinette was, after all, a youthful twenty-four-year-old widow with no children. In short order, her relatives abandoned their suspicions that the wealthy Power had induced Antoinette to marry him with gifts such as diamond and emerald necklaces, forgave her for making light of contemporary mores of mourning, and gave their new in-law a warm welcome. In fact, a few months later, Margaret's niece, Sarah Ann Royston, married James Power, Charles's younger brother, under more socially acceptable circumstances. By then the mood had lightened to the point that Houston didn't hesitate to tease Margaret about the strict line she had taken over their own marriage arrangements. "Will she make him go to Alabama for her? Or marry at the Island [Galveston]? Our relations are more cheap, I fear, than when you would not marry me or come to Texas, but required me to go after you to Alabama."

Adding to the hopeful mood at that time was Houston's announcement that he had switched loyalties from the Presbyterian church he had been attending in Washington, D.C., to the E Street Baptist Church. For thirteen years, he faithfully attended the E Street church whenever he was in Washington and usually summarized the sermon in his letters to Margaret. Sam's revelation that he was inching closer to embracing her Baptist faith filled Margaret with hope. Houston gave her all the credit for turning him into a "sage and regulated" man, but she preferred to see his serenity and sobriety as "the dawning of that change which I have so earnestly sought for you at the throne of grace."

If the Houstons were entering a season of personal calm in the spring of 1846, a storm was brewing on the Texas-Mexico border. In 1845, James Knox Polk, who had run for the presidency as a pro-annexation candidate, failed to secure an agreement with Mexico setting the boundary with Texas at the Rio Grande. In the face of Mexico's refusal to cooperate, General Zachary Taylor was ordered to move his army from Corpus Christi to the Texas side of the border in January 1846, and by the time the United States Congress endorsed the annexation resolution in February, more than two thousand American troops were already at the contested dividing line. Mexico, which considered the American presence an act of war, sent its soldiers across the Rio Grande to attack a small U.S. Army contingent in April, and Polk requested Congress to declare war.

The day war was declared, May 13, Ashbel Smith wrote to Senator Houston that Texans wanted him to lead a company of their citizens against Mexico. Sam assured Margaret that he would accept no commission without "your free voluntary consent." From her vantage in Texas, Margaret witnessed the growing war fever among her neighbors; she wrote that their young nephew Houston Moore was "almost crazy to go" and reported that a local colonel had asked her to supervise the making of a flag for his company. "Perhaps he thinks my connection with you may give it some charm."

As usual, Margaret declined Sam's gambit of giving her veto power over decisions that involved his political career. This time, however, she was unusually frank about her own wishes. She reminded him that in the past she had always "ascertained your views and then coincided with them, let my own sacrifices be what they might." Before leaving the choice to him, however, she stressed two crucial differences: war was riskier business than politics, and now they had a child. "I will not express one word of opposition, but I cannot look around upon my widowed hearth and hear my poor boy's plaintive cry, 'what makes pa stay so long?' and then tell you that I am willing for you to go."

Houston blamed the dark tone of Margaret's June 20 letter on her tendency to "great depression and melancholy." In hindsight, however, he conceded that she was right to object to his taking up arms again.

At this time, Margaret was burdened by her pregnancy, now in its eighth month, which added to her discomfort and apprehensiveness and sometimes confined her to bed. Even when she was feeling well, Margaret's pregnancies were not easy. In an earlier letter, she had joked that when she read that he expected to come home soon, she felt like dancing, but "now from some cause or another it would be a most *ungraceful* exercise."

Congress adjourned in August, and Houston reached Raven Hill before Margaret went into labor. Nancy Elizabeth, whom they called Nannie, was born on September 6, 1846. Thanks to Joshua, who was responsible for nearly every building at Raven Hill and the Houstons' other homes, new structures had sprung up. Near the main house, a kitchen and smokehouse now stood, as well as neat rows of slave cabins, a blacksmith shop, and barns and pens for the livestock. Before the senator headed back to Washington in November, Joshua built a small cabin that was to serve as Houston's office and the library for his books and papers. At least one Houston biographer has commented on how little opportunity he would have to use the cabin office as more than a storage room for his books and papers.

Shortly after Houston departed, a painful breast tumor that periodically troubled Margaret flared up again. The tumor, though painful, did not appear to be cancerous, and it shrank after being lanced. If the lancing failed to cure her, Margaret planned to go to Memphis to have the tumor removed by Dr. Isaac Thomas. She wrote to Sam on November 27 to report on her progress and hopes for a complete recovery and to share her plans for surgery should it prove necessary.

Another illness struck close to home in January 1847 when Margaret was awakened by groans coming from her son Sam's bedroom. When she reached the six-year-old's side, she found him cold, stiff, and shivering, but shortly afterward he turned feverish. When Margaret asked Sam if he was in pain, he would point to his head or neck, and throughout that night the boy was cold and hot to her touch at the same time. In the morning, his skin took on a "dead purple hue." Though scary and myste-rious, the purple color eventually faded, and the boy recovered. She wrote the senator once the danger had passed, "I can give you no idea of the joyful gratitude, that fills my soul this day, for the restoration of my child."

When Sam read Margaret's letter, he immediately suspected that Virginia Thorn, the young ward of Vernal and Mary Lea whom the Houstons had taken in after Mary died in 1845, was somehow the culprit. She was a troubled, difficult child of about eleven, and Houston had never trusted her. Soon after she joined the household, he warned Margaret, "Beware of Virginia. There is no telling what the little *monster* may do." Now he asked whether Virginia might have fed something to Sam that made him ill and hoped that she could be "separated from our dear *jewels*." Catherine Lea, Vernal's second wife, did take Virginia back to Grand Cane in 1848, but the girl was to cause Margaret great distress not many years later.

Senator Houston had an opportunity to shine in the Senate when he spoke in support of President Polk's request for $3 million to be used in peace negotiations with Mexico (presumably to purchase California). "I furnished the world with much new matter and information relative to Texas," he wrote Margaret, mentioning proudly that in the course of his two-hour-long speech, no one left the Senate chamber. Despite the fact that the American armies, led by Generals Zachary Taylor and Winfield Townley Scott, among others, won victory after victory against larger enemy forces, the Mexicans refused to negotiate, and the war dragged on. At the beginning of March 1847, Polk again offered to make Houston a major general in the army, and again Houston declined.

It was about this time that he learned the true seriousness of his beloved wife's tumor. Despite Margaret's avowed plan to go to Tennessee for surgery if necessary, she did nothing until February 1847, when Charles Power, upon discovering that her condition had worsened, wrote to Ashbel Smith, "I believe if you would put your instruments in your pocket and come up here, she would submit herself to you, having confidence only in you in the performance of such a surgical operation."

Ashbel Smith was the trusted friend the Houston family turned to time and again. He had earned undergraduate and medical degrees from Yale and taught and practiced medicine in France and North Carolina before moving to Texas in 1836. He founded the Texas Medical Association and was instrumental in establishing Texas Medical College, in Galveston (1873), and the University of Texas (1883). Though Margaret attempted to downplay the gravity of the procedure, Houston would have trusted no one more than his longtime confidant.

A week after Power's plea to Dr. Smith, Margaret tried to calm Houston's fears by writing that although her pain had made writing too difficult for a while, "the operation will be a mere trifle and easily performed in two minutes." She was preparing herself, she said, "to sit down to it like a soldier." Two weeks later, when her brother Vernal Lea worried that the tumor was continuing to grow, Dr. Smith came back. With a Dr. Bauers to assist Smith, Margaret did in fact tough out the surgery like a soldier. To Antoinette's horror, she refused the whiskey the doctor urged on her to dull the pain, and instead of biting the proverbial bullet, she made it through the operation with a silver coin clenched between her teeth. "Mrs. Houston," Dr. Smith wrote to her husband, "bore the pain with great fortitude."

When Houston came home during the congressional recess, he exchanged Raven Hill for a house closer to Huntsville owned by his overseer, Frank Hatch. He and Margaret both felt that she and the children were too isolated on their "forlorn hilltop," especially when he was away in Washington. While the family was at Raven Hill for the summer, he had the small cabin on the new property, which became known as the Woodland home, enlarged. He kept busy with his law practice and speaking engagements, and toward the end of 1847 started back to the nation's capital. When he left, Margaret was five months pregnant with their third child. They planned to have Margaret join Sam in Washington after the baby was born. "[W]here you are not,

I can not be happy," he wrote, and exhorted his frugal wife not
to worry about the cost.

The Mexican War ended in September 1847, and the Treaty of
Guadalupe Hidalgo was adopted the following February. In it,
Mexico agreed that its border with Texas was the Rio Grande,
and it also ceded California, Arizona, New Mexico, and parts of
Utah, Nevada, and Colorado to the United States.

The treaty had an unforeseen personal impact on the Houstons as well. During their long periods of separation, letters
were the lifeline that preserved their intimacy, and when the
flow of correspondence was interrupted, both feared the worst.
In March 1848, after a long stretch without hearing from Margaret, Sam anxiously wrote, "If you have not time or can not
by any means write to me at length, just write me three words,
'all are well,' and I will be happy compared to what I now am."
When Margaret read Houston's letter, she shot back, "My Love,
you ought not to have said, 'If you have not had time to write.'
I never felt more pained by an expression. Can you believe for
a moment that I would put off writing to you for any other occupation?'"

The cause of her apparent silence was that when the Treaty
of Guadalupe Hidalgo was signed on February 2, 1848, the mail
boats were temporarily diverted to bring American troops back
from Veracruz. When Houston learned the cause, he wrote an
abject apology in which he claimed that in an "excess of love"
he had imagined Margaret unable to write because she was
nursing a sick child. Before that letter arrived, Margaret, with
the same tone as his previous anxious letter to her, expressed
the disquiet brought on by a period with no word from him: "I
must either hear from you regularly, or you must come home,"
she wrote. "I know I ought to conceal every feeling of distress
from you, but I am so disappointed that my heart sickens."

It is easy to forgive Margaret's flash of impatience, which was written on April 9, three days before she went into labor. In fact, she tried to compose another letter on the twelfth but managed only a single line. A healthy girl was born on April 13. Margaret and Sam had been considering various names but hadn't made a choice. On May 8, Margaret wrote, "She is becoming quite a young lady, to have no name." Her letter crossed with one from her husband, who proposed Margaret: "I have no choice, unless it were that we might have a dear little Maggy."

As happened whenever Sam and Margaret resolved to join forces in Washington, obstacles arose. The first setback occurred when Margaret fell ill with pneumonia for several weeks, but she still intended to make the trip—with the new baby girl, Maggie, and Sam in tow—in late May or early June. She was comfortable leaving Nannie at home, in the care of Nancy Lea, but, she explained, "A mother, like a good General, ought to watch that part of her little force which is most exposed to the fire." When the former general read what Margaret intended, he began to see danger everywhere: in her traveling with two young children, in sea voyages as well as poking along in a stagecoach at six miles an hour, and in "the coarseness of stage drivers and car conductors." He proposed waiting until the fall, when he would charter a carriage to take her from Alabama to Washington.

By the time Sam had compiled his objections, however, Margaret had already concluded that the entire project was an impractical scheme designed to distract her from "the dreary range of six or seven months absence from you, but when the subject is brought closely to view, there are so many things in the way, that I do not think it will be possible." As far as she was concerned, it would be as easy to travel to Washington as to Alabama, but she had decided "to remain quietly at home, until you return."

There could have been other reasons, as well. Margaret and the children liked their new Woodland house, with its brick chimneys and glass windows. She decided that some improve-

ments Houston had planned for the house had to be postponed
because of their cost, so instead she planted shrubs and flowers,
many of them dug up from the Raven Hill property. Equally important, because the Woodland house was close to town, Sam,
at age four, could collect the mail from the post office on his
own. "I have never seen such a boy for business and he sees
every thing about the place, that is not just right," Margaret
wrote. People came to stay with them, such as Minerva, Eliza,
and Carry Davis, Raven Hill neighbors and sisters of Catherine, Vernal Lea's new wife. Two of the girls attended school
in Huntsville. Perhaps most important, in Huntsville Margaret
had like-minded friends, notably Tercey Birdwell and Frances
Creath, wife of the local Baptist minister.

Tranquility restored, Margaret turned her attention, as she
often did, to Houston's spiritual well-being. He may not have
been attending church as regularly as he had during the previous session, and she suspected that political distractions might
be the reason. Eighteen forty-eight was a presidential election
year, and Houston's name was one of those on the lips of people
in Washington. Ashbel Smith noted in his diary that "General
Rusk said Houston has behaved very well, and if he continues as
he has done he will 'rent the White House.'" Margaret, fearing
that what she called the "bewitching . . . voice of fame" might
steal her husband's heart from God, prayed "that you may be
kept from the evil of this world and fitted for the joys of the
next." When Houston reassured her that he was not neglect-
ful of religious matters, Margaret revealed that "[t]o see my
husband enjoying the comforts of religion, and to have his aid
in bringing up our children for the Lord would be greater bless-
ings than I can ever deserve."

Houston didn't consider the presidency among the world's
evils, however, although he insisted that he wasn't actively seeking the Democratic nomination. He admitted, in his letters to
Margaret but perhaps not to anyone else, that he would welcome the nomination, and wrote that if he were to occupy the

White House, "it would give new charms to home." Proud as ever, he added that "I will not *truckle* nor degrade my feelings for any station on this earth!" The nomination would have to come to him, and whatever happened, he added, he spent more time thinking about Margaret and their children than any political office. In the event, the nomination went to Senator Lewis Cass of Michigan, who had been Andrew Jackson's secretary of war. Houston refused the vice presidential nomination, and though he also declined to campaign for Cass around the country, he did speak on his behalf in Texas.

When Congress adjourned and Houston was finally able to come home, he met Maggie for the first time and saw the results of the expansion of their house, now a two-story structure with double chimneys on both floors and open breezeways upstairs and down. Their bedroom and a parlor were on the ground floor; the children's bedrooms were upstairs. Margaret had gathered things from their other houses to furnish the Woodland home, but there were still only a few luxurious items: the piano, the marble-top table that had been Houston's desk when he was president of Texas, a serpentine carved rosewood sofa, and a four-poster bed. The grounds, however, were full of flowering plants and fruit-bearing trees, as they were wherever Margaret lived: walnut and pecan trees near the house, and lilacs, roses, irises, syringas, narcissus, jonquils, and Easter lilies in the garden. At the corners of each flower bed stood a crepe myrtle tree, sixteen in all. Behind the main house were quince, apple, peach, and fig trees.

The property covered 173 acres, much of it uncultivated woodlands and meadows. On her own initiative, Margaret proposed adding two "shed rooms" on the south side of the house, one a dining room and the second a bedroom for Nancy Lea. Although Margaret and Houston never ceased vacillating about whether she should join him in the capital, from the time the family settled into the Woodland house she was more inclined to stay put. Because of the coming election, the fall session was expected to be short, so the prospect of separation was less daunting.

In any case, when Margaret thought about living in Washington, she unrealistically imagined "a pleasant boarding house" eight or ten miles outside the city, where "at night I would have your company, without being so much interrupted by visitors." Life was also more economical at home, where they could raise their own fruits and vegetables, cure their own meat, and obtain credit at stores for whatever they couldn't grow or make themselves. In addition, Sam Jr. was now five, and Margaret was responsible for his education; Thomas Gott, the new overseer, had recently arrived; and Vernal's ward Virginia Thorn had moved back in with the Houstons. Their household had thus grown increasingly complex, and in Houston's absence the job of supervising it fell on Margaret's shoulders. For the most part, she managed on her own; occasionally, as when she felt that Gott's success in managing the slaves was lacking, she asked Houston to intervene.

In Texas at this time, most people aimed for as much self-sufficiency as possible. They raised their own crops, built their own houses, often with the help of friends and neighbors, and made their own clothing. Some even wove their own cloth. Like Margaret, many of them had come to Texas from parts of the country with more highly developed cash economies, more manufacturing, and better transportation systems. Moving to Texas in the 1840s usually meant adjusting to a more rudimentary, but also a more self-reliant way of life.

For her part, Margaret Houston, at twenty-nine, had learned a great deal about self-reliance after moving from Alabama to Texas, and she had also begun to gain perspective on her inclination to moodiness when Sam was away. In November, she admitted as much and advised, "[I]f I should be so unfortunate again as to write in a melancholy mood, you must just take it for what it is worth." She increasingly leavened her letters with news of local goings-on. In addition to the children, about whose growth and accomplishments she wrote at length, and other family members, she also reported on visits from friends, her work with the Baptist church and Temperance Society, and even—apologetically—shared her opinions about politics. When Zachary Taylor won the three-way contest for the presidency in November (Martin Van Buren's Free Soil Party siphoned enough votes away from the Democrats to allow Taylor to carry most of the Northeast), she predicted that if Lamar hadn't been able to ruin "poor little Texas," Taylor wouldn't succeed in ruining the United States.

When a problem arose when Sam was away, Margaret generally told him about it only after it had been resolved, or else waited until he returned home. One difficulty that was to plague the family for two years was the attachment that Virginia Thorn formed with Thomas Gott. Early in 1849, the fourteen-year-old Virginia told Gott, who was twenty-six, that she was nineteen, trailed after him by day, and caused gossip by sitting up with him late at night on the Houstons' porch. When Margaret scolded the girl, Virginia was "insolent and ungovernable." Because the girl was a Baptist, Margaret persuaded her to visit the Creaths, the local pastor and his wife, hoping they would be able to curb her behavior. When Houston came home in April, he and Margaret discussed the awkward situation, but they did not take steps to separate the pair by dismissing Gott or sending Virginia away.

Margaret was again pregnant when the time came for Sam to return to Washington in the fall of 1849. Her fourth pregnancy was proving even more difficult than the first three had been. Houston pledged to return before the baby was due in April, but in the spring of 1850, Congress was embroiled in disputes over boundary lines and American slavery that carried profound implications for Texas and the Union. Resolving them involved a cluster of bills collectively known as the Compromise of 1850. This absorbed much of Houston's attention that year and prevented him, at times, from being with his family. As he humorously put it in a letter to Margaret in December 1849, "I am and ever will be for the *Union* and for *our Union!*" His mission, however, to offer a temperate southern alternative to "southern fanatics" who refused to consider compromise, was one he took seriously. He proposed a compromise that he described to Margaret as "the only feasible plan" for preserving the balance between the slaveholding South and the abolitionist North. To make it possible for him to slip away to Texas without abandoning his political responsibilities, he planned to find a Whig senator who would agree to offset his votes so that his absence would not affect the legislative outcome of any critical bills.

To deal with Virginia Thorn's rebelliousness, Margaret's friends Tercey Birdwell and Frances Evans advised her to discipline the girl on her own and not to refer the matter to the church council. Margaret tried to do so, and for a while she thought that Virginia was more content, but near the end of January 1850 she awoke one morning to find that the girl and Gott had slipped away to Cincinnati, Texas, where the Presbyterian missionary and educator Melinda Rankin ran a school. Virginia intended to enroll as a student for one term before marrying Gott.

At about the time Virginia disappeared from Huntsville, Sam, concerned about Margaret's health, left Washington to spend several weeks at home. Hoping to ease Margaret's burdens, he hired a new overseer, Daniel Johnson, to replace Gott. Margaret later found that Johnson had trouble managing the slaves, who took advantage of his lenient disposition. She told Houston that Eliza was the only one among their servants who was unfailingly faithful and helpful.

A month later, Houston was on his way back to Washington. He was absent when their fourth child, a girl, was born on April 9. Margaret's sister, Antoinette Power, was with Margaret for the birth; she wrote Houston that the baby had been named Mary William, after their sister-in-law, the late Mary Lea, and Houston's brother William. For the first month Margaret wasn't well enough to write, and even then, she said, "it seems impossible for me to recover my strength."

Virginia Thorn returned to Huntsville after a few months, moved in with the Houstons' friends B. L. and Jane Wilson, and attended the local school. Stories circulated in town that Margaret had mistreated the girl, and Margaret was of two minds about whether the Wilsons were parties to a scheme to defame her. Houston suspected that the entire affair was an attempt by his enemies to gain some advantage over him by attacking "the females of my family." He assured Margaret that if a plot existed, it was doomed to fail and counseled her to act as if she hadn't heard the rumors. Soon she reported that her relations with the Birdwells and Wilsons were as amicable as ever. "I trust the storm is past."

Efforts to reach agreement about the borders of Texas and the status of slavery in the territories acquired from Mexico in 1848 dragged on through the summer of 1850. Houston had no choice but to remain in Washington while the debate over the future of Texas and the stability of the Union continued. He felt there was too much at stake to leave, especially before the future of Texas was assured; it "would be a desertion of the highest duty of a man and a Patriot." To compensate for his absence from home, he devoted long passages in his letters to the children. When Margaret mentioned that although young Sam was a good reader, he preferred to be read to, Houston began to address letters directly to his son, containing messages for the boy to deliver to other members of the household and giving him work to do on the farm. Margaret had also written that Sam felt outnumbered as the only boy and that the previously sweet-natured child had turned irritable and willful, so Houston added words of moral instruction. "Boys should always be kind and generous to their Sisters," he told his son. "No man is either good or great who is unkind to women!"

The bills that made up the Compromise of 1850 finally passed that September. In return for surrendering its claims to New Mexico and land north of the Missouri Compromise line, established in 1820, Texas received $10 million to pay off the national debt from its years as an independent republic. In other components of the compromise, California was admitted to the Union as a free state, and the New Mexico and Utah territories were given the right to determine whether to be slave or free by popular sovereignty; a stronger Fugitive Slave Law was enacted; and the buying and selling of slaves—but not slaveholding itself—was prohibited in Washington, D.C. With the passage of legislation that benefited Texas and is generally credited with preserving the Union for ten years, Houston was finally free to go home.

At Thomas Gott's urging, Virginia Thorn had accused Margaret of physical abuse when she lived with the Houstons, and before Houston returned to Texas, a grand jury met to consider the charges. Houston had engaged his friend Henderson Yoakum as Margaret's attorney. In his diary, Yoakum noted laconically, "He is somewhat troubled about some domestic matters." Based on Virginia's testimony, Margaret was indicted and a trial set for September 1851.

When Yoakum reported in November 1850 that the Texas legislature had voted to accept the federal terms setting its boundaries in return for monetary compensation, Houston told him, "I may now retire then, for it is consummation of what I have struggled to attain for eighteen years past." Of course, he didn't retire, and when he went back to Washington in January 1851, Margaret returned to the idea of joining him there. Houston pledged never to endure another long congressional session like that of 1850 without Margaret and wrote that he had begun to inquire about a house large enough for the entire family.

A short legislative session in the new year made it possible for Houston to spend much of 1851 in Huntsville. This put to rest, at least for a time, talk of his retiring or of Margaret and their children relocating. He came home laden with gifts—dresses, bonnets, and parasols—because he wanted, he told Margaret, "not only to see you smile, but to keep you smiling." During an uncommonly leisurely summer, Houston and Margaret had time to travel to Houston, Galveston, and Cedar Point, where they were able to see their friends and relatives.

On the last day of September, Margaret's trial on charges of having assaulted Virginia Thorn was held in Huntsville. In her testimony, Virginia claimed that when Nannie started crying while Virginia was dressing her, Margaret said that Virginia had hurt the child and then shoved Virginia against a bedpost and struck her perhaps twenty times with a cowhide whip. As a result, she said she suffered bruises on her wrist and elbow. Thomas Gott, who Virginia conceded had proposed bringing a complaint against Margaret, told the court that he had seen Virginia's bruised wrist and heard Margaret threaten the girl with another beating if she didn't behave. "That cowhide is still there," Gott claimed she had said.

Margaret did not testify, but her brother, Vernal Lea, Virginia's legal guardian, said that the girl had always behaved poorly, and a neighbor of Vernal's added that she could be governed only with strong discipline. A number of other witnesses, including Frances Creath, Melicia Baines, Frances Evans, Martha Ransom, and Thomas Parmer, acted as character witnesses for the defendant. The jury was unable to reach a verdict, and the case was referred to the Baptist Church for investigation. A month later, the church exonerated Margaret, but the affair had cost her two formerly close friends, Jane Wilson and Tercey Birdwell, who had sided with Virginia and who the Houstons suspected may have encouraged Gott and the girl to take legal action against her former benefactress.

Margaret's fifth child was due in January 1852, so when Houston left for Washington in November, there was probably no doubt that he would not be present for the birth. From all appearances, Margaret and her family settled placidly into their domestic routine after his departure. They had hired a nurse, Isabella, for the children, who was said to have "bewitched" them into exemplary behavior. On November 28, Margaret summarized a typically harmonious day in her household.

> We all arise with the sun, and so soon as we are dressed, assemble for worship, an exercise in which the children engage heartily. When that is over, we proceed to break-fast which Eliza is getting ready, while Perlee and Nash are milking. Soon after breakfast, Isabella and myself sit down to our sewing, while the children are engaged with their lessons. We do not confine them long to their books, but allow them an abundance of time for exercise. Thus one duty after another is taken in regular succession, and all confusion is avoided. We have supper before dark, that the children may be present at evening worship [a daily custom in the Houston household]. After they are asleep, I often take a book and read until late.

The night before Margaret composed this letter, she added, Sam, who was eight, decided to read aloud to her from a history of Queen Elizabeth, "and I became interested in that, for he reads quite well enough now to entertain me very agreeably." She tried to keep Houston abreast of all the children's antics and progress, from Nannie's incipient bad temper and Maggie's high spirits to Mary Willie's resemblance to the portrait of Houston painted when he was a young man of twenty-one.

When Antoinette Power Houston, known as Nettie, was born on January 20, 1852, her father was pleased, as always, but young Sam was disappointed: he had been lobbying for "a little brother to play with." But the proud father was also weighing his prospects for the presidency in this election year, and as usual Margaret gave him free rein: "I do not wish you to do any thing that you will afterwards regret. It is an important year with you, and if you think it will be more favorable to your prospects to remain at your post, distressing as the loss of your society would be, I will try to summon fortitude and take care of our little ones at home." For herself, she had no great desire to live in Washington, where she was "not surprised that you see the nothingness and vanity of all around you" and was pleased that he assiduously attended church and read the Bible.

Houston very possibly believed that his chances of winning the presidency were better this year than they had ever been. Although there was political opposition to his candidacy within the Democratic Party, he insisted that "wherever I go, the enthusiasm among the people is manifest," and he found strong parallels between the current status quo and 1824, the year Andrew Jackson first ran for president: "He had the politicians against him, and the people for him." He predicted, accurately, that the Whig Party would pass over the incumbent, Millard Fillmore, and nominate General Winfield Townley Scott as their candidate, "and if the Democrats, wish to succeed they will have to run, a military man, or they will be beaten." Houston was nominated by the Texas Democratic State Convention as a favorite-son candidate, but the party's nomination went to Franklin Pierce, who although he had served *under* Scott in the Mexican-American War and was little known as a politician, won handily in November.

If Houston claimed not to be disappointed by his failure to receive his party's nomination, Margaret was positively relieved. "Strange and wonderful are the ways of Providence," she wrote, adding that little Sam opposed his candidacy as well, "lest it keep you from home." During the summer and fall, Houston stayed close to home, but he did campaign for Pierce in Texas, and the family made use of the new yellow carriage, large enough for the entire family, Margaret had asked for.

In December 1852, at about the time that Houston left Huntsville to return to the Senate, the first of a series of sad reports reached the Houstons. Margaret heard that her brother Vernal had died of lung disease (most likely tuberculosis) on December 17. She wrote that "Mother is completely crushed in spirit," and she too must have been devastated. Margaret had

not worn mourning when her brother Martin committed suicide in 1843 or after Houston's sister Eliza Moore died in 1850,
because her late father had objected to the practice. After Vernal's death, however, she told Houston, "as I feel now, I could
not bear to wear any thing else." A few months later, Houston
heard from Margaret's cousin Columbus Lea that Margaret's
brother-in-law, Varilla's husband Robert Royston, was dying; he
passed away on March 11, 1853. When Houston wrote to Margaret about Royston, he added, "Death is making inroads in
our family, and I pray Heaven, that we may all be ready, for the
summons, when it shall come."

Margaret, who not long afterward also learned that her
brother, Henry Lea, was gravely ill (he died in 1854), turned her
thoughts about death and eternity into a plea to her husband to
work on his conversion and salvation: "Oh begin now the mighty
wrestling that shall prevail with God! You must come to it at
last. Even the lofty spirit of General Jackson entered there, and
none have ever entered or will enter in at the 'straight gate' that
does not first struggle and strive." At this time, Houston not only
attended church faithfully but also delivered frequent addresses
at Baptist churches, never charging a fee except when he under-
took to raise the cost of a bell for the Huntsville Baptist Church.

Perhaps it was a desire to be closer to the members of Margaret's family who were still alive that prompted Houston to
leave Huntsville for Independence, Texas, when he came home
in 1853. He and Margaret may also have wanted to take advantage of the town's excellent primary schools, run by Baylor University. Whatever their reasons, in June, Houston purchased a
house on 365 acres opposite the Baylor campus. Nancy Lea's
small house was just a few minutes away, near the Baptist
church; Antoinette and Charles Power lived a short distance
out of town; and Varilla Lea was close by as well. In addition,
George Baines, Lyndon Johnson's great-grandfather and Houston's "strongest friend in religious matters," and his wife, Melicia, were in Anderson, a short ride from Independence.

Rufus Burleson, Baylor's president, was also the local pastor.
He and Houston rarely agreed, but they carried on a spirited
intellectual debate. Burleson's sermons sometimes grew out of
topics the two men had discussed, and on at least one occasion
Houston interrupted Burleson in church in order to take issue
with the morning's address. Margaret believed that the religious disputes stimulated her husband, and it is likely that she
hoped that his frequent encounters with Burleson and Baines
would hasten his conversion.

Notwithstanding the spiritual riches Independence offered,
living there was costlier than it had been in Huntsville. "What
has become of your copper mine?" she asked Houston shortly
after he went back to Washington at the end of 1853, and she
wondered whether Cedar Point, despite its relative isolation,
wouldn't be more economical. What she really wanted was for
Houston to resign from the Senate and come home. When he
reminded her that he saved more of his Senate salary ($240 a
month) than he could earn in Texas, she wasn't persuaded. "I
would live on bread and water, or make any sacrifice of comfort
rather than give you up again."

Margaret, pregnant for the sixth time, was drained by events
of the spring and summer of 1854. With Houston at home for
only one week in all that time, she nursed Nettie through a bout
of scarlet fever and then took care of her mother, who had also
fallen ill. In addition, she was dissatisfied with Sam's schooling
and decided to teach him at home. "I will not annoy you with
the various reasons" was all the explanation she gave Houston, but at the same time she worried whether she was up to
the challenge of educating their precocious eleven-year-old son,
and wanted Houston to resign from the Senate. "I know the
country needs your services," she wrote, "but when we calculate
the sacrifices which must be made at home, is it not a question,
which has the strongest claims upon you, your country or your
family?"

On June 21, 1854, young Sam finally got his wish: Margaret

was delivered of a boy, who was named for Andrew Jackson. Houston was not home for the birth, but family lore has it that the arrival of a second son inspired him to discuss baptism with George Samson, pastor of the E Street Baptist Church in Washington. He decided, however, to reserve a decision until after he had returned to Texas. When he came home in October, Margaret made up her mind that he must be baptized before he returned to Washington. In fact, Houston had almost certainly been thinking about his faith throughout the year. When the Senate debated the Kansas-Nebraska bill, which Houston rightly saw as a threat to the geographical balance between slave and free states and territories that held the Union together, he had defended the more than three thousand ministers from New England who had signed a petition opposing the bill, calling them "harbingers of peace" and expressing the hope that they would not be insulted on the Senate floor again. Houston was the only southerner to vote against the Kansas-Nebraska bill, which passed by a margin of three to one. His principled opposition made him a hero in the North, where he was nominated for the presidency by a New Hampshire convention, but in Texas it alienated him from his own party. Houston vociferously defended his vote when he returned to Texas, but he admitted to Burleson that his opposition to the Kansas-Nebraska bill was the most unpopular stance he had taken as a politician. He insisted, however, that it was also his wisest and most patriotic action. Years later, Houston's defense of the ministers' petition would also be the cause of an almost miraculous instance of good fortune to the family.

Baptism was very much on Houston's mind that fall, but despite Margaret's urging, he held back. He might not be worthy, he told her, of taking communion. One day in October, George Baines stopped by on his way to Brenham, and Sam offered to accompany him. As they rode, Houston told Baines, "My wife and other friends seem anxious for me to join the church, and I would if I could," but he feared that if he took communion without being truly saved, he might be damned. He traced his concern to a sermon on Corinthians that he had heard as a young man. Baines assured Houston that the interpretation he cited "missed entirely the true teaching of the inspired apostle" Paul and suggested that he read another New Testament passage. When Houston had done so, he agreed to be baptized.

An ecstatic Margaret sent word to all their nearby relatives, and the baptism was scheduled for November 19 in Kountz Creek, where a coffin-shaped baptistery had been carved out of limestone. During the night of the eighteenth, however, some pranksters filled the pool with tree limbs, stones, and mud, and the ceremony had to be moved to Rocky Creek, a chilly stream a mile from the church. At noon on the appointed day, during a "blue norther" that froze both pastor and baptismal candidate, Houston walked out of the water a Baptist. When Burleson told him all his sins had been washed away, he quipped, "If that be the case, God help the fish down below!" Although he put off taking communion, he wrote to Margaret that he had finally committed to taking that step at Dr. Samson's church on March 6, and would try to spend as much time as possible with Brother Samson.

Just two years after moving to Independence, the Houstons decided to return to Huntsville. The reasons for their change of heart are unclear, but after spending the summer in Cedar Point, where the breezes afforded some relief from the heat, they reoccupied the Woodland home. Without her mother and other Lea relatives nearby, Margaret sometimes spent too much time brooding, feeling that a "dark cloud hung over me, threatening to fall upon me and extinguish the feeble light of my soul." Of course, she still had friends in Huntsville, especially Frances Creath, who was often able to lighten Margaret's moods and with whom she enjoyed discussing scripture. In January 1856, however, Frances fell gravely ill. Margaret spent a great deal of time with her friend during her last days, reciting psalms and hymns with her and offering comfort. After Frances died, she wrote to Houston about Frances's leave-taking from her family, especially from her husband, the Reverend Joseph Creath. "Oh how often have I thought that his condition would be yours! but here I am, still spared, while the good, the great, and the useful are taken."

Among the good, great, and useful people close to the Houstons who succumbed during this period were Mary (Polly) Rusk, the beloved wife of Houston's Senate colleague Thomas Rusk, and Henderson Yoakum, close family friend and attorney and author of the *History of Texas from Its First Settlement in 1685 to Its Annexation to the United States in 1846*. Both died of tuberculosis, Polly Rusk in April 1856, and Yoakum seven months later.

In May 1857, Houston failed to win the state Democratic Party's nomination for governor and decided to run against the nominee, Hardin Runnels, as an independent Democrat. With no party apparatus behind him and little support from the press, Houston relied on friends to organize rallies—speeches followed by a barbecue—and made sixty-seven such appearances during two months of campaigning. Because of his unpopular votes in the Senate (for example, his opposition to the Kansas-Nebraska Act), the stage companies refused him passage and livery stables would not rent him a buggy. Fortunately, Ed Sharp, a plow salesman, saw an opportunity to advertise his product to the large crowds that gathered at each campaign stop by offering to drive Houston around the state at no charge in a buggy emblazoned with WARWICK'S PATENT PLOW in gilt letters on the sides. Despite his efforts, Houston lost to Runnels—the only election he lost in a career that spanned more than four decades. When the report of the voting results reached Huntsville in August, it is said that Houston was sitting on the porch with Margaret, whittling a scrap of pine, as he often did for relaxation. For a few minutes after he heard the news, he remained silent, then said calmly to his wife, "Margaret, wait until 1859." In November 1857, he returned to Washington to complete the Senate session.

Just a few weeks before he lost the race for governor, Houston suffered a personal loss. In July 1857, Thomas Rusk, whose wife's death had plunged him into severe depression and who had a cancerous tumor on his neck, committed suicide in Nacogdoches. Some of Houston's detractors blamed him for Rusk's suicide because of the difficult choice that was placed upon his colleague after Houston declared himself an independent candidate for the governorship. Rusk was forced to decide between throwing his support to his friend or campaigning for the Democratic nominee, Runnels. When Houston heard that Rusk had consented to speak against him when he appeared in Nacogdoches, he asked, "Is it possible that my dear old friend Rusk has become my enemy?" But when the two of them met face-to-face on the speakers platform, they "embraced each other and 'sobbed like women.'" Then, without saying a word, they walked to Rusk's carriage and drove to Rusk's home together. No doubt having to choose between his deep friendship for Houston and his loyalty to the Democratic Party was agonizing for Rusk, but it was only one of many concerns that plagued him at the time. The true cause, as he wrote to his children shortly before taking his life, was his overwhelming grief at losing Polly.

After their seventh child, William Rogers Houston, was born on May 25, 1858, the family went to Cedar Point for the summer, where they hoped the climate would relieve Margaret's asthma and help the sickly newborn to gain strength. In the fall, Houston returned to Washington. When he left the capital for the last time in March 1859, an editorial in the *Washington Evening Star* stated, "No other public man ever made more . . . sincere friends here, nor was severance of a gentleman's connection with American public affairs ever more seriously regretted than in his case." Despite his 1857 statement to Margaret, for two months Houston said nothing about the upcoming gubernatorial election. But in May he suddenly went into campaign mode,

predicted that "the people will elect Houston," and sought support for his candidacy. He first approached Ashbel Smith, whom
he asked "to serve your old and devoted friend, General Houston. The constitution, the Union, the frontier, state reforms,
and a large debt of gratitude demand his services." In contrast
to his energetic effort of two years earlier in a losing cause, this
time he barely campaigned—he made only a single speech, in
Nacogdoches in July—and defeated Runnels easily.

The people may have rekindled their love of Houston, but
the politicians remained hostile. The Governor's Mansion in
Austin, a yellow-brick, two-story Greek Revival building with
Ionic columns, had been completed only three years earlier. It
was a large house by contemporary standards, but scantily furnished. The legislature, however, refused to appropriate funds
to buy adequate furniture; one member scornfully quipped that
the public should not pay to house a man who had lived in a
wigwam. Houston nonetheless managed to secure enough furniture to accommodate the largest, liveliest first family in the
state's history. All of the children were living at home, except
for Sam, who at sixteen was a student at the Allen Academy in
Bastrop. The girls, who were all of school age, attended primary
school in Austin and often invited friends to visit. One friend,
the story goes, even taught a group, including Governor Houston, to dance the Pigeon Wing (so called because it consists of
shaking one's leg in the air, the step was incorporated into min-
strel shows, vaudeville, and the cancan), until Margaret, who
disapproved of social dancing, put a stop to it.

Much of the mischief could be traced to Andrew, who loved
to play pranks. Not yet old enough for school, he often trailed
along to the capitol with his father, where he sometimes visited Eber Worthington Cave, Adolphus Sterne's son-in-law and
Houston's secretary of state. Once, after Cave had scolded the
boy for misbehaving, Andrew wandered upstairs to the Senate chamber, locked the door from the outside, and hid the
key. When the senators discovered that they were trapped,

they called for help through a window. The predicament was brought to the governor's attention, who surmised that Andrew was the culprit, recovered the key, and liberated the lawmakers. According to family legend, Houston afterward told Margaret that Andrew had handled the legislature better than he was able to, and this prank may have prompted him to write to his son Sam, "I have to keep Andrew at the office some days, as they can't manage him at home."

Houston wrote many letters to Sam, letters full of advice about education, news of the family, and—perhaps anticipating the political storm that was brewing—exhortations "to love and revere the union. Mingle it in your heart with filial love." In 1860, he seriously considered running for president as an independent after failing to garner support for his candidacy within the Democratic Party. His main concern was that a Republican victory would precipitate secession by the southern states, and he embarked on a two-month speaking tour to promote his ideas for the preservation of the Union, individual freedom, and slavery, in part by turning Mexico into a slaveholding American protectorate, but this time the people did not rally behind him. A week after Margaret gave birth to their eighth child, Temple Lea Houston, on August 12, 1860, Houston withdrew his candidacy.

Rumors of assassination plots somewhat unnerved Margaret, who was slow to recover from the strain of childbirth, but she concurred with Houston's cardinal rule of conduct—"To be honest and fear not is the right path." She made an effort to carry on a normal life, attending concerts and church services, sometimes with the children in tow. To put as much distance as possible between their son Sam and the secession fever that was spreading through the state, she and the governor agreed to take him out of school and send him on a geological expedition in Mexico with Francis Moore, whom the governor had appointed state geologist.

Even after Abraham Lincoln was elected, Houston contin-

ued to favor remaining in the Union as long as the president
obeyed the Constitution. "To secede from the Union and set up
another government would cause war," he said in a speech in
January 1861. "If you go to war with the United States, you will
never conquer her, as she has the money and the men. If she
does not whip you by guns, powder, and steel, she will starve
you to death. . . . [I]t will take the flower of the country—the
young men." Margaret told her mother, Nancy Lea, of hearing
her husband at night, "agonizing in prayers for our distracted
country."

The Texas legislature was bent on secession, but Houston
cast about for some means to prevent it. He declined Lincoln's
offer to send federal troops to Texas, but only after conferring
with four of his close Unionist friends, Benjamin Epperson,
James Throckmorton, David Culberson, and George Paschal.
Of the four, only Epperson thought Lincoln's stratagem might
work. Houston bowed to the political reality but told the four
men, "If I were twenty years younger, I would take Mr. Lincoln's proposal and endeavor to keep Texas in the Union." Then
he burned the letter.

Seeing how bleak the prospects were, Margaret expected no
miracles. As she wrote to her mother, "I cannot shut my eyes
to the dangers that threaten us. I know that it is even probable
that we may soon be reduced to poverty, but oh I have such a
sweet assurance in my heart that the presence of the Lord will
go with us wherever we may go, and that even in the wilderness
we may erect an altar of prayer." At the same time, Houston
tried to keep what he regarded as the wilderness at bay by holding off convening the legislature until the last possible moment.
Then, on January 21, just a week before a secession convention
was to meet, he called the legislature into session. The legislature voted to allow the convention to take place but ruled that
the referendum on secession had to conform to its own independent decision. When the results of the referendum were announced, Nannie and Maggie, who were at home at the time,

observed their father's reaction. "Houston's face turned ashen. His head dropped to his chest and his whole being shook with emotion." Then he said to Margaret, "Texas is lost. My heart is broken." According to the two girls, it was then that Houston's health started to fail.

Houston worked every stratagem he could think of to prevent secession. He tried to persuade General David Twiggs, the United States Army commander in Texas, to surrender his troops to the governor. When Twiggs declined, he argued that in the case of Texas, secession meant that it reverted to its status as an independent republic. Finally, he refused to recognize that Texas was part of the Confederacy. The convention ignored his efforts and on March 15 sent a delegate to announce that at noon the next day he and all other government officials would be required to swear their loyalty to the Confederacy. Houston told the messenger that he needed time to think about the ultimatum and explained to Margaret that he was worried about the repercussions on his family if he should refuse to take the oath. She promised to support his decision and suggested that he seek divine guidance.

Neither of them slept that night. Margaret sat up in a chair, waiting until dawn, when Houston came downstairs and told her, "Margaret, I will never do it." Then, after she went to bed, he returned to his desk to compose a statement explaining his reasons for refusing the oath. It was published in the *Southern Intelligencer* of March 20, 1861. Although he disagreed with the people's decision to secede, Houston wrote, he would "stand by Texas in whatever position she assumes . . . and go out from the Union with them." He would not take the oath, but he would not resort to violence to remain in office, despite the fact that his authority was being usurped, because "I love Texas too well to bring civil strife and bloodshed upon her."

Later that morning, Houston went to his office at the capitol, where he sat whittling quietly, ignored the summons to come upstairs to the convention, and left after Lieutenant Governor

Edward Clark had been sworn in. Two days later, he demanded that the legislature dissolve the convention, but instead it seconded the convention's ruling that when Houston refused to take the oath, he had vacated his office.

On March 19, as the Houstons were packing to leave Austin, some friends visited the mansion with a plan to disperse the convention by force. Houston told them he was grateful for their gesture but asked them to abandon their plan. "Go tell my deluded friends," he said, "that I am proud of their friendship, of their love and loyalty, and I hope I may retain them to the end. But say to them that for the sake of humanity and justice to disperse, to go to their homes and to conceal from the world that they would have ever been guilty of such an act."

The Houstons had lent their Independence house to Baylor University, so they stayed with their friends Asa and Elizabeth Hoxey. When Sam Jr. returned from Mexico, Houston and Margaret were determined to keep him from enlisting. Hoping to distract him with work, Houston made Sam overseer at Cedar Point and peppered him with advice about planting, animal husbandry, and managing the hands. He labored to persuade the young man not to join the Confederate army, at least not yet; the time was not right, he argued, and it was the wrong war: "It is every man's duty to defend his Country, and I wish my offspring to do so at the proper time and in the proper way. We are not wanted or needed out of Texas, and we may soon be wanted and needed in Texas. Until then, my son, be content."

Unbeknownst to his parents, in the early spring Sam and his cousin Martin Royston, who was the overseer at Ashbel Smith's farm near Cedar Point, had stolen off to drill with Smith's Bayland Guards. When they learned what Sam had done, Houston and Margaret hoped that he would return once the training ended. Meanwhile, Houston renewed his efforts to persuade his son to remain at home to defend Texas. "She can look for no aid from the Confederacy and must either succumb or defend herself." He tried to pull rank by insisting that Sam mustn't commit himself to another power without Houston's consent. Finally, he warned that the name Houston would not be popular in the Confederacy.

Margaret was "beyond consolation" at the prospect of young Sam's going to war on any front. When she learned that his company was being sent to Mississippi, she wrote to Nancy Lea, "I thought I would lie down and die. . . . I did not love him more than the rest of my children, but he absorbed all my anxiety, all my hopes and fears." She added that she hoped that Varilla, Martin's mother, whose son had enlisted along with Sam, would join her to "mingle prayers and tears."

Houston did his best to assuage Margaret's fears, writing that "God can shield him as He has his father before him," but Margaret refused to be comforted. When Ashbel Smith stopped at Cedar Point before leaving for Mississippi, Margaret had him take a small Bible to Sam, which she inscribed to him. She wrote to her mother, Nancy Lea, "My weakness gave him the opportunity to display traits of character that made his father's heart swell with pride," and she worried that she would never see him again. "I cannot forget that my boy, my darling, he that was to be the prop of my old age, is gone from me, probably never to return."

Margaret found little comfort in the letter her cousin Columbus Lea wrote from Mississippi saying that Sam was "in robust health." Houston did act on Lea's suggestion that he secure a lieutenancy for Sam, but he sent his request to William Oldham, by then a Confederate senator from Texas, just a day before the battle of Shiloh. On the first day of the battle, Ashbel Smith was wounded and Sam narrowly escaped serious injury when he was hit by a minié ball. The bullet lodged in the Bible that Sam carried in his knapsack; according to family lore, it came to rest at Psalm 70, whose opening words are "Make haste, O God, to deliver me; make haste to help me, O Lord."

On the second day of the battle, Sam was not as lucky. He was wounded in the groin and left on the battlefield by his comrades and the Union soldiers, who thought he was either dead or beyond saving. A Union surgeon merely glanced at him before passing by, and Sam was certain that he would not be rescued. At evening, according to the family's story, a Union chaplain stopped and noticed that Sam was still breathing. In Sam's knapsack, he found the Bible, and when he read the inscription—"Sam Houston from his Mother, March 6, 1862"— he asked the young soldier whether he was related to General Sam Houston of Texas. The chaplain was one of the New England preachers whose petition against the Kansas-Nebraska Act Houston had praised on the floor of the Senate. He stayed with Sam until he was taken to the field hospital, where his wounds were treated. After the war, the Houstons attempted to learn the identity of the minister who had saved Sam's life, but they were never able to trace him.

When reports of the battle were published, Sam was listed among the "dead and missing" Confederate soldiers. Margaret prayed that her son had somehow escaped death and had been taken prisoner, but it would be months before she discovered that he was alive. In the meantime, conflicting and overlapping reports and rumors reached the family: that Sam had been killed; that he had not been wounded but had collapsed during the retreat after having had nothing to eat for two days; that he had been captured and was a prisoner. Margaret wrote to Maggie that Houston took heart from the reports that Sam had been the last to retreat.

As a prisoner of war, Sam was sent to Camp Douglas, Illinois. While Margaret wrote a hopeful poem, "A Mother's Prayer," imploring God, "Be thou his guardian, guide and shield / And save him, in the last great day!" her son was composing verses of his own: "I know my mother's weeping for her long lost wandering boy / Does she know that still I'm living—even that would give her joy." Sam's poem ends with a vision of a lonely death "far away from friends and kindred." But he would see his family again.

He was released in a prisoner exchange on September 23, 1862, promoted to lieutenant, and made an instructor of tactics. Too weak even for such limited duty, he was granted a medical discharge less than two weeks after his release.

At Cedar Point, Houston and Margaret had as yet no definite word of Sam's fate or whereabouts. Meanwhile, a steady stream of ill and injured soldiers returning from service passed their house, often stopping to rest before continuing their journeys. One October day, Houston was not at home when Margaret saw a pale young man on crutches making his way toward the garden. As she approached him, thinking to offer something to eat or drink, she heard the soldier say, "Why Ma, I don't believe you know me." She hadn't recognized her own son. Home at last, Sam recounted the details of his ordeal to his parents and showed them the Bible that had saved his life.

Not long after Sam's return the family moved back to Huntsville. Houston wanted to repurchase the Woodland home, but when that couldn't be arranged he rented "the Steamboat House," so called because it resembled a riverboat. It was there that he and Margaret decided not to wait for the Emancipation Proclamation to take effect in January 1863 before granting freedom to their slaves. On a Sunday morning they gathered their entire household in the yard and Houston read aloud the text of the proclamation, explained its significance, and announced that he was exercising his legal and God-given right to free his slaves immediately. He invited all of them to continue working as they had always done, but for wages, and he offered to help them whenever he could. Joshua, who had already purchased his freedom, said that he intended to keep working for the Houstons, and many of the others followed his lead. The faithful Eliza, whom the children always called Aunt Eliza, feared that she would be forcibly separated from the family and asked not to be emancipated, and Margaret reminded her of their mutual pledge never to part as long as they lived.

By 1863, the years and the trials of the last few years had

taken their toll on Houston. No longer the tall, rugged figure of his portraits, he had trouble climbing stairs or riding a horse, tired easily, and was often in pain from his old wounds. But even as his health declined, his composure never wavered. At one point, Houston took sick and didn't think he would recover, so he summoned his family and the servants to his bedroom, where he gave each of them advice and then asked Margaret to read a psalm and Nannie and Maggie to sing a hymn. As she had done for Frances Creath, Margaret performed bravely, but the girls' efforts to sing were stifled by their tears, so Houston finished the hymn for them and then sent everyone back to bed. A few days later he was better and instructed a friend, Hamilton Stewart, "Tell my enemies I am not dead yet."

As she had done when Houston was away in Washington, Margaret continued to shield her husband from upsetting news, especially when it concerned their children. When Maggie had to drop out of Baylor after contracting scarlet fever, Margaret said nothing to Houston until she was well enough to come home from Independence. Maggie's recuperation would be a long one, so in Huntsville she took over from Margaret as Houston's secretary. A more disturbing development was their son Sam's decision to leave Baylor, in order to reenlist in the Confederate army. Houston learned of his plans, of course, but one biographer believes that Margaret never showed him the "disrespectful" letter Sam wrote after his father remonstrated with him over his plans. To make matters even worse for the perpetually cash-strapped Houstons, Sam had run up bills at an Independence store without telling his parents, and now that he was leaving school, his account would have to be settled. To Sam she wrote sternly that notwithstanding his wounds and war record, he was still a boy. Somewhat morbidly, she added, "The time will come soon enough when you will have no one to admonish you when you do wrong. . . . Do let us be gentle and affectionate with each other the little while we have to live." About his bills, she was equally stern. "I do not think your father has the remotest idea that you have made any bills," she told Sam. "Do not get any thing more, I beseech you."

Margaret thought that Houston might have tuberculosis and urged him to go to Sour Lake for the mud baths that were thought to be curative. Houston went with Jeff, his personal buggy driver, who became his inseparable companion from the moment Houston first laid eyes on him, a forlorn child being tormented by a group of white children at a Huntsville slave auction. He purchased the boy on the spot. Writing from home, Margaret urged her husband to remain at Sour Lake as long as the treatments were helping him: "If you find that you are improving at Sour Lake, I would not . . . change it for any other place." Sour Lake did nothing for his symptoms, but the indomitable Houston managed visits to Galveston and Houston City before going home.

Stoical to the end, Houston said little to Margaret about how he felt, but he admitted to Jeff that he didn't think he would survive another two weeks. He had pneumonia, and the hot, dry July weather made it exceedingly difficult for him to breathe. His doctor suggested placing his bed in the middle of the room to increase the ventilation. Jeff, who never left Houston's side (he slept on a pallet in the room), constantly worked a fan above the patient's head and Margaret often sat nearby. One day Jeff dozed off on his feet and dropped the fan on Houston, who calmly said, "Margaret, you and that boy go and get some rest. There is no use both of you breaking yourselves down."

On July 25, as Houston wavered between consciousness and coma, Margaret sent for their friend Colonel Thomas Carothers, superintendent of the Huntsville penitentiary, who came with Austin College president Samuel McKinney. For a while Houston was alert, and the men discussed the war and the slavery issue. But he quickly grew weak again. As he was fading, Rev. McKinney inquired about the state of his soul. "All is well, all is well," Sam answered.

He slept through the night, and the next day, a Sunday, Margaret was in his room, reading the Bible aloud. Maggie later recounted that her father's voice was weak, but "we caught the words 'Texas! Texas!' in a voice of entreaty." Margaret then took his hand, "and his lips moved again. 'Margaret,' he said, and the voice we loved was silent forever."

According to a family story, Margaret removed her husband's gold ring, which his mother had given him fifty years earlier, and showed her children its one-word inscription: HONOR. The year after they married, Houston had written to Margaret, "If I leave no other legacy on earth but love and honor, they shall stand and remain pure and unsullied as the moon beams which play around our cottage home."

During the night, Margaret composed a poem of farewell, "To My Husband," which the Reverend J. M. Cochran read at the funeral, held the next afternoon at the Steamboat House. Its closing stanza reads:

> And now may peace, within thy breast,
> From him descend, and there remain!
> Each night oh mayst thou sweetly rest,
> And feel thou hast not liv'd in vain.

Despite a steady rain, a large crowd gathered to pay their respects, and the line of mourners that followed Houston's coffin, which was borne by a group of Masonic pallbearers, stretched from the house to the grave site.

Houston's will named Margaret sole guardian of their minor children, and most of his personal items he left to her as well, but he gave his San Jacinto sword to Sam, with the stipulation that he was to draw it "only in defense of the Constitution, the Laws, and the Liberties of this Country." By "country," Houston meant Texas and the United States, but Sam had his own ideas of where his loyalties lay, and within a month he had enlisted as a private in the Confederate cavalry, making no mention of his previous rank and service. His return to the army only served to deepen Margaret's despondency. She visited Houston's grave daily, and Nannie and Maggie worried about her health. Nancy Lea managed to talk her daughter into visiting her in Independence. Margaret did so, but only because she rationalized that it was there she could arrange for her sons to be educated as their father had wished.

The Houston family's financial situation was not good. Beyond the constraints that affected everyone in the Confederacy during the Civil War—high costs and widespread shortages—the estate was worth only half the original estimate of one hundred fifty thousand dollars, and most of that was in land, difficult to sell at the time, and loans to people who were as short of cash as Margaret. Fortunately, she was able to rely on her brother-in-law Charles Power and E. W. Cave, their close friend who as secretary of state in 1861 had joined the governor in refusing to take the oath of loyalty to the Confederacy. Margaret also asked Sam to request a furlough, claiming that she needed his views on finances as well, but this was probably a ploy to get her son away from the dangers of the war.

In any case, Sam did not obtain a furlough, but Margaret visited him in Galveston, where he was training. Afterward, she wrote to him often. Her anguish at the time—her sense of bereavement over Houston's death compounded by her terror that she might lose Sam in the war—is palpable in her letters to her son. She feared for his soul "if you should fall in battle" and pleaded with him to attend a revival in Galveston: "[G]o where God is pouring out his Spirit, and try to have your sins forgiven." She had always imagined that Sam would step in as the man of the family when her much older husband was no longer with her. When Sam returned to the army and an uncertain fate, she felt doubly abandoned and cried, "I am but dust and ashes! A few more days and this feeble frame shall cease to suffer."

Cave was perhaps the most loyal of Houston's friends, and his practical help at this time was also the most beneficial to Margaret and the children. He engineered a trade of some of the Houstons' Independence farmland for a two-story colonial house in town, not far from Nancy Lea's home. It had two bedrooms upstairs and Margaret's room and a parlor on the ground floor. The parlor was large enough to accommodate two pianos and a poster bed. The rooms had rock chimneys, and a double chimney connected the main structure to the kitchen and dining room, which were in a separate building. After another four months in Huntsville, where Margaret visited Houston's grave every day, bringing flowers and shedding tears, she moved the family into the new house in Independence. The older girls were already there; they had returned in September when school started. Not long after Margaret arrived, Joshua, the former slave who was now a successful blacksmith, visited with a gift: a bag containing his life savings, two thousand dollars in gold, to help Margaret provide for her children. He had heard that the family was in financial straits and wanted to help. Moved to tears by Joshua's offer, Margaret declined; instead, she told him to use the money as Houston would have wanted him to: to give his own children good Christian educations. Joshua followed her advice, and one of his sons later became president of the Sam Houston Manual Training School in Huntsville.

Margaret had hoped that her presence in Independence would allow her to care for her mother, but barely three months after the move, Nancy Lea suffered what was vaguely diagnosed as a "stomach affliction." She died on February 7, 1864. In one of the many letters Margaret wrote to Sam during this period, she reported that her mother had been laid to rest as she had wished, in the tomb she had constructed on her property, but added, "I am sure you will not be surprised to know that I had not the strength to be present." To his credit, Sam wrote frequently to Margaret even when he was at the front, enclosing sketches and poems with his letters. She encouraged Sam's literary and artistic efforts, but thinking of the many families who had lost sons in the war, she insisted that there was a reason he'd been spared. "Take care that you do not bury your talent," she admonished. Sam tried to reassure her, writing after one battle that "God is good and is on our side."

A letter from Sam was an occasion in the Houston household. At dinner, one of the girls would read it aloud, and their contents were often entertaining and even racy, especially measured against Margaret's standards. When his regiment was preparing to depart from their training camp, Sam wrote of bidding farewell to his "acquaintances." "The prettiest one threw her arms around my neck and said, 'Houston, I guess I had better kiss you for I know you are not coming back to see me'—of course I had not the slightest objections."

In at least one letter home, Sam revealed his reasons for his stubborn insistence on proving himself as a soldier, and how difficult it was to live up to the legendary name he bore. From Wills Plantation, Louisiana, he wrote on July 5, 1864:

Ma I was reckless and ambitious, and I was restless when out of hearing of the boom of the cannon—it almost seems to me now that the death groan and bursting shells had a music for me—I was proud that I could ride fearlessly through it all, and show to friend and foe that I was not afraid to die. Ma it was not for myself alone—I was proud of my name and I wanted to show the world that the blood of a Houston ran untainted.

Neither mother nor son knew it at the time, but Wills Plantation was to be Sam's last battle, although many months would pass before the soldiers stationed at Alexandria, Louisiana, were able to return home.

At home, Margaret was especially concerned about "boisterous and unmanageable" Andrew and urged Sam to come home in order to take his younger brother in hand. Andrew had started visiting the local school that her daughters attended, and Maggie had told Margaret that he was attracted to older girls. She considered sending him to a school out of town, hoping he would benefit from a stricter regimen and discipline. The two younger boys, on the other hand, were angels: "Willie and Temple are the sweetest little companions for me in the world. They are such perfect opposites that it makes their conversation very spicy and interesting."

Margaret's spirits never completely revived after Houston died. Always inclined to sobriety, she was sometimes discomfited by her children's natural ebullience. In one poem written late in 1865, she wrote about trying to maintain a cheery disposition around her family—"But thy children gather round, / And my sorrows I must hush, / For the merry step must bound / And youth's joy I would not crush"—while she herself continued to harbor grief and loneliness. One day Nettie came home from school to find her mother, unaware of her daughter's presence, staring into the fire with a look of "deep longing" on her face. Margaret didn't emerge from her reverie until she heard her daughter say, "No wonder my father loved you so."

If an undertone of melancholy infected Margaret's life after July 1863, there were joyous times, often associated with her children, as well. Sam's return from military service—suffering from nothing worse than exposure—was one such occasion. Another was Nannie's marriage to Joseph Clay Stiles Morrow, a Georgetown, Texas, merchant she met in Independence. Their wedding, on August 1, 1866, was performed by William Carey Crane, Baylor's president and pastor of the Independence Baptist church. After an extended honeymoon that took them to New York and Washington, D.C. (where they visited President Andrew Johnson), they settled in Georgetown. By then, Nannie was pregnant. She spent the last weeks of her pregnancy with Margaret, and the baby was delivered in Independence, with Margaret and Eliza in attendance. Margaret's first granddaughter, Maggie Houston Morrow, was born June 4, 1867.

When Nannie left to rejoin Joe in Georgetown, north of Austin, she tried to induce her mother to come to live with them, but Margaret declined. She did insist on sending Eliza as the baby's nurse, however. And Margaret felt relief when her daughter and son-in-law proposed having Andrew move in with them. Joe was able to harness Andrew's high spirits, and Margaret was grateful that he was being taken in hand. "I am truly glad that Nannie feels such a maternal interest in my dear Andrew," she wrote. "I know you both will give him good advice."

On August 1, not long after Nannie's wedding, Maggie became engaged to Weston "West" Lafayette Williams, a young man who had lived at Nancy Lea's while a student at Baylor. West Williams owned a plantation in Labadie Prairie, Washington County. This time Margaret tried to entice the couple to settle in Independence by offering them Nancy Lea's small house and wasn't happy when they refused. Four of her children were still at home—Mary Willie, seventeen; Nettie, fifteen; Willie Rogers, eleven; and Temple, seven—but the family was beginning to disperse, and the unease this development produced in her intensified when Sam left to attend medical school in Philadelphia.

Financially, matters improved for Margaret when the postwar legislature voted to pay Houston's gubernatorial salary for the portion of his term after he was forced to relinquish his office. In addition, some of their debtors repaid their loans in part, but Margaret continued to be short of funds. To pay Sam's fees at the University of Pennsylvania, Cave signed a note for two hundred dollars, and Margaret wrote to Joe Morrow that she had taken two sides of bacon from one of his supply wagons when it passed through Independence, but "I did not pay for them, for the simple reason that I had not the money."

Safeguarding Sam Houston's legacy was of great interest to Margaret. The governor, Andrew Jackson Hamilton, asked Margaret's advice about a portrait of Houston to be hung in the Texas House of Representatives. Perhaps most gratifying to Margaret during this period, aside from family matters, was that in Rev. Crane she thought she had found the ideal biographer for her husband. When she first proposed the idea of writing a life of Houston to Crane, he hesitated. But he came around quickly, and Margaret gave him access to the trove of Houston's papers that he had amassed over a lifetime and suggested people who had known him whom she thought he should contact, including Andrew Jackson Hamilton, Ashbel Smith, and George W. Samson. Some consented to share what they knew with the author, but others demurred, because they felt that the time was not right for a biography of Houston. Margaret requested only that at least one chapter discuss Houston's "religious character."

The resulting *Life and Select Literary Remains of Sam Houston* suppressed some of the facts, for example, Tiana Rogers (Houston's Cherokee wife), but not others, such as Houston's alcoholism. Publication was delayed for nearly twenty years in part because many of Houston's acquaintances declined to assist the author. One wrote to Crane that "it does not seem to me that there is any pressing urgency to present the Life and Labors of General Houston to the world. It is true that they will possess a paramount interest so long as the Republic or State, or Country of Texas, whichever it may be, shall possess an interest for men; yet even in this view there is an advantage in bringing out a book in an opportune time." That response infuriated Margaret, who started to burn Houston's papers in view of Crane and her children. Some accounts claim that she did not destroy materials indiscriminately but only burned some items she felt were too intimate or not worth preserving. In any case, a great deal was spared from the flames, and Crane later returned to the project. People also began to argue about whether Crane, a genteel Whig from Virginia and of the kid-glove school, was the right biographer for Houston, "a plain, rugged frontiersman, of intense earnestness." The biography, the first full-dress account of Houston's life—and the first of any kind since Charles Edwards Lester's work of 1846, which was essentially a campaign biography—was finally published in 1884.

In September 1867, a yellow fever epidemic descended on Independence and other sections of the state. White "quarantine" sheets hung from houses throughout the town, and Baylor University shut down. Margaret sent Willie and Temple to stay with the Morrows in Georgetown, while she went to Labadie to look after Maggie at her plantation home near Brenham. From there she wrote that "nearly all our [Huntsville] friends have died of the yellow fever." Grateful for being spared, she wrote, "I am amazed at the Lord's goodness and mercy. Oh, Why am I so blessed while so many households are made desolate?" Hoping that the performance of their "religious duties" would protect her children, she told them to "form a habit of singing hymns while you are working."

When the weather turned cold in November, the contagion ebbed and Margaret returned to Independence. She was planning to spend Christmas in Georgetown and remain there until the spring. She was keen on getting back to "the pure air of Georgetown," but one night while she was still in Independence, she had a dream in which "Ma [was] standing at the foot of my bed, and she said, 'Margaret, in two weeks you will be with me.'"

In fact, yellow fever had returned, and this time Margaret came down with it. She tried to persuade her daughters Mary Willie and Nettie to escape to Georgetown with their two younger brothers, but the girls refused to leave her. Margaret was already suffering from delirium, and there was no longer a doctor in town. It may have been Cave, who had visited faithfully ever since Houston's death, who brought Dr. Bingley from Brenham, but by the time the doctor reached Margaret's bedside on December 3, she was dead. Because the risk of contagion was so great, she was buried that night in a grave next to Nancy Lea's tomb, with only Nettie, Mary Willie, Dr. Bingley, and one servant present. The girls covered the grave with evergreens.

Eliza, the shadowlike presence who had been part of Margaret's life longer than anyone besides Nancy Lea, now shuttled between Nannie's and Maggie's homes, helping to raise another generation of Houston children. Because Eliza was illiterate, the girls wrote letters to their siblings for her. Aunt Eliza was a fixture in their lives and those of their growing families. In a letter Nannie wrote to Maggie, "Often I think of a remark which dear Wes made about her—that 'she was an example to all of us.' She never forgets the comfort or fancies of any one and is a mother to everything on the place."

According to Madge Thornall Roberts, Margaret and Sam's great-great-granddaughter, the Houston children did their best to repay Eliza's kindnesses to them. When Eliza suffered her own final illness, she was living with Maggie in Houston, where Maggie had moved after West Williams's death. The doctor said that Eliza wouldn't recover, and Maggie explained to Eliza that her condition was fatal. She replied that she understood, "that her feet had 'already touched the chilly water of the Jordan.'" She asked only to be buried next to Margaret, and when she died in 1898, her wish was granted. Her simple epitaph reads, AUNT ELIZA—FAITHFUL UNTO DEATH.

Part VII

TRAIL DRIVES AND RANCHES

1860s–1920s

Kate Malone Medlin

Bettie Matthews Reynolds

Amanda Nite Burks

Hattie Standefer Cluck

Eliza Bunton Johnson

Molly Dunn Bugbee

Margaret Heffernan Dunbar Hardy Borland

Lizzie Johnson Williams

Mollie Taylor Bunton

Henrietta Chamberlain King

Molly Dyer Goodnight

Henrietta King   *Molly Goodnight*   *Bettie Matthews Reynolds*

Eliza Bunton Johnson   *Lizzie Johnson Williams*   *Mollie Taylor Bunton*

The popular image of the cowhand is invariably of a man—sometimes young and restless, at others mature and weather-beaten, but always hardened, tough, and solitary. The same is true of the rancher, who may be either a cowhand with ambitious hopes or a well-heeled frontier entrepreneur, although he is permitted to have a wife stationed demurely in the background. Given the demographic imbalance in the West during the nineteenth century, most ranch hands, trail drivers, ranchers, and cattle dealers were undoubtedly men, but not all. Against the odds and the prejudices of the times, a surprising number of women took up these vocations as well, and some of their stories have survived.

However devoted Texas ranchers were to ranching as a way of life, to stock raising and breeding, to the landscape, and to their comrades, from the humblest vaquero to the so-called cattle barons and queens who sometimes attained the status of aristocracy, in nineteenth-century Texas the cattle business was above all a business—difficult, precarious, and dangerous even in the best of times. Weather, disease, price fluctuations, and predators—human and animal—were constant threats to solvency, well-being, and even life on the cattle trails. This was especially true when the markets for beef on the hoof shifted increasingly to destinations north and west of the ranches in Texas and elsewhere in the Southwest.

Ranching was introduced to Texas by the Spanish in the early eighteenth century, initially to provide beef for the missionaries, soldiers, and settlers in San Antonio and a few other locales, and later by entrepreneurs who secured large land grants. A small number of these early ranchers were Mexican women or members of families from the Canary Islands who settled in San Antonio. María Bentacour, Rosa María Hinojosa de Ballí, and Ana María del Carmen Calvillo were among the women who acquired large landholdings, often through inheritance, and raised cattle. But the roots of the boom in Texas ranching were implanted a century later, when settlers from the United States and Europe began arriving in large numbers.

The destination of the first cattle drives from Anglo Texas was Louisiana's markets, and some herds were shipped over water to New Orleans. By the mid-1840s, however, the preferred destinations were in Kansas, Missouri, Colorado, Ohio, and other points north. At the end of the decade, the discovery of gold in California created a profitable market on the west coast that was interrupted only by the Civil War. Sales could be lucrative, but drivers had to cross long arid stretches where water and grazing were scarce and predators plentiful. Stockmen risked losing their cattle and trail hands their lives to Comanche and Apache raiders and American rustlers.

The potential profits led to a proliferation of trails, most of them leading north to Missouri and Kansas (see map, p. xxiii). Drives followed routes named for the men who had blazed them or made them popular, but many of the trails had long been familiar to generations of anonymous Indians, traders, immigrants, and travelers. A few of the most renowned were the Shawnee Trail, which wound from South Texas through Austin, Waco, and Dallas, crossed the Red River at Preston, and ended in Missouri; and the Chisholm Trail, which went through San Antonio, Austin, and Fort Worth and terminated in Kansas. The Goodnight-Loving Trail took a route off the Chisholm to Young County, then turned west through New Mexico, ending in Colorado. Right up to the start of the Civil War, cattle were sometimes trailed all the way to Chicago or the east coast; Walt Whitman wrote of watching herds enter Washington, D.C.

Resistance to the drives from Texas was not long in coming. In Missouri, fear of the spread of tick-borne "Texas fever" to local cattle prompted local farmers and cattle-raisers to demand an end to the drives, especially after the disease appeared in Missouri herds in the mid-1850s. Texas cattle had developed immunity to the microscopic protozoan responsible for the contagion, but in other cattle it killed the animals by destroying their red blood cells. Some herds were prevented from entering the state, and farmers threatened to kill cattle originating in Texas. To circumvent the problem, Texas stockmen gravitated to more westerly routes, through eastern Kansas to Kansas City, or, after 1859, to the rail link at St. Joseph, Missouri, from where cattle were hauled to Chicago. Other cattlemen, notably Oliver Loving, trailed their cattle to Colorado, sometimes via Kansas.

Kate Malone Medlin

Born in Missouri in 1839, Kate Malone was the second of six daughters of Perry and Polly Malone. The family moved to Texas in 1844 and eventually settled in the Hill Country, in what became known as the Missouri Colony. By the middle of the next decade, the Malones had added five more children, including two boys. During the same period, many members of their extended family and that of Hall Medlin settled in the area. Strong-willed, devout Baptists like their neighbors, the Malones and Medlins were among the founders of the Lonesome Dove Baptist Church.

The support of their tight-knit community wasn't enough to prevent tragedy from visiting Kate's family. When she was sixteen or seventeen, a neighbor, identified only as a member of the Hill Country's large German enclave, shot Polly Malone in a rage after she refused his request to marry Kate. A distraught Perry grabbed the man's gun and beat him to death with it. Two years later, Kate married Jarret Medlin, one of Hall Medlin's sons. They had two children before the outbreak of the Civil War, during which both families endured hardship, as did many settlers throughout the region. The economy was mostly based on barter, and Indian raids threatened whatever modest wealth people managed to accumulate. Hall, the Medlin paterfamilias, sought more tranquil surroundings in Travis County. Kate and Jarret followed, but they were soon left behind when Hall led a wagon train of Medlin family members to California, where he hoped to strike it rich in the gold fields.

When war was declared, Jarret and his brother Marion joined the Confederate army, and Kate, who was pregnant with her fourth child, was left to care for their growing family and provide for its needs. During the war, manufactured goods of any sort were in short supply throughout the South, and Kate later recalled how the women wove the cloth to make dresses for themselves and their daughters. "They looked awfully coarse and shoddy, as many of us had never woven any cloth, much less worn such shoddy looking goods," but they made the best of it. By war's end, Jarret was dead—a casualty of measles and exposure—and when Kate's father-in-law returned to Texas to recruit family members for a cattle drive to California, where Texas beef was commanding "fabulous prices," the twenty-nine-year-old widow and her four children joined three dozen Medlin relatives for a drive from Hays County, outside Austin, to Los Angeles. They set off on April 15, 1868, in seven ox-drawn covered wagons. "I made the start to California with great hopes. It was like starting to fairyland, and I thought I had counted the cost and could see what the hardships and trouble would be but I soon found I had no idea what was coming, but still braved the storm. I thought when I arrived in California with my money and got to my relatives, it would be all right with me."

Starting out with no cattle, the Medlin party purchased 1,800 head and 150 horses on the Texas frontier, and set off in early May in a company that included many women and children but too few men to tend the animals or safeguard the wagon train, its occupants, and the herds. Hall Medlin planned to add trail hands with guns at a fort or town en route, but the man he had appointed captain of the drive argued that it was more important to follow a route that led to pasturage and water than to worry about safety and hiring experienced vaqueros. Since "he had traveled the road a number of times and had never seen an Indian, he did not think it necessary to bother about the guns, and the other road was better for our stock. . . . We did as our captain advised, and did not equip ourselves for the dangers ahead of us."

"I often wish I had taken a diary of the trip as we progressed," Kate said years later, "but I was a widow, my husband having been killed in the Civil War, and I had lots of work to do, having four children to take care of, and cook for several men, who helped care for our stock. I gathered most of my own wood by walking along by the wagon, gathering what I could find and placing it in a cowhide we had fastened under the wagon to carry wood and cooking vessels, so you see I was always very tired when the stops were made."

The women generally weren't responsible for the cattle, but they were constantly busy on the trail. Whenever the group stopped near an abundant source of water, the women did laundry and refilled the water barrels. Kate was a small woman weighing less than one hundred pounds, but she "was strong and was able to work hard all day, and all night, if necessary." She later scoffed that "the women of California don't know what hard work is. We women of Texas had worked both indoors and outdoors when needed, which was often during the Civil War."

When the drive reached the Llano Estacado (Staked Plains)—an arid eighty-mile stretch with no freshwater at all—the Medlin party's inexperience with trailing cattle took its toll. They traveled only at night, when it was cooler, but the cattle were nonetheless parched. Several miles before they reached the Pecos River, many of the cattle were poisoned after drinking alkali-laden water that accumulated in nearby mud holes. At the steep riverbank, the cowhands were unable to control the frenzied animals, who pushed one another into the quicksand, "so wild that they ran over anything in their way."

Once across the Pecos to the north bank, the Medlin group met another party of herders who were also headed west; these men were traveling without families, and the Medlins arranged to shadow them in hopes of being safer. After a few days, however, the two groups split up when they couldn't agree on the best route to follow. Once again, it was the Medlins' trail boss who was at fault. He refused to believe reports—or even his own eyes—that Indians had seized "a large herd of cattle only three days before, but I did, as we could see fine beef cattle along the roadside. The Indians had secured them from the

train ahead and had let them scatter out on the range to feed."
When the two herds went their separate ways, two men in the
Medlin group decamped as well. That left only thirteen men,
one a mere boy of fifteen.

To improve the chances of getting their herds safely to market, savvy trail drivers always attempted to maintain contact
with the herders ahead of and behind them. Even separately
owned herds established communication for their mutual benefit. Sometimes, a large herd owned by a single stockman or
cattle company would be split into two because two thousand
head was considered the optimal size for trailing, even if running two herds was costlier, requiring separate trail bosses and
crews, remudas (herds of horses used by the trail hands), and
chuck wagons. Three or four horses per man was the rule; to
avoid overworking the mounts, riders changed horses every afternoon and always started the day with a fresh one. For night
duty, the hands would ready their horses before going to sleep,
to avoid the time-wasting chores of catching and saddling their
mounts in the dark. The cowboys themselves wasted little time
with preparations; when they slept, they rarely "undressed" beyond removing their hats and boots.

When there was little danger of rustlers or Indian raiders,
the horse wranglers and wagon drivers sometimes doubled as
scouts, riding out ahead of the herd to find water and grazing
land, set up camp for the night, and cook the meals. Otherwise,
the entire party traveled as a unit, pausing at midday to rest
and allow the cattle to graze, and stopping again for the night
when they reached a spot with ample water and herbage.

In the mountains ahead, the Medlins soon spotted the Indians' campfires. As the party drew near them, Kate's brother-
in-law, Joseph Bradford, was injured while trying to free a
wagon that had bogged down in the mud. The Medlins tried to
continue, but when Bradford grew weaker, the group camped

at Independence Springs, where there was freshwater, hoping
that rest would speed his recovery. It was then the Indians confronted the wagon train.

When Kate saw the Indians approaching, she feared for her
children, "and my heart sank as I saw no help, no one near and
so few men, short of guns and ammunition but I said I would
fight until they killed me. Some of the women began to wring
their hands and cry. I said, 'What is the use of crying, it will
not help matters any.' But they said, 'Oh! They will kill us!'
I told them that crying would not keep them from killing us.
So I quickly placed my children and my sister's children in my
wagon and put my feather beds over them, as I had heard that
bullets would not go through feathers. The Indians had a few
guns and plenty of bows and arrows."

At first Kate grabbed her Enfield rifle—"I . . . was going to
guard my wagon, but one of our men come and wanted it." Instead, the women were told to mold bullets for the men's guns
and rifles. "I kept busy melting the lead and molding three
kinds of bullets for the different varieties of guns, as our bullets
were giving out, one pointed kind for six-shooters and the other
two round. All this time the arrows fell thick around me, but I
could see them before they got to me and would step back under
the shelter of my wagon. The firing of guns was fast and loud."

The fighting continued until sundown. Then the Indians withdrew, taking more than half the Medlins' cattle with them. The
group decided not to try to recover the livestock but to guard the
rest of the herd. "We thought of sending some of our men back
to see if the other train of cattle was coming our way, but we
were afraid if we divided up the Indians might cut off our men
and kill them and then return to us women and kill us."

In the morning, the Indians returned for the remaining
cattle, but still they didn't leave. The Medlin party was help-
less to stop them. Around noon, an Indian woman approached
the circled wagons, coming as close as twenty feet, riding the
horse the raiders had seized from the captain the previous day

and holding a long spear in her lap. The Indians were taunting the Medlin party—and testing them—daring them to fire at the woman. "If we had killed the young squaw that would have opened the war. But thank God, who was protecting us, no one shot her. The Indians came closer and closer, I could stand on my wagon and count sixty. I did count that many, but later more came." The men did shoot at the raiders, but in the evening, the Indians told them they could leave, after warning them that Apaches were lying in wait to kill them at the next watering hole, and headed back into the mountains.

During the day's fighting, Bradford died; his injuries had turned gangrenous. He was hastily buried inside the circle of wagons. The group then moved on, not stopping until they reached an old fort where they made camp and rested for a week. While they recuperated, a second party of twenty-two armed men joined them. They told the Medlins that Bradford's body had been dug up, scalped, and speared. They themselves had lost half their cattle to the Indians and later fought a group of Apaches, a battle that ended when they managed to kill the warriors' chief.

At Franklin, a town in the mountains north of El Paso, the Medlin party couldn't afford to replenish their stocks of food because they no longer had any cattle to sell or trade. They considered backtracking in hopes of recovering at least part of their herd, but they were warned that seven hundred warriors encamped in the nearby Guadalupe Mountains posed a threat to their safety. So they stayed on in town, subsisting on handouts, until another group of herders arrived with some of the Medlin cattle, which they had either managed to recapture from the raiders who had stolen them or which had gotten mixed up with their cattle. "We then got enough cattle of ours that had gotten in with their herd to sell and buy enough beans and bacon to bring us into California." By then, only three of the wagons were still serviceable, and the temperature made travel impossible during the daytime. The group finally reached California in November 1868, broke but having lost only Joseph Bradford during their grueling journey. Kate, the first woman known to have participated in a cattle drive from Texas to California, never left the Golden State. She joined her father, who was already living in Los Angeles, married her deceased husband's older brother, Marion, a successful storekeeper and hotel and saloon owner (despite his Baptist faith), and raised her four children there. She died in 1914.

Bettie Matthews Reynolds

When fifteen-year-old Bettie Matthews married George Reynolds in 1867 her dowry included two hundred head of cattle, a gift from her father, Joseph Matthews. He'd come to Texas from Louisiana in the early 1860s and raised cattle from the time he settled. Not long after the Reynolds wedding, George and his brother William became partners in an enterprise they named the Reynolds Cattle Company, adopting the Long X as their brand. It is still in use today. William took part in the fateful Goodnight and Loving drive in 1867, when Oliver Loving rashly attempted to travel through Comanche country in daylight and died of the wounds he suffered when the Indians attacked. At that time, William was trailing a small herd of his own.

Despite the very real dangers lurking on the trail, in settled areas and over short distances, even women often traveled alone. As George's sister Sallie Reynolds Matthews (who was married to Bettie's brother J. A.) wrote, "A woman thought nothing of taking a small child behind her saddle and another in her lap, and riding several miles to visit a neighbor. I've done it many times in my early married life." Not that the area of Throckmorton County near George's Old Stone Ranch was entirely safe. In North Central Texas, near the Oklahoma border, Fort Griffin had been built by the U.S. Army in 1867 expressly to protect settlers from Indian attacks. Bettie not only coped with the local risk—chiefly the threat of livestock raids—she also braved a long cattle drive, together with her husband and a sizable crew, along the Goodnight-Loving Trail in 1868. For their drive, George combined his herd of between seven and eight hundred cattle with Bettie's two-hundred-head dowry, and they set off for the West. She drove a Civil War ambulance (a large carriage similar to a stagecoach) from which two of the benches had been removed to make room for a bed and other amenities. The coach was drawn by teams of four to six mules or horses. George's younger brother, Bennie, and a cousin, named McLean, were members of the trail crew, which included another dozen or so other trail hands. McLean, who suffered from tuberculosis, hoped that a change of climate would cure his disease. George's father, Barber Watkins Reynolds, was trailing his own cattle on the drive.

Their route took them through the arid Llano Estacado. "Water for drinking and cooking was hauled in barrels fastened on a shelf made on the side of the wagon bed, and each wagon carried a barrel. No one dared start across the plains without such a supply of water, and even so equipped, they often suffered from thirst." When the Reynolds party left on July 9, the Concho River middle tributary was dry, so there would be no potable water until they reached the Pecos River, a salty, steep-banked stream, difficult to cross. The crew faced the added challenge of preventing the cattle from drinking the toxic, alkali-laden water commonly found on the Llano Estacado.

At the Pecos, Indian raiders "dashed in and drove off six horses before the night herders could arouse the camp." From then on, the crew redoubled its efforts to keep watch for Indians, who were rarely far from the trail. When George caught sight of a band of about one hundred fifty, Bettie "begged her husband's promise to shoot her if he saw she would fall captive to the Indians," but by next day they had made it safely to Fort Sumner, New Mexico. While the exhausted crew slept, the cattle "wandered away in search of grass," but they were easily rounded up the next morning.

In Bosque Grande (now Roswell, New Mexico), George's father sold his own cattle, as well as livestock belonging to other Texas stockmen he was acting as agent for, and returned to Texas, but all the others, including Bettie, wintered near Red River Station, New Mexico. There they met friends from Texas,

Tom Stockton and his wife, Etta Cuington Stockton. The previous year, the Stocktons had made the same drive, taking their infant child with them. One of the trail hands, Si Hough, was riding alongside Etta's wagon when his pistol accidentally discharged, killing the infant. They buried the child along the trail, with nothing but a quilt to wrap it in.

Tragedies like the death of the Stockton baby were far from unusual on the frontier. Death from illness, accident, or violence occurred frequently, perhaps especially to travelers along isolated routes. As Sallie Reynolds Matthews wrote in *Interwoven*, her family memoir, "These old cattle trails are marked by many graves. Some of them have crude headstones, but not many, as most of them were obliterated as much as possible to keep them from being desecrated. The old Butterfield stage route passes through our ranch, the route which so many wagon trains took during the famous gold rush to California; it has its share of graves."

When spring came, the Matthewses left Red River Station for California, traveling through Colorado, and at the end of the trail made "an extremely good profit" on the sale of their cattle. They remained in California for nearly two years, spending much of the time in San Francisco and Sacramento, and visited Salt Lake City on their way back to Texas in 1870.

Bettie and George made another drive together, in 1871, this time with two herds, one led by brother Will, with help from Bennie Reynolds, and the other by a trail boss named Brice Derrett. George's brother Glenn Reynolds and Bettie's brother Bud Matthews joined their siblings in the ambulance as far as Fort Gibson, in Indian Territory, where they boarded a train to Kit Carson, Colorado. At the Arkansas River, George found an abandoned, half-finished federal project to create an Indian reservation. It included an irrigation ditch capable of bringing water to several hundred acres of land and the walls of two stone buildings "between two hills, a very picturesque spot overlooking a large valley with the river curving around the south side.

The place was called 'Point of Rocks' . . . with miles of open grazing land on the north." The Reynolds Cattle Company stocked the new property with Texas longhorns; it was the start of a Texas-based ranching operation that made cattle drives over a large expanse that included Wyoming, Utah, Nevada, Montana, Nebraska, the Dakotas, and western Canada.

In 1880, George, his brother William, and Bettie's brother John Alexander Matthews, formed a five-year ranching partnership. At the end of that period, the partners decided to dissolve the arrangement and divide their land and livestock into equal parts. The acreage that fell to J. A. Matthews in 1885 lacked a source of freshwater, so he began purchasing additional tracts of land, including parcels on the Clear Fork of the Brazos River and another that included the headwaters of Lambshead Creek. He named his holdings Lambshead Ranch, after the creek, whose name originated with Thomas Lambshead, an English agent for the Butterfield Overland Mail, a stage service that ran from St. Louis to San Francisco between 1858 and 1861, passing through northern Texas.

Lambshead was a fifty-thousand-acre spread and J. A. Matthews was an innovative operator. He led the effort to eliminate Texas fever by dipping cattle in a solution that kills the ticks that carry the disease, and introduced practices to preserve pastureland that are still in use today. After Matthews's death in 1941, management passed to several of J. A. and Sallie Reynolds Matthews's surviving children. The last, Watkins "Watt" Matthews, who ran the ranch until his death at ninety-eight, in 1997, became a legend in his own right.

Watt Matthews, who never married, lived nearly his entire life at Lambshead. Except for four years as an undergraduate at Princeton University, he rarely spent more than a short time away from the land, the cattle, and the way of life he loved. Almost to the end of his life, he was an active rancher, and in 1989, when he was ninety, Laura Wilson published a portrait of Watt in photographs, *Watt Matthews of Lambshead*. He continued the Lambshead tradition of producing pure Hereford cattle, but when the longhorns from Fort Griffin State Park were brought back to Lambshead in 1972, he experimented with cross-breeding them with his Herefords, which he thought would result in easy calving.

Aside from raising its famed Herefords, the Lambshead Ranch was active in efforts to preserve native wildlife, restored the ranch houses that had belonged to members of the oft-intermarried Matthews-Reynolds families, and sustained the annual Fort Griffin Fandangle, an annual musical drama about the history of the region that is performed in a natural amphitheater on the ranch.

The diminutive Watt Matthews (five feet six inches tall) was the last nineteenth-century-born link to the Reynolds-Matthews families' ranching traditions. His funeral was held in the Presbyterian church built on the ranch in 1898, one year before he was born. The service was private, but afterward, a crowd of seven hundred made the fifteen-mile drive from the county road to the family cemetery, next to the amphitheater. There Watt was buried, dressed as he had been for work over nearly a century, in worn denim jeans and jacket, a bandanna around his neck, with his Stetson resting in the coffin next to him.

Amanda Nite Burks

Amanda Nite grew up in East Texas. At sixteen, she met William Franklin "Bud" Burks, when her brother Jim invited him to the Crockett Female Seminary's Christmas ball in 1857. They became engaged before Bud left town a week later and were married the following October. Two years older than Amanda, Bud had begun trading cattle in his teens, and the couple started ranching on Shawnee Prairie in Angelina County shortly after the wedding. Their first child, John, died in June 1860, when he was just nine months old. A year later, they had a daughter, whom they named Lucy. By this time, Bud's sister and four half siblings, Bob, Mark, John, and Margaret, ages nine to seventeen, were also living with them. They had moved in shortly after the death of Bud's stepmother and never rejoined their father, even though he later married for a third time.

After the South seceded from the Union in 1861, Bud volunteered for service in the Confederate army, but from the moment he joined his company, he missed Amanda and wrote her often, expressing hope of being granted a furlough before he was sent off to war. His hope soon turned to despair. "I do not know whether I will ever see you again," he wrote. As the war wound down, however, his optimism returned, and he wrote, "I would like to see your face out here do you think you would come to me if I was to write to you? I think you would come." His letters were also full of advice about farming, stock raising, and looking after their daughter and his siblings. "Make the children mind you," he advised, "and if they won't do right whip them and make them."

Late in the war, Bud served under Colonel John Salmon "Rip" Ford in Nueces County, on the coast of the Gulf of Mexico, where he saw land he thought was ideal for cattle raising. "This is the best country I have ever seen in my life," he wrote, and he resolved to move there, if Amanda agreed, after the war. Before his discharge, Bud did manage to get home on furlough in early 1865, and when he left, Amanda accompanied him for the first day of his ride back. During her brief absence, four-year-old Lucy suddenly sickened and died. She was buried next to her brother in the Jonesville cemetery.

Discontented with Texas under Reconstruction, Bud decided to relocate to Mexico. Amanda went along with his decision, although she later called leaving the community where her two young children were buried "the darkest day of her life."

The Burkses didn't make it all the way to Mexico, however. When they reached Banquete, in Nueces County, Bud was apparently as taken with the region as he had been two years earlier. They bought 151 acres outside the town, built a five-room house on the property—"quite a mansion in those days"—planted a garden, and returned to raising horses and cattle. For the next several years, Bud regularly drove livestock to Louisiana, and from the trail he wrote faithfully to Amanda, as he had during the war. These letters, like his earlier ones, alternated between offering practical advice and lamenting their separation.

By 1871, the market for beef was poor in Texas and Louisiana. When a steer was slaughtered, only its hide and tallow had commercial value; the meat was good only as pig fodder. In the north and east, however, the demand for beef was stronger, so William Burks assembled a herd of one thousand of his best cattle and set off for Kansas in April. For safety, he traveled in tandem with Jasper "Jap" Clark, who was trailing his herd to market at the same time. Burks and Clark each had ten or so trail hands, most of them Mexican vaqueros, and a cook.

A day after Bud left Banquete, he sent his brother-in-law, Marcus Banks, back with a message for Amanda: he wanted her to join him. Because the Burks cattle covered only ten miles or so a day, in order to fatten en route, Amanda quickly caught up with the herd. She brought Nick, the Burkses' servant, along in her buggy, which was drawn by two ponies. Nick prepared meals for Amanda, pitched her tent in the evenings, and spelled Amanda when she wanted relief from driving the buggy. That was rarely necessary, however, because the ponies mostly followed "the slow-moving herd unguided, and I would find a comfortable position, fasten the lines and take a little nap." Although Amanda was a skilled horsewoman, she made the entire trip to Kansas in her buggy.

When cattle passed through forested areas with thick undergrowth, the trail crew tried to keep them moving quickly, to take advantage of their habit of following the lead of the animals ahead of them. If a steer got lost in the woods, it was often impossible to recover it, and near Lockhart, Texas, the Burkses lost thirty head in the timber. During the one stampede (perhaps caused by Indians, though no cattle were stolen as a result), which affected both the Burks and Clark herds, it took a week to round up all the animals, and more days passed before the two herds were completely sorted out.

Of all the dangers facing cattlemen, stampedes were the most feared. Difficult to prevent and impossible to anticipate, one might be caused by an unfamiliar animal—a tame dog, a timid rabbit, or even one of the drive's own horses—that got in among the steers. The noise from a flock of birds taking flight in the morning, the bolting of startled deer, or the peal of thunder during a storm could cause a chain reaction of panic that set the cattle running. Raiders and rustlers, of course, intentionally caused stampedes by showering arrows down on the herd or firing their weapons. To reduce the risk, the cowhands kept watch over their herds day and night, because even after the animals had been bedded down for the night a slight disturbance might trigger a stampede.

When the herd was on the move, the hands rode alongside them, and at night the crew worked in shifts, riding slowly around the resting herd. As they rode, "they would whistle and sing to the cattle and the cattle, being used to hearing their voices and the movement of the horses, would lie contented." In addition to calming the cattle, singing also helped the night herders, who spent long days in the saddle for the several months a drive typically lasted, to stay awake. Thanks to round-the-clock vigilance, stampedes were the exception, but if cattle were lost because a cowhand had fallen asleep while night herding, he was likely to be fired on the spot.

Stampeding cattle raced ahead at breakneck speed, usually in as straight a line as possible, and were almost impossible to stop. Attempting to head off a stampeding herd was futile, even suicidal; the cowboys would therefore gallop alongside, as close as possible to the herd, until the cattle started circling and eventually ran themselves out. With calm restored, the hands would hunt down the strays that had separated from the main herd. Recovery could take days, and they didn't always succeed in finding all the missing animals. If the owners were lucky, their strays would be picked up by drivers of herds that came up the trail later and returned to them when they reached the railhead.

Stampedes aside, the Burks party experienced its share of hardships, especially when it stormed and "the lightning seemed to settle on the ground and creep along like something alive." During one torrential storm of rain and hail, Bud led Amanda's buggy to shelter in a heavily forested spot and unhitched the ponies. Then he returned to help the hands keep the cattle, who were easily spooked by storms, from bolting. "Cold and wet and hungry and all alone in the dark," Amanda wrote, "this was the only time of all the months of my trip that I wished I was back on the old ranch at Banquete."

In fact, extremes of weather caused greater difficulties on the drive than did any human adversaries. Besides the rain and hail, Amanda reported that the Trinity River at Fort Worth was so flooded that she counted at least fifteen herds waiting to cross. Beyond the Red River, they encountered insufferably hot days and chilly nights, but fortunately there were no serious attempts to raid or rustle their livestock. Some Indians did come into their camp to trade, and Amanda confronted a couple of would-be rustlers, who were throwing rocks at the grazing herd. "Don't you know you'll stampede those cattle?" she yelled, and one of them replied, "That's what we're trying to do," but when some of the hands approached, the intruders fled.

In the parched landscape, fire was a constant danger. One night, a candle left burning when the Burkses went to sleep set a box of Amanda's personal items alight. Early one morning, the crew escaped a spreading prairie fire by racing to a zone that had recently been burned in another blaze. A few days later, Amanda recalled lighting a fire for cooking that quickly "blazed higher than a house and went straight ahead for fifty miles or more." When the investigators learned that a woman was the responsible party, they were forgiving, but she sensed that a man would not have gotten off so easily.

Amanda's other misdemeanors were more innocent. To discourage her from wandering off in search of wild plums, Bud sometimes claimed that dangerous Indians were lurking nearby, but at the Canadian River, where a profusion of red, blue, and yellow plums lured her away from her buggy, she lost her bearings and thought the horses had run off. They were right where she had left them, however, and that day the entire crew feasted on plum pie. On other occasions, the trail hands, eager to please the only woman in the party—and the boss's wife, to boot—would present her with gifts of fruit, grouse, or even antelope tongue they had found or hunted.

After three months on the trail, the Burks and Clark herds reached Newton, Kansas, where they discovered that cattle prices had dropped sharply. Like many of the other recently arrived cattlemen, they decided to wait for the market to recover. At first, Bud put Amanda up in a hotel in the town of Elsmore, but after a fire broke out at the hotel, she decided to return to camp with her husband and the crew. Prices remained

depressed, however, and then winter set in. During the first severe snowstorm, nine of the horses died, and to water the cattle
they had to haul ice from nearby streams. The cold discouraged
Bud, and in December he decided to return to Texas. "He met
with no discouragement of his plans from me, for never had I
endured such cold." He and Amanda took a train to St. Louis,
"dressed as if we were Esquimaux, and carrying a bucket of
frozen buffalo tongues as a souvenir for my friends in Texas."
From St. Louis, they continued to New Orleans, where they
boarded a boat for Corpus Christi.

Despite the occasional hardships, Amanda never regretted
her drive up what she called "the old Kansas Trail." As she
wrote, "[W]hat woman, youthful and full of spirit and the love
of living, needs sympathy because of availing herself of the opportunity of being with her husband while at his chosen work in
the great out-of-door world?"

Bud Burks continued to drive cattle to Kansas for another five
years, during a period that saw much of the open range fenced
in. Searching for territory that was still open, he chose La Motta,
in La Salle County, halfway between San Antonio and Laredo:
"beautiful country; great wide expanses of prairie bordering a
wooded stream and shady lakes." He and Amanda dismantled
the Banquete house and used the lumber to build a new one at
La Motta. Only six weeks after they arrived, however, Bud, who
had contracted tuberculosis in the Civil War, died. He was only
thirty-seven. Before his death, he advised Amanda to concentrate on raising sheep; he thought a woman could manage them
better than horses and cattle. She followed his advice and sold
off their horses, some of which were purchased by James Gor-
don Bennett Jr., publisher of the *New York Herald* and founder of
the country's first polo club, to stock his stable of polo ponies.
They are said to have been the first horses from Texas to be
exported to New York.

Amanda hung on at the ranch and fended off the depreda-
tions of bandits, Indians, and even wild animals that preyed on
her livestock. Later, when her sister-in-law Rhoda and Rhoda's
husband, John Baylor, died in rapid succession, Amanda, as she
had earlier done with Bud's brother and sisters, became mother
to the three Baylor children.

Falling prices for wool, drought, and the displacement of
prairie grass by brush made sheep raising uneconomical in the
1890s. Amanda then sold off her flocks and switched backed to
raising cattle. She also enlarged her house at the ranch, which
had grown to forty-three thousand acres.

The Texas writer J. Frank Dobie, whose uncle Jim was
Amanda's neighbor in La Salle County, based a number of his
stories on tales Amanda had told him; they appeared in the
books *Cow People* and *Coronado's Children*. She faulted him for
altering details in some of the stories and wasn't satisfied when
he explained that his changes were made to make the tales
more appealing to readers, but he saluted her as "a remarkable representative of frontier womanhood." Amanda's greatest
claim to fame was almost certainly as the prototype of Taisie
Lockheart, the heroine of Emerson Hough's novel *North of 36*.
When an interviewer inquired whether the novel was true to
the cattle drives, she said, "I have read that great and truthful
book. On many pages, I saw evidence of Mr. Hough's careful ex-
amination of our records [published in J. Marvin Hunter's *The
Trail Drivers of Texas*]. 'North of 36' seems to me as true a work
of fiction as can possibly be." Asked about Taisie's resemblance
to her, Amanda modestly replied, "How could anyone lay claim
to such an honor?" Nevertheless, she conceded, "some of our
experiences were very similar."

When *North of 36*, which had been adapted as a silent film in
1924, was remade in 1938 as *The Texans*, starring Randolph Scott
and Joan Bennett, some of the scenes were shot at La Motta.
Amanda's great-nieces, Virginia Bell Sturges and Amanda Bell
Newman, and her great-nephew Frank Newman were stunt

doubles and extras in the film, and a number of the Burkses' friends appeared as extras as well.

Amanda died in 1931, at the age of ninety. The *Cotulla Record* summed up her life in these words: "In her there was tenderness with strength; refinement with courage; contempt for a coward, but pity for the weak; intolerance for the indolent, but charity for the poor. She dared, but with charming modesty that disarmed her foes. She was truly a gentle-woman."

Hattie Standefer Cluck

*Trail hands were superstitious about having women along on cat-
tle drives, which is doubtless one of the reasons they were mostly
all-male affairs. But a few women refused to be left behind. One of
them was Hattie Cluck, who was three months pregnant when she
accompanied her husband, George, in the spring of 1871. Twenty-
four years old and already the mother of three young children—
Allie Annie, seven; Emmet, five; and Minnie, two—Harriett
Standefer Cluck piled her children into a buggy drawn by two
ponies and left Brushy Creek in central Texas in early April. One
day before her twenty-fifth birthday, on April 23, they crossed the
Brazos River heading north toward Fort Worth.*

Hattie may have been the first woman to make a drive
trailing three young children and pregnant with a
fourth. As she explained years later, "There was nothing else
[for George] to do with me and the babies but to take us with
him. He took all he had in the world with him, and we wanted
to be together no matter what happened." Her granddaughter
Mary Griffin recounted a different version of the tale, in which
George didn't want Hattie to go along, "but she told the men
to get out the wagon and put it in the line of the cattle." By the
time her husband saw the wagon, Hattie was ready to travel.
"So they went."

The drive was made in tandem with a second rancher (most
likely Dudley Snyder), with a crew that totaled fifteen or sixteen
men. Hattie didn't take active part in the drive itself, of course;
she had her hands full looking after her children. Mostly, she
traveled in the buggy, but where the water was wide and deep,
such as at the Red River, she switched to horseback, and the
children rode with George and some of the hands on their

horses. To get the wagon across the river, they strapped logs to its sides for flotation and guided it across the water, with the ponies pulling it along.

In Indian Territory, a gang of would-be rustlers demanded a share of the herds, but George Cluck was not cowed. Accounts of what happened next may have been embroidered and amplified in the course of many retellings by raconteurs and journalists, but in some versions, Hattie, who helped load the guns for the sixteen cowboys who were trailing the Cluck and Snyder herds, announced, "If any of you boys doesn't want to fight, come here and drive the hack and give me your gun." For his part, George is said to have replied to the outlaws' demand, "You won't get any of our cattle. I have sixteen as good fighters under me as ever crossed the Red River, and they are all crack shots. When you get ready, open the ball, but us Texans will dance the first set." The gang leader, after talking things over with his men, led them away empty-handed.

On October 17, after the drive had ended, Hattie gave birth to a son, Euel Standefer, near Abilene, Kansas, where the Clucks had sold their cattle. In no rush to return to Texas, the family spent the winter in Kansas and stayed until spring 1872. Throughout the fall and winter, George traded cattle in Kansas and was involved in several lawsuits—probably related to his cattle dealing. In addition, there was friction with local farmers, who thought that the Texas cattle damaged their crops. The locals wanted to put an end to the cattle drives that terminated in Abilene.

Back in Texas, the Clucks bought a small ranch on Running Brushy Creek near Georgetown, and Hattie was appointed postmistress of Running Brushy. Between 1874 and 1889, Hattie had six more children, the last one when she was forty-three. Over time, George and Hattie enlarged their small ranch to nearly nine hundred acres, farming and quarrying stone as well as raising cattle on their property. Stone from their quarry was used in the building of the state capitol in Austin.

Eliza Bunton Johnson
Lyndon Johnson's grandmother
The Bunton-Johnson family tree appears in the appendix.

*Eliza Bunton was born to Robert Holmes Bunton and Priscilla
Jane Bunton in Russellville, Kentucky, June 24, 1849. The family moved to Texas when she was about ten years old. Her father's
older brother, John Wheeler Bunton, had arrived in Texas in 1835
and became a leader in the revolution against Mexico.*

The Bunton family were prosperous in Tennessee, but John
had been lured to Texas by the availability of land and
the opportunity to make his fortune on his own terms. Two of
his sisters and his two brothers, Robert Holmes and Desha,
later followed him to Texas, settling in central and western
Texas. The Bunton brothers made a good living on their land
and retired in comfort.

Eighteen-year-old Eliza, Robert and Priscilla's fourth child,
married Sam Ealy Johnson in Lockhart, Texas, on December
11, 1867. She moved into the log house Sam and his brother
Tom had built on the Pedernales River near Johnson City.
Their cattle operations had been successful throughout the
1860s, and the Johnson brothers were among the largest ranchers in central Texas.

When Rebekah Baines Johnson, Eliza's daughter-in-law and
the mother of Lyndon Johnson, wrote the family history, *A Family Album*, she described Eliza as tall, with a patrician bearing,
raven hair, piercing black eyes, and magnolia-white skin. Tell-
ingly, Rebekah added that Eliza hated flattery and insincerity.

Living conditions were primitive in this western outpost.
Noted Texas historian T. R. Fehrenbach described frontier life
in these terms: "hardy, dirty, terribly monotonous, lonely and

damagingly narrow." The weather was cold and rainy, muddy and grim, or too hot and unrelentingly dry. The constant fear of Indian raids in the sparsely populated areas that settlers lived in was terrifying. The "Comanche moon" was known to be the most dangerous time. When the moon was full, attacks were brutal. Women were raped and scalped; men were similarly tortured, and children were not spared.

On August 15, 1869, a neighbor couple of Sam and Eliza went fishing after dinner near Cypress Creek and were ambushed, scalped, and killed by Comanche Indians. According to Robert Caro in the first volume of his biographical series on Lyndon Johnson, Lyndon's grandfather, Sam, was among the men who rode out to find the Indians. Eliza was left alone with her baby, Mary. When she saw Indians riding horses through the woods, she "snatched up the baby, and crawled into the root cellar. She closed the trapdoor, and then stuck a stick through a crack in it, and inched a braided rug over the trapdoor so that it couldn't be seen."

When Eliza heard the Indians entering the house, she tied a diaper over baby Mary's mouth so she couldn't make any sound. Caro wrote that Eliza could hear the Indians smashing their wedding gifts in the cabin before going back outside, stealing horses from the Johnson corral, and riding away. Lyndon's daughter Luci told me the story after I had visited the house where Eliza and Sam lived in Johnson City. Eliza stayed in the cellar until it was dark and she heard Sam entering the house. The story passed down through the generations is that Sam wailed, "Oh Eliza, I would take you away from this if I could." On being assured it was Sam and not the Indians returning, she emerged from hiding. In fact, the next year they did move away to a more secure area, Buda, in Hays County near San Marcos and Austin. They had nine children who were reared and went to school in Hays County. The fifth child, and first son, born in 1877, Sam Ealy Johnson Jr., was Lyndon Johnson's father.

Though the family now resided in relative safety away from the Indian raids, the ranching operations continued back on the Pedernales River.

In another Lyndon Johnson biography, *The Formative Years*, a veteran cowboy, A. W. Capt, was quoted as saying about one of the Johnson trail drives in the spring of 1870, "I got my best experience from Sam and Thomas Johnson, then the largest individual trail drivers . . . and [with] headquarters at Johnson's Ranch on the Pedernales River. The roundup . . . usually gathered . . . a herd of from 2,500 to 3,000 head of cattle," which they trailed to Kansas.

Cattle drives, as these frontier portraits attest, were not for the faint of heart. Eliza Johnson was equal to their challenges. It took months to reach Colorado or Kansas, and Eliza rode with her husband through the long days, facing torrential rains and dust storms, camping out every night. Despite the risk of Indian raids, which were common during this period, Eliza would help scout ahead of the herd to look for water and grazing.

A young cowboy, Horace Hall, wrote letters to his father in Illinois after being hired by the Johnsons in Abilene, Kansas, to return to Texas where he was to work on the ranch and become a trail rider. In 1871, on another drive to Kansas, Horace wrote, "I am the hero of our camp. Riding out with Mrs. Johnson some 8 miles in advance of the train . . . I shot a deer."

But 1871 began a run of bad luck. The Johnsons, gambling on a continuing good market for Texas cattle, bought as many as twenty thousand head, mostly on credit, hoping to make a killing when they reached Abilene. But during the unexpectedly harsh winter of 1871, many cattle died, and in the spring, pasture was sparse and there was little rain. Their cattle were thin when they headed up the trail, and when they reached Abilene, they found a market glutted with Texas longhorns. Stockmen waited in vain for a good price for their herds, but a recession in the Northeast only depressed beef prices even further. Unable to make payments on their notes, the brothers lost most of their land—in Austin, Fredericksburg, and Gillespie and Blanco counties—and their cotton mill. They managed to salvage some of their holdings by arranging sales to a nephew, and in another court-ordered sale, the buyer who had bid only pennies on the dollar immediately sold the tract back to the Johnsons. Despite the immense losses they suffered, Sam and Thomas immediately started forming another herd to drive to market the following year.

Devoted to her family, Eliza was a solid and savvy helpmate during the difficult times. Her motto was "charity begins at home," and she was known as a tough bargainer when she sold her eggs and butter. She salted away her earnings, and, Rebekah wrote, "from the depths of the big zinc trunk, which held her treasures and her meeting clothes, she would bring out an old purse, holding the egg-and-butter money carefully saved for the purchase of a new black silk dress, and count out the exact amount needed by the child temporarily financially embarrassed. Sometimes the purse was left empty, but she eagerly assured the recipient of the loan of her happiness to be of service and her own lack of present need." To try to recoup the losses of land, Eliza sold the fine carriage and matched horses, a gift from her brother-in-law Thomas, and made a payment on the place in the Hill Country that became the family home. When the children had been educated and were grown, Eliza and Sam were able to move back to their beloved Hill Country and Pedernales River in 1888, to a small farm near Stonewall.

In "Heroines of the Hills," an article that appeared in *Frontier Times* in October 1940, T. U. Taylor described Eliza as one of the leading women among the pioneers. "Eliza Bunton was gently reared but she took to the frontier life like the heroine she was, and became a member of that hall of fame that should be erected to the heroines of the highlands of Southwest Texas. She often saw horses dash into the pens near the house with arrows sticking in their flanks."

In *A Family Album*, Rebekah recalled that on a February

morning in 1912, Eliza suffered a stroke while sewing a button on one of Sam's shirts. She never fully recovered and died in 1917.

She was born into a family of public figures. Her uncle John Wheeler Bunton was a hero of the battle of San Jacinto, a delegate to the convention that wrote the constitution of the Republic of Texas, and a member of its congress. Her cousin Joseph Desha had served as governor of Kentucky. But she could not have imagined that her grandson, born on their farm in 1908, whom she had cuddled and held in her arms, would be the most famous of them all. Or could she?

Molly Dunn Bugbee

After two years spent hauling lumber in Silver City, Idaho, in 1868, Thomas Sherman Bugbee teamed up with his friends Cornelius Shea and George Miller to buy cattle in Texas and drive them to Idaho, where they were fetching forty-five dollars a head. On their first drive, they brought twelve hundred head of cattle north with a crew of eight, fending off Indian attacks en route and realizing a handsome profit. The next year Tom drove one herd to Colorado and another to Rice County, Kansas, west of Abilene. By 1871, he'd already led several lucrative drives, and that year he met eighteen-year-old Mary Catherine "Molly" Dunn in Peace, Kansas, while he and a crew were fattening steers near Sterling and building corrals for the horses. Tom had gone to the Dunns' house to borrow an ax and, legend has it, was so smitten with Molly that he left without remembering to ask for the ax.

They courted by riding on the plains around Peace, were married in 1872, and spent their honeymoon driving a buggy to Great Bend, Kansas, where they joined up with Tom's herd and five-man crew. From there they drove the cattle to Colorado. At the time, Tom didn't have a specific destination; he was searching for good grazing land and abundant water for his herd.

In an account given by their daughter, Helen Bugbee Officer, Molly stayed at the Great Bend Hotel for a week and then joined the drive, following Thomas's herd of 750 steers. She insisted that Thomas ride in the chuck wagon with her and have Frank, the cook, ride a horse, because, she said, Frank was too dirty. Thomas must have been keen to oblige Molly, because almost as soon as they set off, she lost her sunbonnet, and they had to turn back to recover it. Later, she was sitting on a sack of flour in the chuck wagon; it burst, spilling the contents. One evening, after a long day of driving, she jumped down from the wagon when they stopped to make camp, and "the flutter of her gingham dress and the flying sunbonnet strings frightened the cattle into a stampede."

They slept out of doors, under the wagon. Going to bed after one hot day, Molly felt something dripping on her head. It was the bacon; the heat had liquefied the fat. She shampooed her hair in the morning, and the next night they slept with their heads at the opposite end of the wagon, where the molasses dripped on her hair. Thomas somehow escaped unmolested on both occasions.

After returning from Colorado, the Bugbees settled near Larkin Station in western Kansas, where they dug a one-room house into the side of a hill and stretched a buffalo hide across the front opening. To support their ranching operation while they waited for favorable market conditions, they hunted buffalo and sold the hides, which were in great demand.

After several years in Larkin Station, the Bugbees decided to move to Texas. It was 1876, and on that trip, Molly is said to have insisted on transporting a door, in order to have a real front door on their house in Texas. Thomas, saying it was too bulky and heavy, tossed the door out of the wagon a couple of times, until Molly had the men tie it underneath the wagon, where Thomas wouldn't notice it.

On this drive, because of stampeding, they had difficulty keeping their herd together, and they lost half their herd and many of Molly's household goods as they struggled to cross the swollen Cimarron River. "Molly Bugbee sat on the bank of that river, holding her two small children—Ethel and Thomas Everett—in her arms, and watched horses flounder, wagons break loose and cattle fight helplessly against the current. . . . But Molly did not stop to regret or complain."

Their new home, in Hutchinson County, in the Texas Panhandle, was another dugout, with buffalo hides on the floors, mud-daubed pickets on the front, windows made of thin deerskin, and walls coated with a plaster-like compound made of crushed baked gypsum and water. In this modest house the Quarter Circle T Ranch, the second ranch in the Texas Panhandle, was founded. Molly was just the second Anglo woman to settle in the area; the third, who arrived a year later, was Molly Goodnight, seventy-five miles away. "Molly Bugbee, who was a fine rifle shot, could stand in her door and kill buffalo as they grazed near or came thundering by. They were so numerous that they were exceedingly troublesome, and for two years men were regularly hired to drive buffalo off the range."

After years of dugout living, the Bugbees built the "Stone House" on the north side of the Canadian River, with the help of some Portuguese stonemasons who fortuitously turned up to work at the ranch. It was a relatively spacious five rooms, with floors covered by the hooked rugs Molly made from old flannel underwear. Here Molly's third child, Ruby, was born—two days' ride and seventy-five miles from the nearest doctor. Over a section of the spring that ran through the property, Molly built a "milkhouse" (or springhouse), where water was channeled through troughs to cool their milk and butter, and from where it ran down to irrigate the garden.

When Tom was offered $175,000 for his herd in 1881, he was prepared to sell, but Molly counseled him to "hold out a little longer." A year later, after a "waterspout" (a combination of tornado and cloudburst) destroyed their springhouse and garden, Molly had a change of heart about selling. This time the offer for Tom's 12,500 head of cattle was $350,000, double the previous year's bid.

In Helen Bugbee Officer's telling, "Her [Molly's] uniform kindness to the cowboys of that wild region won for herself and her husband their hearty good will. It became generally known that no wearied or belated cowboy could pass by the Bugbee Ranch without being invited to dismount and partake of food and rest. If their business called them on, there was always a glass of cool water or of rich, refreshing milk to moisten their parched throats before resuming their journey over the sun-baked plains. All this kindness, bestowed without care or reward, was by no means misplaced, for cowboys, as a rule, are quick of perception and warm of appreciation. No matter how far the 'Quarter circle T' cattle might wander, they were invariably well cared for and returned to their owner."

After the Bugbee herd was sold in 1882, Tom offered Molly her heart's desire. She'd never been to Missouri, but she knew that it was close enough to Texas to allow Tom to return to the ranch every spring, and that in Kansas City there were good schools for their children, so Molly asked him to buy a fruit farm there. Tom purchased a ten-acre farm on the outskirts of Kansas City and a second farm in Kansas, and he and William States also entered into partnership in a ranch near Dodge City. By 1883 he was actively engaged in the cattle business in Texas, Kansas, and the Indian Territory, but until 1897, Tom and Molly kept their house in Kansas City, where she gave birth to five more children—Bliss, Kate, Stella, John Sherman, and Helen—in addition to caring for six nieces and nephews who came to live with them. In the city, Molly was a popular figure among the local elite, but after fifteen years she suddenly grew weary of the long absences from Tom and wired him in the Panhandle: "Get us a house. Family Coming to Texas."

The house Tom found for them in Clarendon had only three rooms, so even with an additional "collapsible" house bought for added space, the quarters were so tight that for the first year, until their large home on Bugbee Hill was completed, their piano sat on the front porch. Under the Bugbee aegis, the town quickly took on the trappings of community; Tom and Molly helped found schools and served on the school board; attracted doctors; and opened local banks, one of which Tom served for many years as a director and chairman. For eight years, he was also president of the Panhandle Stockmen's Association. Among their friends and neighbors, "it was Molly Bugbee who was sent for when help was needed"; she advised the careworn, ministered to the sick, and helped her neighbors through the pangs of birth and death.

Tom Bugbee's great passion remained cattle ranching, and he shared that love and the prosperity it brought him with his children. Through the Bugbee Livestock & Land Company, they all received shares of the profits from the business. He increasingly left the running of the operation to Thomas Everett Bugbee, their eldest son. But when Thomas Everett died, at forty-two, in 1917, the tragedy broke his father's heart. Thomas Sherman Bugbee sold his cattle and thenceforth leased the land to other ranchers. He and Molly soldiered on, but he spoke of the years until his own death in 1925 as "borrowed time," and Molly survived her husband by just three years.

Margaret Heffernan
Dunbar Hardy Borland

The details are uncertain, but in early 1836, not long before Mexican forces withdrew from Texas after the battle of San Jacinto, Margaret Heffernan's father, John, was killed, probably by Indians, while helping his brother, James, plant his crops on land near Poesta Creek in Southwest Texas. Their cousin John Ryan, along with James's wife and their five children, were also murdered. Margaret's mother, also named Margaret, was left to care for her four children. In May, as the Mexican army made its way to the border, an officer, José Enrique de la Peña, briefly stayed with the Heffernans. In his diary, he wrote, "I was quartered in the house of John Stefferman [Heffernan], a man who had unfortunately been murdered by the Indians last April together with his brother, the brother's wife, five nieces and nephews, and a cousin. Mistress Margaret was left with four orphaned children, among whom one's attention is drawn to Miss Mary, whose amiability and misfortune touched my sensibility." The elder Margaret Heffernan, who died in 1849, never remarried.

In 1843, young Margaret married Harrison Dunbar, of Victoria. They had one daughter, Mary, before Dunbar was killed in a pistol duel. In October 1845, she married Milton Hardy, whose family had come to Texas from Tennessee in 1822. Hardy was an upstanding citizen and a member of the Victoria city council. In 1847, they had a daughter, Eliza, and a year later, a second daughter, Julia, was born, but Eliza died at about the same time. Another daughter, Rosa, followed in 1852, and finally a boy, William. Milton raised cattle, wrote a will that provided for the emancipation of his slave, Louisa, and her children upon his death, and filed claims on the Heffernan estates, seeking compensation from the state for the "property destroyed and lost by the Mexican and Texian armies" in 1836. Then he contracted cholera and died, on August 24, 1852, and their son, William, also fell victim to the same epidemic. Milton Hardy left twelve hundred head of cattle and "several tracts of land." In the end, Louisa, the slave, wasn't freed but remained with Margaret, who was now a widow with three girls—Mary, eight; Julia, four; and Rosa, nearly one—as well as the young son of her brother John, also named John, who moved in with Margaret after his parents died when he was an infant.

In 1856, Margaret wed for the third time, to Alexander Borland, a wealthy Victoria County rancher. By 1860, their cattle holdings were the largest in the county: eight thousand head. Some of the cattle were likely Margaret's, inherited either from her father or from Milton Hardy—for many years she continued to use his "H" brand. Among the Borland ranch hands were Margaret's brother James and nephew John. Meanwhile, she had four more children with Borland: Alex Jr. (1857), Jesse (1859), Willie (1861), and Nellie, born in 1864, when Margaret was forty. With prosperity also came the accoutrements of wealth: a piano, walnut furniture, linens, china. According to her son-in-law Victor Rose, husband of Julia Hardy, "she had, unaided, acquired a good education." He presumably knew a cultured woman when he saw one; his great-grandmother was Mary Washington, George Washington's niece.

Alexander Borland didn't serve in the Civil War; while the conflict raged, he expanded his ranching operation and may have enlarged his herd by "adopting" some of the five million wild longhorns that by then proliferated in Texas. But in 1867 he fell ill, went to New Orleans to consult a surgeon, and died before he was able to return home. Margaret moved her family into Victoria and took over management of the Borland business. That summer also saw a yellow fever epidemic; it claimed all three of Margaret's daughters from her first two marriages: Mary, Julia, and Rosa. Son-in-law Victor also suffered a bout of yellow fever, but he survived. The widower gave his six-month-old daughter over to Margaret's care. Meanwhile, in September, her youngest son, six-year-old Willie, also died.

After these bereavements, Margaret increasingly turned her attention to business. Her cattle holdings grew—by some accounts she owned as many as ten thousand head in the early 1870s—but prices in Texas were low, a factor that very likely influenced her decision to trail her cattle north, where the markets were more favorable to sellers. In the spring of 1873, with cattle fetching twenty-four dollars a head in Kansas, three times as much as in San Antonio, she decided to set a precedent by becoming the first woman trail boss on a drive to Wichita, with a herd that totaled slightly more than one thousand. In addition, Margaret planned to take her children—Alex, sixteen; Jesse, fourteen; Nellie, eight; and her grandchild Julia Rose, six—along. By now the boys were old enough to work as trail hands, and the girls, including little Julia, would help with chores. She had other, more experienced trail hands as well, of course, and a cook.

Records are sparse, but the drive was concluded without serious mishap, and by the beginning of June, Margaret had reached Wichita, Kansas, and checked into the Planter House. According to the *Wichita Beacon*, "She is the happy possessor of about one thousand head of cattle, and accompanied the herd all the way from its starting point to this place, giving evidence of a pluck and business tact far superior to many of the 'lords.'" Evidently, she had lost virtually none of her cattle on the trail. The same paper later remarked on the impression she made thanks to "her lady-like character." Margaret shopped for clothing at an establishment reputed to be the finest west of Kansas City, and she must also have pondered what to do with her cattle, the market being glutted. If she considered wintering the animals in Kansas while waiting for prices to rise, her plans likely changed when she took sick later in the month. On June 25, 1873, J. L. Cunningham was summoned from Victoria to act as Margaret's agent, if necessary, and less than two weeks later, in Wichita, Margaret died. It's not clear what the cause was; the symptoms mentioned included "agitation and delirium," and her fatal illness has been variously described as "congestion of the brain," "trail driving fever," and even—in the July 9 *Wichita Beacon*—"mania, superinduced by her long, tedious journey and over-taxation of the brain." In other words, the responsibility of a cattle drive was too much for a woman—a judgment that ignores what Margaret had already lived through: the Texas Revolution and the death of her father in an Indian raid by the time she was twelve, and, in adulthood, the deaths of three husbands and six of her children.

Margaret's body was returned to Victoria for burial, and her estate divided equally among her three surviving children, Alex, Jesse, and Nellie, and her granddaughter Julia. The thousand head of cattle she had driven to Wichita were almost certainly sold at a loss in late summer or early fall; livestock prices dropped precipitously during the financial panic of 1873, when many owners were forced to sell in order to pay off loans for which they had put up their livestock as collateral. Alex and Jesse, however, made careers in ranching and trailed herds up the Western Trail as far north as Wyoming and South Dakota. John B. Kendrick, later governor of Wyoming and a three-term United States senator (1917–33), was Jesse's partner on those drives.

Lizzie Johnson Williams

As her niece, Willie Greer Shelton, attested, Lizzie Johnson Wil-
liams "was one of the few women ever to go up the Chisholm
Trail . . . the only [woman] to ever go up it who owned her own
cattle and ran them under her own brand. She went up the trail
two or three times after 1879 when she married Hezekiah Wil-
liams, but she had been in the business several years before they
were married." Despite Willie Shelton's pride in her aunt's ac-
complishments, Lizzie wasn't alone in driving a herd that she
owned and that bore her own brand, but it's possible that no other
woman ever did so with quite as much panache.

Lizzie "was intimately involved in all aspects of the cattle business for most of her lifetime"—from buying to selling and keeping track of the profits. Her relationship with her husband took the form of a friendly rivalry; after his death in 1914, "much of the joy in her life clearly departed as she settled into widowhood . . a solitary life in a darkened room on the second floor of Austin's Brueggerhoff Building, which she owned."

Lizzie was the daughter of strict Presbyterian teachers from Missouri who founded the Johnson Institute in San Marcos, near Austin, in 1853. Lizzie was educated there and at Chappell Hill Female Institute. When she completed her studies, she returned to San Marcos to teach in her parents' school, as did, over the years, her brother and two sisters. Her subjects included arithmetic, bookkeeping, French, grammar, spelling, and music. Her talent for figures would eventually lead her into the cattle business, which she learned about early on because her father moonlighted as a cattleman. Until 1871, Lizzie taught at schools in Lockhart, Pleasant Hill, and Manor, Texas, and that year she joined the Johnson Institute faculty. In 1870 and 1871, she passed the examinations that qualified her for a "Teacher's Certificate of the First Class." Meanwhile, her brother John Johnson invested in land for both of them and also worked as a bookkeeper for William H. Day, a friend who ranched in Hays County.

As early as 1864—and quite possibly earlier—Lizzie received offers of marriage but turned them down. Will Day, thirty-one, proposed to twenty-four-year-old Lizzie in a romantic letter promising not wealth, but that "a true hand, and *loving heart*, is yours, if you but think me worthy of your affections." Lizzie apparently didn't think so, but the two remained friends and business associates, and Will Day later proved himself one of the sharpest traders and innovative businessmen in the Texas cattle business of the 1870s and '80s.

At about the time of Will Day's proposal, Lizzie began investing in cattle, partly with her earnings from stories she published, anonymously or under a pen name, in *Frank Leslie's Illustrated Newspaper*, a popular weekly. Another lucrative sideline that supplemented her teaching salary was handling the bookkeeping for local cattlemen, whom she got to know in Lockhart and Austin. At first she may have invested in cattle trading firms like the Evans, Snider, Bewell Cattle Company of Chicago, which quadrupled in value in three years, but she soon owned livestock of her own as well. Although her brother John, who had been overseeing their investments, died in 1871 from complications of a Civil War wound, Lizzie was able to purchase her own home in Austin a year later. After John's death, she also took over her brother's duties for the Day brothers' cattle operation, where she learned the ins and outs of cattle brokerage and made investments in both cattle and land on her own.

Employing the "CY" brand she acquired when she bought out that owner's entire stock, Lizzie hired hands to round up wild longhorns that proliferated after the Civil War—a practice known as "brush-popping"—and mark them with her brand. She hid her commercial ventures from her family—easy enough to do, since she was still teaching and managing the books for the Days and other cattlemen—but was already having her own cattle trailed north to market in 1879, if not earlier.

Eighteen seventy-nine was also the year that Lizzie finally took a husband. She had not lacked for suitors in her twenties and early thirties—as Will Day's letter and at least one other attest—but she seems to have been immune to all offers of marriage until she met Hezekiah Williams, a stock driver who had been a Baptist preacher, and who despite his religious vocation also gambled and drank. Prior to her wedding, Lizzie had Hezekiah, who had four sons from his previous marriage, sign a prenuptial agreement stipulating that her property and any profits she earned would continue to be hers alone. She kept her teaching job, wrote for publication, managed cattlemen's books, and invested in property and cattle. In addition, she and Hezekiah were partners in a ranch in Hays County, but they kept their cattle separate. They also made their livestock purchases separately, even when they were buying from a single herd. Their foreman, Bill Bob, claimed that they competed so fiercely that Lizzie ordered him to brand Hezekiah's calves with her brand, while Hezekiah told him to do the exact opposite.

The competition—despite the fact that Lizzie's aptitude for the cattle business was far superior to her husband's—seems to have had no adverse effect on their marriage or Hezekiah's affection for his wife. They made some drives together (how many is uncertain), trailing their separately branded cattle as one herd, and sharing a horse-drawn buggy. On one drive that Hezekiah made to Colorado on his own, he wrote to Lizzie asking her to send proof that his cattle had been inspected for Texas fever so that they would not be quarantined, and worrying that he might lose his herd. But, he promised, "I am going to sell every one I can get a dollar for, put the money in my pocket and bring it home to my pet."

Even when Lizzie wasn't driving her own cattle up the trail to market, she went north to St. Louis nearly every fall to manage the books for other cattlemen, a lucrative sideline she never abandoned. Her travels—to Kansas City, St. Louis, and even New York—afforded her the opportunity to shop for stylish clothes, which she bought in abundance but often never found occasion to wear. "You never saw dresses any more beautiful than the fancy silks Lizzie bought in New York and Kansas City," her niece Willie said. "Such brocades! Why, after she died we filled three trucks with boxes of clothes. Many of those old silks had never been unpacked, but they were so old they crumbled in our fingers when we tried to lift them from the store boxes." Her appetite for luxury extended to jewelry as well. On one trip to New York she spent ten thousand dollars on a pair of diamond earrings, a tiara with a three-carat center diamond surrounded by nine half-carat diamonds, a sunburst pin set with eighty-four diamonds, and a diamond and emerald ring.

When a lucrative market for American cattle opened in Cuba, Lizzie and Hezekiah began shipping cattle there and even bought a farm near Camaguey, Cuba, where they lived for several years early in the twentieth century. It is rumored that Hezekiah was kidnapped and held for ransom while they were in Cuba and that Lizzie immediately bought his freedom for fifty thousand dollars, but it is possible that the tale is merely a legend intended to illustrate how much she doted on her husband. One writer even mentions a tale that the chronically cash-strapped Hezekiah had staged his own kidnapping in order to pocket the ransom money. Both versions are probably fanciful, but there is evidence that Lizzie purchased a talking parrot in Cuba and brought it back to Texas in 1905.

Hezekiah's moneymaking schemes, such as building Hays City on part of their ranch near Driftwood (he hoped to move the county seat there from San Marcos), rarely turned a profit. Hays City, which had only two streets, Williams and Johnson, ceased to exist not long after it was laid out. Hezekiah himself, after a long illness, expired in El Paso in 1914. Lizzie collected on his last notes to her after his death (she was, in any case, executor of his estate), but she also lavished six hundred dollars on his casket, and when she paid the undertaker's fee, she wrote on the bill, "I loved this old buzzard this much." During her remaining ten years of life, she continued to take an interest in business, but she dressed exclusively in widow's black and, according to her niece, "didn't care much about herself or anything anymore." Lizzie lived so frugally (partly the result of increasing senile dementia) that few of those who knew her in Austin in those years had any idea that she was a wealthy woman. In fact, many thought she was destitute. She spent her final decade living in a single room in the Brueggerhoff Building, subsisting on little more than orange juice, a daily bowl of soup at the Maverick Cafe, and cheese and crackers, and she begrudged every penny she had to spend for her sustenance.

Lizzie's niece, Willie Shelton, worried that her aunt was starving herself, arranged to have the restaurant in the Brueggerhoff Building "send dinners up to her every day. She thought [the restaurant employee who delivered her meals] was the nicest man because she thought the dinners were free. She never knew that we paid for them." In early 1924, Willie had her aunt move into the Sheltons' home. When Lizzie died in October, she left an estate valued at a quarter of a million dollars, almost all of it earned through her hard work and shrewd dealings in a business thought to be the exclusive province of men.

Mollie Taylor Bunton

Mollie Taylor, born in 1862, daughter of wealthy Austin physician Matthew Taylor, attended fashionable Elmira Female College in upstate New York, where she learned to play the harp and acquired other feminine graces as well as a good education. But when she returned to Texas in the early 1880s, instead of following in the footsteps of her sisters Harriett and Elizabeth and marrying a lawyer from St. Louis or Austin, she chose James Howell Bunton, whom some writers have described as a "coarse and common" cowboy from West Texas. In fact, Mollie's sweetheart was the genteel son of John Wheeler Bunton, signer of the Texas Declaration of Independence and a hero of the battle of San Jacinto. Howell, as he was known, simply preferred raising cattle on his modest Bar S ranch near Sweetwater to practicing law. After the couple married in 1885, Dr. Taylor obligingly treated the newlyweds to a two-month honeymoon on the east coast, but the couple was met with a cruel welcome when they returned to Texas: a series of blizzards blowing down from Canada in which most of their herd perished. All across the West, from Montana to Texas, the blizzards wiped out the fortunes of many a cattle baron, along with that of Mollie's young husband.

Howell Bunton immediately set out to rebuild his herd by buying cattle in South Texas, which had been spared by the storms. Using credit he secured from two Austin banks, he planned to buy five thousand head and trail them to Kansas, to take advantage of the shortage of beef in the North and Midwest that resulted from the interruption to the supply chain from the South. Mollie and Howell went out to the ranch on Sweetwater Creek, where the young bride was surprised to discover that their "house" was a dugout carved into the south side of a hill, with a fireplace and chimney at the back and the opening in the front the only source of light and air. It was a far cry from the luxurious Taylor home in Austin, but Mollie never complained. "To add to my comfort while on the ranch, a small room of lumber was built and I was told that this was the first house of lumber ever built on Sweetwater Creek." Unlike a dugout, however, which maintained a year-round temperature of seventy-five degrees despite the extreme seasonal fluctuations, the aboveground room was hot in summer and cold in winter.

While Howell and his agents were buying up cattle and trailing them to the Bar S, Mollie, who was already a skilled horsewoman, absorbed the lore of cattle herding—roping and branding and living on the trail—from the cowboys at the ranch. When she admired the bridles one of the hands fashioned out of thin rawhide strips, he presented her with a quirt and bridle. She called them "things of beauty and a joy forever, for I used them the entire ten years I lived on the ranch." She was also fascinated by the ropes the cowboys wove from the hairs of horse's and cow's tails; they were laid around the hands' outdoor pallets at night to keep snakes away, "as the snake's body was supposed to be entirely too sensitive to crawl over a hair rope." From another of the cowboys Mollie learned to shoot a rifle and was soon bagging quail and even the occasional deer, which abounded in the region.

Mollie's mother had sent her a pair of riding britches and boots, and the first—and perhaps last—time she wore them caused a commotion among man and beast. The men made such a racket that it frightened the cattle into a stampede. "One 'old-timer' near by observed me on that memorable first occasion, and rising in his saddle, with his long white whiskers flying in the breeze, his arms outstretched, exclaimed: 'My God! I knew she'd do it! Here she comes wearin' the britches!'" In 1886, most Texas women still rode sidesaddle, though a few on the ranches were beginning to adopt the male style of riding astride.

The trail boss Howell had engaged to lead the drive was

laid low with an eye ailment, and he, unable to find a capable replacement, decided that he must "take charge of the herds" himself. He had never before made a long cattle drive, much less acted as trail boss. But his future as a stockman was on the line, as well as his creditworthiness in the eyes of the bankers in Austin. "I fully realize that with my little experience I am undertaking a Herculean task," he confided, "but I can find no other solution." Apologizing, he suggested that Mollie visit his cousin in Sweetwater while he was gone or return to their house in Austin, but Mollie had other ideas. "I do not want to stay in that little town of Sweetwater, and I am not going home without you. I know what I am going to do, and I guess you will think that I am having a 'brain storm,' but I have already made up my mind. I am going up the trail with you."

Howell lectured her on the physical hardships and even mortal dangers of a long cattle drive, painting as dismal a picture as possible of two months of constant exposure to the elements, but Mollie refused to be discouraged. When all arguments failed, he unwittingly stiffened Mollie's resolve by blurting out, "Besides, I have never heard of a woman's going up the trail," which "just made me eager and more determined than ever that I was going." After further cajoling and a few tears, Howell relented and promised that if she changed her mind, he'd put her on the train back home. "That settled the question, but I knew that I would not be taking that train for home."

Sounding like a character in a modern romantic comedy, Mollie exclaimed that she had "nothing to wear"—nothing suitable, that is, for weeks on the trail, far from modern conveniences and constantly on the move. Howell's Sweetwater cousin solved that problem when she generously offered to lend Mollie "a dark green woolen cloth 'riding habit' and several wash dresses of hers that fit me perfectly." As optimistic as she was fun-loving, Mollie also packed a single evening gown, "to be prepared for the social affairs of civilization when we reached the end of the trip."

When Howell presented her with a Concord buggy ("the last word in buggy comfort") and the team of "spirited" bays he chose for it, Mollie withheld the fact that although she was a skilled rider, she had never driven a team of horses. "As Mr. Bunton's duties were very arduous on the trail, I had to drive or ride alone almost all the way." To mask her apprehensiveness, she named her team Darling and Beauty, and after a few days, horses and horsewoman had gotten used to one another. For her saddle horse, she chose a cream-colored Spanish pony. With her usual stubbornness, she ignored warnings that it was unruly with everyone but its previous owner, who had spoiled it.

He proved a joy and was the best gaited saddle pony I ever rode. However, he would never let a man ride him or even catch him if he was loose. . . . Finally, I laid down the law to them, one and all, that none of them was ever to get on his back again. When they attempted to saddle him for me to ride, he would paw, kick and fight every man that came near but the minute he heard my voice he would neigh for me and as soon as I was in the saddle he was gentle and obeyed the slightest touch of my hand on the bridle. I had ridden him many times as much as thirty-five or forty miles on certain occasions and the going was so easy that I was not fatigued and my pony was none the worse for the trip.

As the nights grew warmer, Mollie and Howell abandoned their tent and slept under "the blue sky, spangled with millions of stars for our canopy, and the cowboys riding around the herds at night, singing their soothing songs lulled us to peaceful slumber." During the day, she generally rode ahead of the lead herd, which she remembered as "several thousand head of heifer yearlings, all red Durhams of the same size, age, and color," purchased from the King Ranch. "It was a novel sight to see those immense herds of cattle slowly wending their way along the trail. . . . To me it looked as if a dark-red velvet carpet with its wide border of green grass was stretched just as far as the eye could see." Even at that late date travelers happened on occasional herds of buffalo, "silently grazing on the distant plains or joyously galloping about in the full pleasure of their freedom."

In her memoir, Mollie consistently described their route as following the old Chisholm Trail. Some critics insist that the name applies only to the portion of the trail that lies in Indian Territory and Kansas, north of the Red River, but in popular usage many trails, from the Rio Grande to the Kansas railheads, were considered parts of this most famous route. During actual drives, the herds wandered far from the trail itself in order to graze, converging only at river crossings. Perhaps because the individual herds were spaced out, Mollie rarely mentioned the other herds that were traveling in proximity to the Buntons'. Instead, her eye was drawn to the local flora and fauna. Fascinated by unfamiliar varieties of wildflowers, she wove them into the horses' bridles and into wreaths for her hair and chaplets for her shoulders. To humor her, the cowboys would bow and cry "Hail to the cowboys' beautiful queen of the flowers."

Daily progress on a drive was leisurely even by the standards of nineteenth-century travel. The cattle, who poked along when they weren't stampeding, never covered more than ten or twelve miles in a day, and they weren't prodded to speed up, since one purpose of the drive was to fatten the steers on the free pasturage to be found along the trail. They rarely went faster, unless they were being driven through a desert zone in order to reach water as soon as possible. At those times, "when they came near enough to water to smell it, they would break into a run and there was no holding them back. They could smell it for miles, too, when they were starving for it." For the trail hands, in contrast, an area with abundant grazing and water often meant a chance to relax a bit, take a bath, and wash their clothes.

Mollie marveled at the profusion of wildlife. "I was always

looking for the Bob-Whites calling from the tall grass or listening for the mocking birds singing their songs in beautiful
old trees. Ofttimes, leaving the trees, they would fly higher and
higher while a trail of song floated back as if to cheer me on
my lonely way, long after the clouds had hidden the birds from
view." As the herd made its slow way northward, Mollie was
able to pass her time wandering through a forest if she was in
the mood. She wrote of searching for a stream where she might
catch fish and instead came upon a nest of partridge chicks,
just emerging from their shells. As she was watching the hatch-
lings, she suddenly noticed that she was not alone: a coiled
rattlesnake was keeping an eye on the nest as well, "evidently
waiting for an auspicious moment to make a delicious meal."
Frightened, her first reaction was to bolt, but then she decided
to use her fishing rod to kill the rattler and save the chicks, "so
I gathered some stones that were near, to arm myself further,
for I knew they would be quite a help in beating off the snake's
head." When she returned to camp, she displayed the snake's
rattles to the crew, trophies of a successful hunt. From that day
the trail hands stopped teasing her for being a "tenderfoot" and
"dubbed me a 'seasoned veteran.'"

Her encounter with the rattlesnake was just one moment of
the "darker side" of Mollie's adventures on the trail. There were
also "unknown wild animals, the queer sounds at night and the
prospect of wild Indians roving near." One day while searching
for a creek where Darling and Beauty could drink, she nearly
collided with a group of Indians relaxing in the mud and water,
but the horses, standing in water "clear as crystal" up to their
knees, retreated before Mollie even saw the men. Despite being
thirsty, "they never even lowered their heads to drink."

It was the natural sights and sounds that terrified her most.
"I dreaded to hear the lonely hooting of the owls at eventide
and, too, how frightened I was the first time I saw a sleek, spotted leopard stealthily creeping through the underbrush close
beside me as I rode the trail . . . [or heard] the human-like

screams of a panther calling to his dead mate which some ruthless hunter had killed."

Although by the time Mollie made her drive up the Chisholm Trail in 1886, deadly Indian attacks were very nearly a thing of the past, small bands of Indians sometimes materialized, to wheedle, demand, or steal cattle or food and occasionally commit acts of violence against herders and settlers. Even on this trip, Mollie reported seeing a group of people gathered around a small cabin near the trail. Curious to learn what was going on, she stopped. "To my horror, I saw there a man, his wife, and a little child that had been murdered and scalped by the Indians and then dragged into the cabin, their blood still fresh on the doorstep!"

The Bunton party was never seriously menaced, but on more than one occasion small parties of Indians demanded food or cattle. One time the cook gave the visitors a large tin of scraps he'd been collecting throughout the trip, in order to be prepared if Indians came begging. Near the Red River, when a band of Indians showed up and demanded a share of the livestock, Howell, knowing that the Indians were familiar with the territory, offered a cow in exchange for their help finding a good river crossing for the herd and a campsite on the far side.

Perhaps the most unnerving of the actual dangers the Bunton group faced were the storms, especially one that struck not long after the drive reached Kansas. Throughout the day they watched storm clouds gathering, above an open prairie where there was no shelter for the crew or the cattle. The only cover was in the chuck wagon, where Mollie spent the night while Bunton and the hands circled the herd on horseback, keeping the steers calm by calling and singing to them. In that weather, a stampede would almost certainly have meant the loss of livestock and quite possibly injury or even death to one or more of the trail hands. To reduce the risk of being harmed by the "freaky Kansas storm," the hands removed their pistols and spurs, and they told Mollie to take the hairpins out of her hair and her rings from her fingers. Terrified as she was, when Mollie saw the lightning flash she was also fascinated by the sight. It was "as if millions of fairies in glittering robes of fire were dancing in mad glee over the backs of the cattle and jumping from the horns of one steer to another."

When the couple reached Coolidge, Kansas, where Howell decided to sell his cattle, they were greeted by several friends, Texas cattlemen who had preceded them up the trail, including John Blocker, Ike Pryor, Bill Jennings, and Bill Pumphrey. When the Buntons rode up, the men lifted Mollie out of her buggy and carried her into the hotel, all the while acclaiming her the "Queen of the Old Chisholm Trail." Although Coolidge was at the time said to be a lawless frontier town, Mollie thought of nothing but the hot bath and comfortable bed that awaited her after two months of roughing it. That night their friends held a banquet and ball in her honor, where she was finally able to wear the evening dress she had brought from Sweetwater. Then Howell sold his herds and paid off the men, and he and Mollie rode on to Kansas City, where they sold the buggy and horses and boarded a train to Texas. Their servant, Sam, drove the chuck wagon home from Coolidge, trailing Mollie's beloved pony along with him.

The Buntons lived on the Bar S for ten years, and though Mollie never made another cattle drive, she took part in the round-ups at the ranch and, later, on the fifty-thousand-acre Kinney County spread, west of San Antonio, on the Rio Grande Plain, that she and Howell managed for Matthew Taylor. There, in the early 1890s, ranching was still a dangerous livelihood, with rustlers sometimes attempting to steal cattle. Mollie and her ranch hands defended themselves against would-be rustlers, and she refused to take refuge in Austin even after the state adjutant general ordered her to. Instead she wired Dr. Taylor, who persuaded Governor James Hogg to send three Texas Rangers after the rustlers. When Matthew Taylor died in 1909, Mollie inherited the ranch, and she and her husband continued to run it, although by that time they were spending most of the year in Austin. There they were part of Austin society, and she was celebrated as "Queen of the Cattle Trail." After Howell died in 1923, Mollie leased the ranch to her nephew, David Holding. In 1927 she was made an honorary member of the Old Trail Drivers Association, and in 1939 she published her memoir, *A Bride on the Old Chisholm Trail in 1886*, "the only description of the cattle trail told from a woman's point of view." When the film *Red River* opened in Dallas in 1948, Mollie, then eighty-five, was celebrated as the only woman to have made the cattle drive from Texas to Kansas. That she wasn't the only woman—or even the first—we now know, but Mollie was one of the few, and she may well have been the one with the keenest eye for the splendors and delights of the natural world.

Ranching on a Grand Scale

Henrietta Chamberlain King

The King family tree appears in the appendix.

Henrietta Chamberlain was born July 21, 1832, in Missouri. Her mother, Maria, died bearing twins when Henrietta was not yet three years old. Her childhood was lonely, and when at the age of thirteen or fourteen she was sent to school in Mississippi, she wrote her father that she was very homesick. Her father, Hiram Chamberlain, a Presbyterian minister, wrote her a letter admonishing her to study hard, love God, and do her duty; happiness would be in heaven. He stated that she was well prepared to meet whatever would come in her life with faith and fortitude.

The family moved to South Texas several years later, where Hiram Chamberlain founded the first Presbyterian mission and church in the region. Before the church and his own home were constructed, he installed his family temporarily on a decommissioned ship, the *Whiteville*, which was docked in the Brownsville harbor. Henrietta joined her father and stepmother in Brownsville, where she taught school.

At first glance, Henrietta Chamberlain, the genteel schoolteacher, and Richard King, who stowed away on a ship bound from New York to Mobile, Alabama, when he was eleven and became a riverboat pilot at nineteen, appear an unlikely match. The traditional story is that Henrietta, on board the Chamberlains' temporary home in the Brownsville harbor, overheard King cursing as he maneuvered his riverboat, the *Colonel Cross*, around her vessel, which was blocking the path into his mooring. The rough-hewn, hard-drinking captain, twenty-six at the time, was instantly smitten with the diminutive, demure—but outspoken—eighteen-year-old. They courted for nearly four years before marrying in December 1854, perhaps because it took that long for Hiram Chamberlain's feelings about his prospective son-in-law to soften from "a certain cold abrasiveness" to admiration for the "young captain's sterling qualities and strong personality."

Even allowing for some embellishment of that first meeting and of the romance that followed, there is in it a strong element of the attraction of opposites. That Henrietta had suitors whose backgrounds were similar to her own is certain, as there were references to young men who paid respects to her. However, at about the time Richard entered the picture, the mention of others faded away.

Richard King certainly challenged Hiram Chamberlain's ideas of a suitable husband for Henrietta. She was an associate of Melinda Rankin, a Presbyterian missionary who founded the Rio Grande Female Institute with Hiram Chamberlain's help. In fact, a teaching position at the institute was Henrietta's last job before she and Richard married. To overcome the family's objections, Richard—who had been born into an Irish Catholic family but was not a churchgoer—began attending the Reverend Chamberlain's church services. To improve his chances of winning over Henrietta and her family, Richard quite possibly profited from his friend Mifflin Kenedy's counsel. Kenedy, six years older than King, and a Quaker, was King's business partner in steamboat and ranching ventures, and he too chose a pious bride, Petra Vela de Vidal, a Catholic widow from Mier, Mexico, in 1852.

By the time Hiram Chamberlain presided over Henrietta and Richard's wedding at the First Presbyterian Church of Brownsville, King had been acquiring land and cattle in the Nueces Strip—the territory between the Nueces and the Rio Grande—for at least a year. Two large pieces of the Santa Gertrudis grants dating from Spanish colonial and Mexican imperial

times were in his portfolio by 1854. They would form the ker-
nel of what grew into the sprawling King Ranch. It was there
in a tiny wood-frame jacal, on the banks of Santa Gertrudis
Creek, that Henrietta and Richard began their married life.
Henrietta, who not long before had called the small boat on
Brownsville's waterfront her home, was not put off by the primitive accommodations.

"When I came as a bride in 1854," she later recalled, "the
little ranch home then—a mere 'jacal' as the Mexicans would
call it—was our abode for many months until our main ranch
dwelling was completed. But I doubt if it falls to the lot of many
a bride to have had so happy a honeymoon. On horseback we
roamed the broad prairies. When I grew tired my husband
would spread a Mexican blanket for me and then I would take
my siesta under the shade of the Mesquite tree." The newlyweds most likely spent quite a bit of their time outdoors in those
early months; inside the jacal, space was tight. "I remember
that my pantry was so small that my large platters were fastened to the walls outside."

It may well be that the great passions of Richard King's life
were land, cattle, Henrietta, and their children. The first brand
used on the ranch was an *R* bisected by a horizontal arrow, but
the first brand Richard recorded after the King Ranch was
established was the linked *HK*, Henrietta's initials. Neither of
them seems to have been overly attached to the outward trappings of wealth. For example, despite Henrietta's recollection
that she spent only "months" living in the jacal, the Kings did
not build a large ranch house at the Santa Gertrudis until after
Robert E. Lee's 1857 visit, when Lee chose what he considered
the ideal site for the house. Not only did they follow Lee's advice about where to build, but Lee was also said to have been
the person who advised Richard never to sell land, a policy that
King followed religiously throughout his life. Later, Henrietta
oversaw the construction of her Victorian house in Corpus
Christi, a more lavishly appointed home than their ranch dwell-

ing. Henrietta, though, never ceased to be the modest woman who, after Richard gave her a pair of diamond earrings, had the stones covered with dark enamel, "to avoid the vanity of their display."

It is not known to what degree Henrietta advised her brilliant but unlettered husband about practical matters, but she undoubtedly softened his rough edges. Their friend John Salmon "Rip" Ford, the legendary Texas Ranger, commented that Henrietta "raised the cattle ranch from a bachelor establishment to a first-class married establishment, indicating good sense and refinement." It wasn't that she lacked her own brand of sternness. The isolation of the King Ranch made it a tempting target for thieves and rustlers, and over the years many precautions were taken to protect the property and its inhabitants, but it was said that "the outlaws and renegades who infested the neighborhood preferred to approach the house when Captain King was at home rather than try it when his wife was there alone."

Henrietta's fearlessness and calm in crises revealed itself throughout her life. On one occasion, in 1856, she and Richard were traveling with their infant daughter, Nettie (Henrietta Maria). At night, as they camped near the trail, they were approached by a Mexican who asked to spend the night. King asked the newcomer to gather wood for the fire he was preparing to light, and the visitor went off. As King bent over the kindling, some movement must have caught Henrietta's eye. She looked up from where she was tending to Nettie and shouted, "Captain King! Behind you!" King turned just in time to catch the arm of the knife-wielding man about to stab him, wrestled him to the ground, and disarmed him. Frontier law would have considered King within his rights if he had killed his attacker on the spot, but instead he threw him out of the camp with a warning.

Even when she was alone, Henrietta faced danger calmly. At about the same time, Nettie lay in her cradle near the door of

the Kings' Santa Gertrudis jacal while Henrietta baked bread
in the oven at the back. On this occasion, it was an Indian,
"half-naked," who suddenly materialized at the door, moved
swiftly to the cradle, and stood over it with a club in his fist.
Gesturing at the bread with his free hand, Henrietta understood that he wanted it. She quickly filled his arms with fresh-
baked loaves, and he disappeared.

During the Civil War, Captain King told Henrietta he had
to go on a trip and he did not say where he was going. He asked
his trusted hand, Alvarado, to stay with Henrietta, who was
pregnant, while he was away, as a later letter stated, "chasing
Mexican cattle thieves while dodging Yankees." The Yankees
approached the King Ranch home, their weapons at the ready.
When Alvarado ran to the door, saying, "Don't shoot—there
are only women and children here," a Union soldier shot and
killed him just as Henrietta joined him at the entrance. While
the intruders ransacked the ranch house and the area around it,
Henrietta had someone hitch up her coach and she started for
San Antonio. She got as far as San Patricio, about fifteen miles
from her home, where she stayed with friends until her son,
Robert E. Lee King, was born. Eventually Henrietta reached
San Antonio, where she and her children stayed until the end
of the war.

Henrietta's protective impulse extended far beyond her family to embrace the communities in which she lived. In the isolation of the Santa Gertrudis ranch, she looked after the ranch
hands, known as Kineños (Spanish for people of King Ranch),
and their families. Most of the hands were originally from the
town of Cruillas, in the Mexican state of Tamaulipas, where
King had purchased the cattle of the drought-stricken stockmen, who then followed him back to Texas. To them, Henrietta was known as La Madama or La Patrona. She saw to their
medical needs, the education of their children, and even their
religious lives.

Over the years, especially after the town of Kingsville was

founded on land donated by Henrietta, she helped fund the establishment of many churches and schools. The town's first church service, conducted by a Presbyterian minister, was held in the unfinished building that became the Kingsville lumber-yard. Soon afterward, she donated the site and funds for the construction of the Presbyterian church, the town's first church, and when other faiths—Baptist, Methodist, Episcopalian, Catholic—built churches of their own she provided them with land. The Masonic lodge also stood on land that Henrietta had given. Perhaps her most significant gifts were the twenty-two-room, two-story brick schoolhouse, built in 1909 and entirely underwritten by Henrietta, and her donation of 700 acres for the construction of the Presbyterian Texas-Mexican Industrial Institute, a vocational school for Mexican boys in 1910. Else-where in the region, she supplied the land in Corpus Christi on which the new Spohn Hospital was rebuilt after a 1919 hurricane destroyed the original Spohn Sanitarium structure. She also donated the site of the South Texas State Teachers College (now Texas A&M University–Kingsville).

Of the Kings' five children, it was the youngest, Robert E. Lee King, born in 1864, who took naturally to ranching and seemed destined to succeed his father. But Lee, as he was called, died of pneumonia at nineteen, and his parents fell into despair. For the only time since he had begun to assemble his ranch-ing empire, Richard considered selling out. After some months, however, his resolve returned, and even when he was dying of stomach cancer, in 1885, his instructions to his agent were to keep buying land.

During his final illness, Richard, who despite Henrietta's dis-approval had never entirely renounced alcohol, drank heavily to kill the pain. But when Dr. Ferdinand Herff, the San Antonio specialist the couple consulted in February 1885, told Henrietta that the whiskey was shortening her husband's life faster than the cancer was, she asked Herff to order King to stop drink-ing. "Tell him with a smile that I need him a while longer," she said. When Herff passed the message on to his patient, Richard stormed into Henrietta's room, growled "Etta. Did you say you needed me a while longer?" and quit drinking on the spot. He died two months later.

Henrietta inherited Richard King's entire estate—the ranching empire alone was said to consist of about half a million acres of land—but also half a million dollars of debt. To help manage the ranch, Henrietta turned to Robert Justus Kleberg, whom King had engaged as his attorney after losing a lawsuit—over land, of course—in which Kleberg represented King's adversar-ies. To return the operation to solvency, Kleberg temporarily suspended King's proscription against selling land, but before long the acreage was growing again, eventually exceeding one million acres. Kleberg, who married the Kings' daughter, Alice Gertrudis King, in 1886, consulted Henrietta about major deci-sions but enjoyed her full confidence.

Captain King had discussed the need for finding a perma-nent source of water with young Robert Kleberg and others. After the Captain's death, Kleberg was eventually able to find a man with the equipment to drill more deeply for water. Mrs. King encouraged and paid for bringing this man to Santa Ger-trudis, where he drilled and brought in an artesian well. More wells followed on the Kings' property and ranches to the south of theirs. Mrs. King and Kleberg were then able to interest rail-road development from Corpus Christi to Brownsville. Mrs. King dedicated land to "development" and to the railroad right of way. Kenedys, Armstrongs, and Yturrias, and many more ranchers gave right of way land as well.

One crisis that highlighted Henrietta's stoical calm as well as her close, trusting relationship with her son-in-law occurred on January 4, 1912, when the main ranch house, a two-story wooden structure, burned to the ground, in a fire apparently set by a mentally disturbed gardener at the ranch who had a history of committing arson. As family members and guests scrambled to escape from the burning house, Henrietta emerged, dressed in black as she usually was after Richard's death, carrying two small bags, one containing medicines and the other some valuables. Robert Kleberg rescued some papers from the office inside the house, but when ranch employee Sam Ragland wanted to go after the piano, Henrietta forbade him. "Let nobody get hurt," she said. "We can build a new home. We can't replace a life."

With no means of fighting the fire anywhere near the ranch, the wooden structure was soon destroyed. A family member who was present later remembered, "I can see her now. All dressed in black with a little black bag in her hand. She turned and threw a kiss at the burning house."

About the ranch house that replaced the original, Henrietta insisted to Robert Kleberg only that it must be a house that anyone wearing boots could walk into. True to the spirit of Richard and Henrietta King, her son-in-law created a monument to their hospitality. Broadly modeled on the Mexican hacienda, the twenty-five-room, fireproof mansion incorporated a riot of architectural styles—Mexican, Moorish, California Mission, Long Island, and Wild Horse Desert. Despite Henrietta's personal modesty, it was a lavish place, but welcoming, with wide verandas, a patio surrounded by plants, a grand salon decorated with murals, a dining room accommodating fifty guests, Tiffany stained-glass windows, and a marble interior stairway. And yet, splendid though it was, the house welcomed "anyone in boots" as surely as the Kings' earlier houses had done, no questions asked. Legend has it that early in the days of the King Ranch, a stranger rode in one evening on a handsome gray stallion, stayed for dinner and spent the night. Richard King complimented the visitor on his horse, but nothing more was said. When the man left in the morning, King had one of his hands ride out to the trail with him, and when the vaquero was about to turn back, the stranger insisted that they switch horses. He sent the gray back to his host, "with the compliments of Jesse James." Helen Kleberg Groves, Henrietta's great-granddaughter, has written that descendants of that gray stallion were used on the King Ranch to near the end of the twentieth century.

When Henrietta died on March 31, 1925, at ninety-two, an honor guard of two hundred of her vaqueros, on quarter horses bred on the ranch, formed a cortege that followed the hearse, and at the cemetery, each rider made a circuit around her grave. Unlike numerous other ranching women, Henrietta was never acclaimed a "cattle queen," but she may have been as close to royalty as Texas has produced.

Molly Dyer Goodnight

When Mary Ann "Molly" Dyer married Charles Goodnight in 1870, he was a successful cattleman whose base was a ranch in Pueblo, Colorado. Together with his partner Oliver Loving, he had already blazed the first leg of what became known as the Goodnight-Loving Trail from central Texas to eastern New Mexico and through Colorado to Wyoming. Larry McMurtry's popular novel Lonesome Dove *was said to have been based on Goodnight and Loving: Goodnight the prototype of the character Woodrow Call, and Loving the character Gus. This conjecture has been denied by the author, though there are obvious similarities of facts and relationships, as noted by Charles Goodnight's biographer William Hagan.*

Molly Dyer was born in Madison County, Tennessee, September 12, 1839, where her father, Joel Henry Dyer, was a prominent lawyer. The family moved to Fort Belknap, an army post in north-central Texas, in 1854. By 1864, both her father and mother, Susan Lynch Miller Dyer, the great-granddaughter of John Sevier, Tennessee's first governor, were dead, and it fell to Molly to raise her three younger brothers, Leigh, Sam, and Walter, who were between eight and fifteen when their mother died.

In 1860, at eighteen, she was teaching school in Young County, Texas. Molly, however, had never attended school herself. As she told her niece Phoebe Kerrick Warner years later, "I don't know what it is about me that makes people ask me where I went to college. Why, I never went to college at all or to any other school. There were no colleges in Texas nor public schools either when I was a girl. My only teachers were my father and mother, both of whom were well educated for their times. Then too, I learned a lot from Nature." Molly's self-reliance served her well throughout her life.

Molly and Charles had courted for more than five years before they were wed in Hickman, Kentucky, where Molly's closest relatives lived. Molly told Goodnight that she wanted the boys to move in with them after the wedding, and Goodnight agreed. All three of the boys (as well as Albert, one of Molly's older brothers) worked in the Goodnight cattle ventures, and Leigh became a rancher in his own right.

Goodnight's business interests in and around Pueblo, Colorado, eventually extended to urban real estate, including an interest in the opera house and a meatpacking plant; the Stock Growers' Bank; and mining. In agriculture, he introduced innovations such as an irrigation scheme using water from the Arkansas River to water his farmland and apple orchard. His prominence was such that people began addressing him as "Colonel," although the storied onetime Texas Ranger had never held a commission. When Molly expressed a desire for church services, Charles and some of his colleagues built the first Methodist church in the region.

The couple's life in Pueblo did not get off to a promising start. Soon after they arrived, Molly objected when Goodnight reacted insensitively to the hanging of three cattle rustlers (he supposedly replied that it hadn't hurt the tree any). She told him, "I used to think I knew you in Texas, but you have been out here among the Yankees and Ruffians until I don't know whether I know you or not, and I want you to take me back to Texas, I won't live in such a country." Goodnight, who truly was as rough around the edges as he was brilliant in business, managed to convince Molly to wait until she'd rested up from the voyage out before leaving; in the interval, he took pains to introduce her to all the area's gentlefolk. Molly relented, and they stayed in Pueblo.

Within three years, however, drought and the financial crisis of 1873 had bankrupted Charles Goodnight, and to make a fresh start he chose the Palo Duro Canyon, one of the most beautiful parts of the Texas Panhandle. The area, long a Comanche and Kiowa hunting ground, became safe for settlement in 1875, when the Red River War ended the tribes' nomadic way of life. Molly, who had gone to live with relatives in California while Goodnight struggled to turn his businesses around, saw that Charles didn't plan to "leave the Panhandle and come out to civilization," so she resolved to join him there.

In 1877, the Irish financier John Adair, who was married to Cornelia Ritchie, a widow from New York, proposed a partnership that would make possible the large-scale ranching operation that Goodnight envisioned. Molly joined Charles in Colorado, and the two couples traveled to the Palo Duro together. From the railhead at Trinidad, Colorado, they covered the remaining four hundred miles on horseback and by wagon, followed by four cowhands who were trailing the 100 Durham bulls Goodnight had purchased with an eye to upgrading his stock. During the weeks-long trip, they crossed the desolate Llano Estacado without meeting a single traveler. At the Palo Duro, reaching the valley floor of the canyon took eight days. The Indian trail was too steep and narrow for the wagons, which had to be taken apart and lowered on ropes, along with all their contents.

Although the terms of the Adair-Goodnight partnership heavily favored Adair, they permitted Goodnight to amass considerable holdings in the Panhandle. At the end of the decade, he decided to move the ranch headquarters twenty-five miles east, to be closer to the growing settlement of the region, to the railroad, and available supplies. It was Molly who chose the site for the new JA Ranch buildings, which included a large house for the Adairs, although they spent little time at the ranch (at Adair's death in 1885, he had visited the ranch only three times). When the initial five-year term of the partnership ended in 1882, Adair persuaded Goodnight to extend it for another five. They had already realized a profit of more than half a million dollars.

The Palo Duro may have been ideal for ranching, but the prolonged solitude was a strain on Molly. Except when the Adairs made one of their infrequent visits, Molly spent much of her time alone. The ranch was about fifty miles from Mobeetie, where Tom and Ellen O'Laughlin had a boardinghouse, and eighty miles from Molly and Tom Bugbee at the Quarter Circle T Ranch. With no children of her own, Molly earned her sobriquet, "Mother of the Panhandle," by looking after the ranch hands, who worked far from the main house. She patched their clothes, ministered to their illnesses and injuries, sent food to the men at distant camps, and rode along with the hands, using the two-horned sidesaddle custom-made for her in 1870 by Goodnight's friend S. C. Gallup in Pueblo, Colorado. Safer and more comfortable than conventional sidesaddles, the design was widely adopted by women in the United States and Europe. (The original is now in the Panhandle-Plains Historical Museum.) On longer trips, such as when she accompanied her husband on drives to Kansas along the Palo Duro–Dodge City Trail, she usually rode in a wagon rather than on horseback.

Every week, "Aunt Molly" (as the hands affectionately called her), a former teacher and practicing Methodist, conducted a Sunday school at the ranch. To show their appreciation, a group of hands pitched in to make her a gift of a silver tea service, which they ordered from New York. One gift she especially enjoyed was the three chickens that one of the cowboys gave her in the early years, thinking that they might provide a welcome change from the daily fare of beef. Instead of cooking them, however, Molly adopted the chickens. "No one can ever know how much pleasure and company they were to me. They were someone I could talk to. They would run to me when I called them and followed me wherever I went. They knew me and tried to talk to me in their language." Larry McMurtry clearly knew this story when he wrote *Lonesome Dove*, where he has the character Clara Allen refer to her hens as company, saying, "I'll only eat the ones who can't make good conversation."

Always the teacher, Molly taught many of the Goodnight cowhands to read and write. As the JA Ranch grew, its population also expanded to include the families of hands and other employees who attended the community school and the church and whose homes were scattered across its 1.3 million acres. Molly looked after the families of the Goodnight employees, seeing to their needs and the education of their children, and even raised the son of their housekeeper, Cleo Hubbard.

Although by the mid-1870s, the buffalo had been largely exterminated from the Great Plains, within the Palo Duro Canyon, Charles encountered a herd of about ten thousand. To create grazing space for his cattle, he drove the buffalo deeper into the 120-mile-long canyon. Later, when buffalo hunters had reduced the population almost to extinction, Molly took great pains to preserve the species. From their herd, the Goodnights eventually donated specimens to American and European zoos and Yosemite National Park. (In recent years, the Yosemite buffalo have been the source for the rerelease of the animals to the wild in several areas of their original habitat.) Molly began taking in calves that had been orphaned when their mothers were killed (calves were spared by buffalo hunters because their hides were too small to be of commercial value), and gradually added full-grown animals as well. Thus Molly saved the Southern Plains buffalo from being hunted to extinction. Her one-woman campaign qualified her as a pioneer of the modern conservation movement, although as often happened, the herd became known by her husband's name, the Charles Goodnight Herd. Nonetheless, the inspiration and the initiative were Molly's.

At the end of the last century, the buffalo were relocated to Caprock Canyons State Park.

Even in the Palo Duro, however, buffalo could not always be found. Charles wrote of a visit in 1878 by a large party of Kiowas and Comanches led by Quanah Parker, who claimed that the land, where his people had long hunted, still belonged to them. In his account, the hunters found no buffalo at that time and began killing Goodnight's cattle. To placate them, Goodnight made a treaty with Quanah that allowed the Indians to take two steers every other day until they were able to find buffalo. Called the Treaty of Chief Quanah Parker and the Leopard Coat Man—the Dangerous Man, it also marked a new "title" for Goodnight. The Comanches may have considered him a dangerous man because of his expertise with a rifle. When the Indians were about to return to their reservation, Charles gave them twenty-five beeves to eat on the way to Fort Sill. "Rounding up a large bunch of cattle and picking out the ones which I did not want to keep, I killed the twenty-five and did not miss a shot, and only shot one cow each time. This was a very difficult feat to accomplish because the cattle were milling in a circle on the run, and the Indians were circling around them in the range of the gun. The Indians said I was in league with the Devil, because no one could shoot like that unless he was in league with the Devil."

For his part, Goodnight experimented with breeding a hybrid "cattalo," a cross of buffalo and polled Angus, hoping to develop a source of beef capable of surviving the high altitudes and cold winters to which their hardy buffalo ancestors were accustomed. In later years, he also sometimes invited reservation Indians to participate in staged buffalo hunts, using traditional bows and arrows.

After Adair's death, Goodnight ceded the Palo Duro portion of the JA Ranch to his widow, Cornelia, and moved his own operations sixteen miles north to what became Goodnight, Texas, in Armstrong County. In tow were Molly's beloved buffalo. There, in addition to raising cattle, the Goodnights founded Goodnight College, where local youth could pursue postsecondary education. The college, which began as an industrial institute and grew into a junior college, lasted until 1917, by which time West Texas State Teachers College (now West Texas A&M University) in nearby Canyon and other schools were serving the Panhandle's students. During Goodnight College's existence, Molly extended her hospitality to many of its students, a number of whom boarded with the Goodnights while they attended the school.

Molly died in April 1926. Her epitaph, "One who spent her whole life in the service of others," may well have been an understatement. Charles suffered a serious illness following her death, but Corinne Goodnight, a young nurse and telegraph operator, helped him to regain his health. Corinne was from Butte, Montana; she and the rancher had begun corresponding because of their shared surname, and she later joined him in Texas. On Goodnight's ninety-first birthday, March 5, 1927, he married the twenty-six-year-old Corinne in Clarendon, where he owned a summer house. He sold the Goodnight Ranch, with the proviso that he could continue living there for the rest of his life. After Charles died in December 1929, he was buried next to Molly in the Goodnight community cemetery.

Part VIII

MASTER BUILDERS: A TALE OF TWO CITIES AND TWO CENTURIES

1850s–1950s

Sarah Cockrell
Oveta Culp Hobby

Sarah Cockrell   *Oveta Culp Hobby*

Texas's earliest settlers faced the hardships of primitive living conditions and lack of amenities or even necessities. They cleared the land, fought harsh weather, and lived with deprivation of comfort. In the beginning there was political unrest, during the run-up to the war of independence from Mexico and the Civil War. The brutal attacks by Indians were a constant threat in remote areas. The often nameless, faceless women who confronted these obstacles made a mark on our state as surely as did the men who are celebrated in the history books.

As towns grew and commerce increased, women began to operate businesses in the populated areas. Daughters inherited from their fathers, and widows added significant value to their husbands' estates. Many women had little prior experience, but when tested, they learned by doing and proved equal to the challenge, or more than equal.

The financial successes of women did not lead to their acceptance as civic or business leaders. The first women mayors of Texas's major cities were not elected until the last quarter of the twentieth century (Lila Cockrell, San Antonio, 1975; Carole Keeton McClelland [now Strayhorn], Austin, 1977; Kathy Whitmire, Houston, 1982; Annette Strauss, Dallas, 1987; Kay Granger, Fort Worth, 1991). The first women to chair chambers of commerce or to lead major professional organizations likewise set those precedents late last century. With rare exceptions, leadership was still a "boys' club" for more than 125 years after Texas became a state.

A handful of women were notable for success *and* acceptance in the fullest sense. This is the story of two of them. Sarah Cockrell was not just the mother of Dallas; she was a founder and builder of early Dallas in the second half of the nineteenth century. Oveta Culp Hobby was as respected a business leader as any man in Houston, an integral player in the shaping of that city in the mid-twentieth century. They were two of the women who built a bridge to professional acceptance for women, and their bridge crossed the centuries as well.

Sarah Cockrell
The Bridge Builder of Dallas

Alexander Cockrell never learned to read, but he was quick to spot the opportunities in Dallas after the Mexican War. Born in Kentucky in 1820 and raised in Missouri, his mother died when he was still a child. In his early teens, he set out for the Indian Territory, where he lived with the Cherokees and mastered their language and way of life, including the handling of horses and cattle. For a while, he supported himself by selling the skins and pelts he hunted and trapped, and he entered Texas for the first time in 1845, reportedly in pursuit of runaway slaves. Instead of returning to his former haunts, he stayed with relatives who lived near Mountain Creek, and when war broke out with Mexico in 1846, he joined Ben McCulloch's company of Texas Mounted Volunteers, serving as a scout and courier. In 1847, he returned to Mountain Creek and married Sarah Horton, the twenty-eight-year-old daughter of a neighboring family. Cockrell and Sarah settled on a 640-acre claim bordering the creek, where he traded stock and ran freight between Dallas, Houston, and Jefferson, in Texas, and Shreveport, Louisiana.

Little is known about Sarah's life before her marriage to Cockrell. Born in Virginia in 1819, she arrived in Texas when her parents, Enoch and Martha Horton, relocated with their seven children in 1844. Most women Sarah's age would have been married by then—she was twenty-five; whether she was still single out of choice or for lack of opportunity is a mystery. But it is certain that becoming Mrs. Alexander Cockrell had a profound effect on Sarah's life; as soon as they married, she immediately took an active role in all of her husband's businesses. She kept the books, handled the finances, and wrote the letters and commercial agreements. Sarah is sometimes described as the bookkeeper for Cockrell's ventures. She was that, but it is also true that before his marriage, while Cockrell had shown himself to be independent and resourceful, he had never done anything that hinted at the entrepreneurial brilliance he displayed after 1847. It's tempting to wonder whether the Cockrell success story wasn't all along a true partnership, but one where Sarah kept discreetly in the background, as proper Victorian women were expected to do. She also bore five children in the space of seven years. Logan, the eldest, survived only five months after his birth in 1849, but the others lived into adulthood: a daughter, Aurelia, born in 1850, and three more sons, Robert, Frank, and Alexander Jr., born in 1852, 1854, and 1856.

Whether it was Alexander or Sarah who first foresaw that Dallas was on the threshold of explosive growth after it was designated county seat in 1850, the Cockrells' decisive steps reveal a prescience about Dallas's future that few shared. The town had won the contest for county seat, over neighboring Hord's Ridge, by a mere twenty-eight votes, and at that time, just 430 people lived in Dallas—a few dozen short of the population of Nacogdoches. Its courthouse was a log cabin, and in addition it boasted just one small hotel, a saloon, and little else. Between 1845, when John Neely Bryan founded Dallas and laid out the half-mile-square town grid on the headright he owned, and 1853, when the Cockrells purchased Bryan's unsold acreage and his ferry concession across the Trinity River, only eighty-six of the building lots had been purchased.

Where others had been hesitant, the Cockrells acted boldly. To make it easier for people to get across the river, which became impassable when it flooded, they replaced the sluggish ferry with a wooden toll bridge and causeway. Adjacent to the bridge site on the east side of the river, they established a sawmill where cedar logs were cut into planks on the spot. When the bridgework was completed, they moved the mill to a forested part of their land and started selling lumber to the growing number of people who were building houses, often on land they had purchased from the Cockrells. At the same time, they began investing in new parcels, concentrating on areas they predicted would become the most valuable as the town expanded.

Their gamble paid off. Within a few years, Dallas had progressed to the point where the Cockrells built a two-story brick commercial building on the town square, and they followed it in 1857 with the first three-story structure in town, also of brick, which when it opened was adjudged the finest hotel in North Texas. The horizons of the man who has been called "Dallas's first capitalist" seemed limitless, but he did not live even to see his hotel open for business. On April 3, 1858, City Marshal Andrew Moore shot Cockrell after an argument, and he died less than two hours later. It is not clear what caused the argument, but Moore owed money to Cockrell for a loan he had failed to repay, and Cockrell had taken steps to secure a judgment against the borrower.

Sarah, now widowed with four young children ranging in age from two to eight, doubtless mourned her husband's murder, but she also assumed full control of the family businesses and shouldered her responsibilities as a single parent. One of the first steps she took was a legal action against Moore. Although he was never convicted of homicide (perhaps because Cockrell had also been armed when their fatal confrontation occurred), Sarah's lawyer did secure a judgment against Moore for the amount of the loan. As one early writer put it, somewhat quaintly, "It is in keeping with the firmness of purpose and character of Mrs. C that she carried through her husband's determination to collect an honest debt."

Sarah also completed the hotel, which opened in 1859 as the St. Nicholas Hotel. The name was a nod to the manager, Nicholas Darnell, a friend of the Cockrells and a well-known figure in Texas, a veteran of the Indian Wars and at times speaker of the Texas House of Representatives and lieutenant governor. In a frontier town of the time, a hotel was more than a place for weary travelers to rest before moving on. It was a crossroads for visitors and locals alike, where business was conducted and social life played out. The opening of the St. Nicholas was an occasion for a grand ball that drew a crowd that admired its finely appointed public rooms. Less than a year after its inauguration, the hotel was destroyed in a fire that laid waste much of downtown Dallas, consuming the St. Nicholas's carved chairs and tables, glowing lamps, and regal staircase, but Sarah furnished another Cockrell building as a hotel and had it open for business within a few months.

In fact, Sarah's ability to rebound from reversals would be remarkable in anyone, but especially in a widowed business-woman and mother at a time when a woman could not even enter into a contract under her own name. Four months after Cockrell's murder, the west section of the toll bridge collapsed, and Sarah immediately put the ferry back into service. It had been kept shipshape, for use when the causeway flooded, by the Cockrells' servant, Berry Derrit, who collected the bridge tolls and piloted the ferry until a new bridge was built in 1872. After emancipation, Sarah gave the ferry concession to Derrit, who earned his living from the operation for ten years.

Sarah hadn't expected the ferry's second career to extend into the 1870s. In 1860, she applied to the legislature for a charter to construct an iron suspension bridge—a rarity in Texas at the time—to replace the original wooden one, and it was promptly granted. It was perhaps not happenstance that Sarah's charter request met almost no opposition in the Texas legislature despite a petition from a group of Dallas businessmen to have the county build a free bridge instead: The speaker of the House in 1860 was Nicholas Darnell. Sarah's charter, however, was of little use when the Civil War intervened, making it impossible to find financing for the project until 1870, when the Dallas Wire Suspension Bridge Company started building. Characteristically, Sarah had no publicly visible role in the enterprise; her name did not appear on the papers of incorporation, and she was not an officer or board member (her son, who was a boy of sixteen at the time, and her son-in-law stood in for her), but she was the majority owner, and she ran the company.

The bridge, completed in 1872, made Dallas accessible for the first time from south and west of the Trinity and ensured Sarah a place in the ranks of people who transformed the small town into a bustling commercial center. By this time, the population of Dallas was poised to exceed seven thousand, and many of the people who passed through were guests at Sarah's hotel, now rechristened the St. Charles. Even though Dallas was connected to the rest of the country by rail at about the same time as the bridge was put into service, the span continued to make a major contribution to the area's economic life. And unlike other widows of men who had struck it rich in business, Sarah didn't see her role merely as a steward to what Alexander Cockrell had started. In the 1870s, she bought into what became Dallas's leading industry in the period, flour milling, purchasing one-third of Todd Mills.

In this period, wheat and cotton shared the distinction of being the leading cash crops in North Texas, and the demand for mills was growing. Within three years, Sarah acquired the rest of the company and changed the name to S. H. Cockrell & Company, a not-so-subtle indication of who the boss was. By this time, her son Frank had become a genuine partner in her operations; with him and her son-in-law, Mitchell Gray, she renewed the involvement in real estate that she and Alexander had begun and started buying, selling, and leasing in and around Dallas at an astonishing pace. Some of her projects included housing—notably, the Sarah Cockrell Addition, south of the downtown area—and commercial development, including the Cockrell Office Building, five stories tall in the heart of the city.

She accumulated a list of commercial successes that would guarantee the entrepreneurial reputation of anyone of either sex, including real estate transactions involving businesses, churches, railroads, and the city government that in one year (1889) were completed at the rate of one a week. But Sarah was anything but a coldhearted wheeler-dealer who just happened to be a woman. In fact, she was a devoted mother to her children and a homemaker who seems to have been as proud of her capacious stove—of which she wrote, "I had rather cook for 20 on it than for 2 in the fireplace"—as she was of her iron suspension bridge. She gardened, cultivated fruit trees, grew vegetables, and one year entered her homemade wine in the county fair. It won a prize. Of course, Sarah had plenty of domestic help, including a cook, a laundress, and a maid, but working out of her house—instead of commuting to an office as men did—may actually have made it easier for her to manage her multitasking life (long before that term was introduced into our lexicon).

Evidently possessed of great reserves of energy, Sarah managed a busy life on three fronts at once: home and family, business, and society. She entertained often, both her own friends and those of her children; she herself attended many dinner parties, dances, and church socials (she donated the land on which the First Methodist Church of Dallas stands and contributed to the building fund as well). Her house was often crowded, but she could always find room for guests, as she proved one day when her friend Margaret Bryan and her three grown children turned up unannounced with no place to live. All four of them were sick, so Sarah put them up until she could find a house for them—on which she paid the rent as well.

The portrait of Sarah that emerges from her letters and the recollections of her children and friends is of a kindly, generous woman who wanted to make it possible for her children to rise in the world but who also felt responsible for those who had not been as fortunate as she was. She made certain that her children received good educations, sending Robert, her eldest son, to school in St. Louis, and all three of the boys attended Washington and Lee University, in her native Virginia. She missed her children when they were away, but their father had apparently wanted his children to enjoy the benefits of education, and in 1870, Sarah wrote to a friend, "I would never die satisfied if I did not comply with . . . my promise to their Father."

Aurelia, Sarah's only daughter, did not attend college—something that few young women did in the nineteenth century—but she did excel at the best girls' school in Dallas, the Select School for Young Ladies, run by Lucinda Coughanour. Aurelia exhibited no interest in entering the family business, and it is questionable whether Sarah would have wanted her daughter to jeopardize her status as a proper lady by doing so. The letters they exchanged when Aurelia was staying with relatives in St. Louis and after her marriage to Mitchell Gray are brimming with mutual affection. In one of them, Sarah wrote that she would give her daughter anything that pleased her, "as your happiness is the only thing that can ever make your Ma happy." Unfortunately, Aurelia, sickly and delicate, died in childbirth in 1872, but Sarah and Mitchell Gray maintained close relations as long as Sarah was alive. He was as integral to her businesses as her own sons, and it was he, in fact, whom she appointed executor of her estate before her death in 1892.

Sarah Cockrell's most important contribution to the Dallas community, however, may have had nothing to do with the bridge that made its growth into a major city possible, the local businesses emblazoned with the family name, the children who played prominent roles in its civic life, or the church built on land she donated. Half a century after Sarah died, her grandson Monroe Cockrell opened a trunk containing some of her papers. Inside the trunk, he found hundreds of pieces of paper, notes for loans of cash, grocery bills she had covered, and loads of firewood people who didn't have the money to pay for had taken from her property. On many of them she had written, "paid in full," but she had also marked a number of them "forgiven." Monroe recalled that as a child he had often seen ordinary people, black and white, whose clothing identified them as working class, show up at the house to see his grandmother.

At the time, he had no idea what the visits were all about, but that day in 1943 he realized that in late-nineteenth-century Dallas, people who were struggling to feed, clothe, and shelter their families knew that Sarah Cockrell would not turn them away. She was the only woman acknowledged as a "founder" of the city of Dallas. The working poor who depended on her generosity probably didn't know how she had made her fortune. What they did know was that Sarah would help them without robbing them of their dignity. Unlike her beneficences to the stately Methodist church she helped construct, these were acts of charity that remained hidden from sight, preserved in the memories of their beneficiaries. Sarah's was a life that was truly "paid in full."

Oveta Culp Hobby
The Media Giant of Houston

A generation after Sarah Cockrell helped transform Dallas into a thriving commercial center, Oveta Culp began an odyssey that would take her from Killeen, a small town that formed around a railroad depot midway between Waco and Austin, to prominence in Houston and beyond. The daughter of local lawyer and sometime state legislator Isaac "Ike" and Elizabeth Hoover Culp was born January 19, 1905. Oveta learned to shoulder more than her share of responsibility from an early age. After her maternal grandfather died, she moved in with her grandmother, Cordelia Hoover, to take the edge off her loneliness, but as Oveta later remarked, "Grandmére was too old to have to take on a small child, and I was too young to profit as I might" from her grandmother's high-minded example.

When she was five or six, a temperance delegation descended on Killeen's Sunday school students, urging them to take the pledge against drinking, and distributing white ribbons to those who did. Oveta refused—politely—to sign, but when she came home without a ribbon, her grandmother was furious until she heard the child's reason. "I did not sign because I did not know what the word means—temperance," Oveta explained, an early sign of the thoughtful independence that distinguished her actions throughout her life.

The Culps assumed that Oveta would take on adult responsibilities even as a child, and she unfailingly met the challenges head-on. After school, she routinely made her way to her father's law office, where she eavesdropped on his conversations about politics and the law. By the age of ten, the *Congressional*

Record was part of her regular reading, and within a few years she had read the Bible three times.

When Oveta had just barely reached her teens, she joined forces with her mother to solicit gifts of food, clothing, and cash for Killeen's needy families from the citizens who could afford to help their neighbors. At about the same time, Ike Culp moved his family and his law practice to nearby Temple, won a seat in the Texas House of Representatives, and in 1919, with his favorite daughter in tow, headed to Austin for the legislative session (one of Ike's colleagues that term was Sam Ealy Johnson Jr., Eliza Bunton Johnson's son and Lyndon Johnson's father). Instead of attending high school in the capital, fourteen-year-old Oveta spent her days in the House chamber, where she observed the give-and-take of lawmaking and politicking, and studied with tutors.

After one term in the House, Ike Culp returned to practicing law in Temple, and Oveta completed high school and spent a year at Mary Hardin Baylor College (since 1978, the University of Mary Hardin–Baylor) in nearby Belton. In 1923, when Culp regained his legislative seat, father and daughter went back to Austin. But this time Oveta was not content to be a passive observer of the House's deliberations. She was just eighteen, but she talked her way into a job as a reporter for the *Austin Evening Statesman* (now the *American-Statesman*).

In 1925, Oveta wasn't yet old enough to vote, but she was already such an astute observer of House procedure that she was appointed parliamentarian. After serving in the post for several terms, she published *Mr. Chairman* (1937), a handbook of parliamentary procedure geared to schools and clubs. Later Oveta looked back on her time as parliamentarian as the period that made her future achievements possible. "Twenty is a wonderful age for things to be sparked," she remembered.

One of the positions she held during her twenties was as a clerk for the State Banking Commission, where she helped codify Texas financial statutes. During one busy period, the commissioner asked her to examine a bank in her hometown of Temple. When she objected, "But I'm not a bank examiner," her boss replied, "You are now." And she got that job done.

Certainly the time Oveta spent in and around the legislature whetted her appetite for politics. Later in 1925, she moved to Houston and took a job in the *Houston Post-Dispatch* circulation department. She also became active in the local chapters of the League of Women Voters and Democratic Women's Club. At the 1928 Democratic National Convention in Houston, she organized a breakfast at the Rice Hotel attended by former first lady Edith Wilson, the mayor, the governor, and Jesse H. Jones, the convention organizer.

After Al Smith was nominated, Oveta supported his presidential campaign and also worked to help Thomas T. Connally defeat Earle B. Mayfield, the Ku Klux Klan candidate, in the Texas race for the U.S. Senate. Two years later, already a seasoned political veteran at twenty-five, she ran for the first—and last—time for a seat of her own in the state legislature. She lost to a Klan-backed opponent who vilified her as "a parliamentarian and a Unitarian." At the same time, she supported Walter E. Monteith's successful bid for election as mayor of Houston. Monteith asked her to serve as assistant to the city attorney, and she accepted the job on condition that she would be given time off to resume her duties as legislative parliamentarian when the 1931 Texas House session convened, in Austin.

One important influence on Oveta's views of politics during this period was Estelle Boughton Sharp, who introduced herself after a meeting where Oveta had spoken out to urge women to register and vote. "Mrs. Sharp opened the world to many of us," Oveta later recalled. "She organized a study group and saw to it that we learned about important national and international issues . . . such matters as the League of Nations report on the invasion of Manchuria [by Japan in 1931] and the meaning of the German desire for *Lebensraum*."

Estelle Sharp had been married to Walter Benona Sharp, a

Texas oilman and inventor whose innovative methods for drilling in soft soil and quicksand and, later, hard rock, revolution-
ized the oil industry. With Howard Hughes and J. S. Cullinan,
the founder of Texaco, he formed the Sharp-Hughes Tool Company, to manufacture their rock bit, which is still the standard
around the world. After Sharp's death in 1912, at forty-two, his
widow sold her interest in her husband's enterprises and spent
her time raising her two children and promoting education
(especially of women), social welfare, and world peace. Among
other efforts, she helped found the United Charities in Houston, a forerunner of the United Fund, promoted U.S. entry into
the League of Nations, and was a member of the Texas Centennial Commission. In 1918, she underwrote Rice Institute's
(now Rice University) first endowed lectureship, and years later
was instrumental in creating the Oral History of Texas Oil Pioneers at the University of Texas.

Oveta's later focus on international affairs, about which she
wrote many articles for the *Houston Post*, can be traced in large
measure to Estelle Sharp's tutelage. Oveta's editorial vision
was behind a series of *Post* articles that began to appear in the
late 1930s on topics including the Ottoman Empire, the constitutions of Greece and Turkey, the pact between England and
Egypt, and Afghanistan. Similarly, her interest in issues as di-
verse as education and the rights of minorities also owes much
to Estelle Sharp, who endowed a fund "to benefit the Negro
population of Houston."

Concurrently with her journalistic and editorial duties,
Oveta kept up her involvement in social service, and the problems she confronted often spilled over into print. When she
served on the Texas State Committee for Human Security, an
organization that solicited funds for blind and needy children,
for example, the experience inspired a series about community
welfare—health, child welfare, leisure-time problems, and the
merging of social agencies. These, in turn, prefigured interests
and expertise that Oveta would later reveal as secretary of the

U.S. Department of Health, Education, and Welfare in the Eisenhower administration.

Adept at juggling work and public service, Oveta added marriage and family to her daunting schedule without missing a beat. William P. Hobby, who had been Texas governor when Oveta first went to Austin with her father in 1919, was president of the *Post-Dispatch*. After the death of his wife, Willie Cooper Hobby, in 1929, he renewed his acquaintance with his friend Ike Culp's daughter. They married in 1931. Neither Oveta's new status nor the birth of her children (William Jr., in 1932, and Jessica, in 1937) slowed the pace of her involvement in public service. Shortly before William Jr. was born, she was installed as president of the Texas League of Women Voters, and in the course of the decade she sat on the citizens' task force that developed a bayou drainage system for Houston and joined the board of the Community Chest. Her contributions to culture and education in Houston alone embraced the Houston Symphony, the Houston Art Museum (now the Museum of Fine Arts), the YWCA, the Houston Recreation Council, and the University of Houston's endowment campaign, which she cochaired.

Oveta liked to insist that it was others who deserved the credit for her successes, especially her husband. "Everything that ever happened to me fell in my lap," she said more than once. "And nothing in my life would have been possible without Governor." The access to influential people provided first by Ike Culp and others, especially Governor Hobby, helped launch Oveta's rise in government, journalism, and business, but her achievements were her own. In fact, one reason she threw herself into work at the *Post* when she and Governor Hobby married in February 1931 was that he had suffered financial reversals in the first years of the Depression and was considering bankruptcy. "It would have been very easy for Will to have taken bankruptcy," she later said, "but we weren't going to do that."

Throughout the 1930s, Oveta was also a busy newspaperwoman. Her role at the *Post* grew—advancing from research editor to book editor to assistant editor to executive vice president by 1939, when she and Will bought the paper from Jesse Jones, who also owned the rival *Houston Chronicle*, for four million dollars. Throughout, she was a hands-on journalist, writing book reviews, editorials, and a syndicated column about parliamentary law, as well as editing copy. She also had a role in broadening the paper's scope, increasing coverage of national and international news (which she often reported), adding "women's news," and running more articles about Houston's black community and citizens. Concurrently, her stature in the publishing industry rose. By the end of the 1930s, she was president of the Southern Newspaper Publishers Association and the first woman member of the American Society of Newspaper Editors.

As a formerly all-male organization, no one at the society paid attention to the fact that a dinner meeting had been scheduled at an exclusive club whose foyer was open only to men. Normally, that barred women from attending events at the club, but it didn't stop Oveta. When it came to gaining entry to places that were normally closed to her, she didn't stand on ceremony. Her entrée to Texas politics, after all, had been as the only female on the floor of the Texas House of Representatives at a time when women were not yet permitted to vote. Even after the Nineteenth Amendment became law, many doors remained closed to women. Oveta delighted in unlatching them. At the editors' dinner, she skirted the front door and slipped in through the kitchen. It wasn't the first time she'd used that route to crash an all-male gathering. When Huey Long came to Houston for the LSU-Rice football game in 1932, Mayor Monteith hosted a men's-only brunch in his honor. Governor Hobby was sitting next to Governor Long when a woman dressed as a waitress approached and offered to serve them coffee. The "waitress" was Oveta, who explained that she had wanted to meet Huey Long.

During the Texas Centennial Exposition in 1936, the Hobbys flew to Dallas with Jesse Jones, their friend and the owner of Houston's two newspapers (the *Post* was the morning paper, and the *Chronicle* its afternoon rival), where Jones was to deliver a speech. On the return flight, a fire broke out in their small plane's oil line, and the pilot, Ed Hefley, made a crash landing in a cotton field. Will Hobby was knocked unconscious, and Oveta helped pull him out of the plane and away from the flames, while the copilot, Eugene Schacher, went back to extricate Hefley from the cockpit. A farmworker's car took the injured men to the nearest town, where an ambulance was waiting to rush them to a hospital in Dallas. Throughout the ordeal, Oveta remained so calm that the doctors realized only after they had tended to the other survivors that she had been a passenger in the plane as well and insisted on examining her. Schacher, who suffered severe burns and smoke inhalation, died two days later. In tribute, Jesse Jones created a trust for the Schacher children.

When the Hobbys purchased the *Post* from Jones in 1939, they also acquired KPRC-AM, the Houston radio station. It is believed that in 1941, while Oveta was in Washington, D.C., for discussions at the Federal Communications Commission, General David Searles of the War Department's Public Relations Section contacted her. The country had just introduced its first peacetime draft, and ten thousand letters were pouring into Washington every day from women concerned about the draftees' welfare. Searles wanted Oveta to organize women's activities on behalf of the nation's defense effort. She initially demurred, but her husband convinced her that she was duty-bound to answer the call.

As head of the Women's Interest Section, War Department Bureau of Public Relations, Oveta at first saw her role as providing information. In her first public statement, Oveta said:

For every one of the 1,500,000 men in the Army today, there are four or five women—mothers, wives, sisters, sweethearts—who are closely and personally interested. Mothers are more interested in their sons' health than they are in army maneuvers. They want to know what their man or boy is doing in his recreational hours, what opportunities the men have for training and promotion, about the health of camps and the provisions made for religious life.

This soon changed as American entry into the war loomed closer. General George C. Marshall, the army chief of staff, asked Oveta to draft plans to include women as army auxiliaries who would take over tasks that they could perform as well as or better than men, in order to make more men available for combat roles.

By late 1941, Oveta was regularly shuttling between Houston and Washington. En route to Houston in December, she had stopped in Chicago to deliver a speech when news broke of the attack on Pearl Harbor. Afterward, General Marshall always insisted that Oveta's speech constituted the United States' first declaration of war. She returned to Washington to compose the list of military functions that could be entrusted to women and to prepare a roster of women qualified to command the Women's Army Auxiliary Corps. When she handed her sheet of nominees to Marshall, he looked at the names and said, "I'd rather you took the job."

After some cajoling—on Governor Hobby's part as well as General Marshall's—Oveta agreed. "It would never have crossed my mind to command an army of women," she later said, characteristically modest. The notion ran counter to tradition; previously, the only women to wear military garb were nurses. She convinced army brass that women could handle at least 239 of the tasks formerly performed by servicemen. Oveta then took to the road, selling her plan for the WAAC to audiences around the country. Everywhere she went, she carried an electric fan and iron with her, so that each night she could wash, dry, and press her uniform, in order to present a crisp military appearance the next day. By war's end, more than one hundred thousand women had volunteered to serve.

Despite support from General Marshall and Secretary of War Henry Stimson, the army at large proved less than enthusiastic about letting women into their ranks. When she asked the army's engineers to design barracks for women, she was told that because the WAAC weren't a bona fide part of the army, they would have to design their own barracks. Leading fashion designers donated their time to create uniforms that would appeal to potential volunteers, only to have the Quartermaster Corps reject the pleated skirts because they required too much fabric and the leather belts as being a waste of a scarce resource. The comptroller general declared that because the physicians who treated the WAAC weren't actually military doctors, they couldn't be paid (at Secretary Stimson's request, Congress enacted a special law that authorized the comptroller general to pay the doctors). One camp commandant considered the presence of women such a threat to discipline that he had a fence built around the WAAC barracks and permitted the women to attend the nightly movies only twice a week. Even Oveta, who held a colonel's rank, didn't have a jeep assigned to her. When she needed transportation, she had to request a vehicle from the motor pool. In 1943, Oveta was successful in having the stigmatizing "auxiliary" removed from the name, and the Women's Army Corps (WAC) was official.

If the bureaucrats failed to appreciate the women's contributions, the generals were aware of how valuable they were. The women were twice as efficient as men at tasks that ranged from preparing meals to taking dictation to folding parachutes. Because of their proven talent, women were gradually allowed to perform more tasks as the war progressed. By 1944, six hundred thousand women had been requested from WAC headquarters, three times the maximum strength authorized by law. General Douglas MacArthur praised them as "my best soldiers," more industrious and better disciplined than men. For her efforts, Oveta received the Distinguished Service Medal, the nation's highest nonmilitary award, when she stepped down as head of the WAC. She was the first woman so honored, just as in 1978 she became the first female recipient of the George Catlett Marshall Medal for Public Service by the Association of the United States Army, named for the general who had chosen her to head the nation's first woman's military organization.

In 1945, as the war wound down, "the Little Colonel," as she was called, returned to civilian life, resuming her roles as executive vice president of the *Houston Post* and director of KPRC, which a year later added an FM station and, in 1950, was joined by KPRC-TV, when the Hobbys purchased KLEE-TV from W. Albert Lee and rechristened it with their familiar call letters. She also revived her engagement in politics, throwing her support behind Republican presidential candidate Dwight Eisenhower in 1952, in large part because he supported Texas's claims to jurisdiction over its tidelands and their mineral deposits. These rights were granted to the state in its 1845 annexation treaty with the United States, but their validity had been challenged because Texas seceded from the Union in 1861 and reentered in 1865. (The Texas rights were upheld and are intact today.) Oveta also had met General Eisenhower in England during the war and admired him very much. Knowing the excellent job she had done in forming the WAC, he later asked Oveta to be part of his new administration.

In postwar Houston, Oveta lost no time in putting the lessons of her wartime experience—the refusal of most Americans to acknowledge the contributions and sacrifices of women and minorities to the war effort—to work. When her cochairman of the city's 1946 Armed Forces Day celebration discussed with her his plans for a lavish military banquet, she answered, "Fine, if we understand each other. No celebration of Armed

Forces Day will be held in Houston which is not open to every one who has served in our armed forces—regardless of race." The man's reply has not survived, but Governor Hobby, who had prevented Japanese Americans in Houston from being ostracized and interned during the war as they had been in other communities, dressed him down for his prejudices. In the next decade, when the U.S. Supreme Court was about to decide the question of segregation of the public schools, the *Post* invited religious leaders of all faiths to contribute their opinions and published them as op-ed pieces on page one. By promoting dispassionate and open discussion of the issue, the paper encouraged Houston to pursue a policy of moderation when it desegregated its schools.

After Eisenhower was elected, he appointed Oveta to head the Federal Security Agency. When its functions were absorbed by the newly created Department of Health, Education, and Welfare (HEW), with full cabinet status, Oveta became its first secretary (and the second woman ever to achieve cabinet rank). Her greatest challenge came when HEW and the National Polio Foundation collaborated in overseeing the production and testing of the new polio vaccine developed by Jonas Salk, assessing the results of its clinical trial, and approving its use in advance of the 1955 summer polio season. During her tenure at HEW, she also oversaw a large-scale hospital building effort and an initiative to increase the number of hospitals dedicated to the treatment of chronic diseases; diagnostic, treatment, and rehabilitation facilities; and nursing homes. She proposed the building of schools to educate the children of the postwar baby boom, tightened the enforcement of food and drug laws, broadened mental health treatment, nurses' training, and physical rehabilitation, and put in place a hospital insurance program designed to help Americans cope with rising medical costs. After less than three years in her post, she resigned as secretary when Governor Hobby became ill in order to return to Houston to be with him. "Nothing is as important as Governor," she explained, but some of her Washington supporters were upset at the suddenness of her departure. "What?" Treasury Secretary George Humphrey exclaimed. "The best man in the Cabinet?"

Governor Hobby recovered and continued as chairman of the Houston Post Company for another nine years, until his death in 1964, at the age of eighty-six. Throughout that period, he and Oveta, who was president and editor, occupied adjoining offices at the *Post* and in their Houston home. Although Oveta didn't serve in government after her stint at HEW, she was appointed to numerous advisory boards. During Lyndon Johnson's presidency, she was asked to serve on one advisory group charged with charting the future of the military draft, as well as on the founding board of directors of the Corporation for Public Broadcasting.

Busy as she was with her media company and family after leaving Washington, Oveta was equally active in service to education and other social causes. She joined the Rice Institute board as its first woman trustee. There she allied with a group of like-minded board members to change the long-standing policy that refused to consider African-American applicants. Despite opposition from some alumni, Rice joined the ranks of American colleges and universities with a color-blind admissions process. Overall, Oveta's work on behalf of public and private higher education in Houston, the state of Texas, and around the country resulted in the award of more than a dozen honorary doctorates. Much of this support came through the Hobby Foundation, which William and Oveta created in 1945 to assist educational institutions and charities. Close to home, in addition to Rice University (the name was changed in 1960) and the University of Houston, they lent their support to the Houston Community Chest, local YMCAs and churches, the United Jewish Appeal, the Houston Symphony, and the Museum of Fine Arts. To the museum, Oveta contributed more than one hundred works from her personal art collection, including a number of modern masters, and helped fill gaps in the institution's twentieth-century holdings by underwriting purchases of works by Joan Miro, Arshile Gorky, and others.

In 1983, the Toronto Sun Publishing Company purchased the *Post* from Oveta for $130 million. The company resold the paper later in the decade, and it folded in 1995, just a few months before Oveta's death. The family sold its seven television stations, operating in six states, held by H&C Communications Inc., for $600 million in 1992. After the sale, the Hobbys retained only their original radio station, Houston-based KPRC-AM. According to *Forbes* magazine, Oveta was one of America's three hundred wealthiest people; the magazine estimated the family's wealth at $400 million. Still, she shied away from descriptions of herself as a powerful person. "The world is full of powerful people who render a great service to society, but we never hear of them."

Oveta suffered a stroke in April 1995 and died four months later. Marguerite Johnston, a historian who was also a close friend, called her "one of the greatest leaders the United States has ever produced," pointing to the millions of people whose lives she touched as leader of the first generation of women in the military, secretary of HEW, and publisher and director of the *Houston Post* and other media outlets.

I was one of those whose lives she changed. As a young woman law school graduate, I looked for a job in a Houston law firm in 1969, a time when the big firms didn't hire women. So I decided to try my luck in a different field. I walked into KPRC-TV (the NBC affiliate) without an appointment. Surprisingly, the news director, Ray Miller, came out to the reception room to see me and gave me an interview. He told me they did not have an opening on the news staff, but he was going to try to find a place. I'm told that when he and the station manager, Jack Harris, showed my résumé to Oveta, who owned KPRC, she said, "I should be the first to hire a woman news reporter for Houston television." And the job was mine.

When I saw her years later at a Texas inauguration (her son

Bill Hobby served as lieutenant governor of Texas from 1973 to 1991), she told me she was very pleased to have given me my career start. Of course, I felt honored to have been working in a company owned by such a respected Texas trailblazer.

She was accepted by her male peers as one of the most prominent business leaders in Houston in the middle of the twentieth century, which were important formative years for the city. She put her mark on it, as well as on Texas and America.

Epilogue

In trying to explain the phenomenon of the Texas spirit and the role women played in its evolution, I have reached back to the nineteenth century, when all the elements converged: the harsh land, lack of luxuries or even necessities, deadly Indian attacks, war for independence, building the republic, then statehood, secession, and reunification. And yet, despite all the struggles and obstacles, the settlers who persevered built a lasting economic powerhouse. The positive attitude and can-do spirit has been passed through the generations to the present day.

When Mary Austin Holley captured the confluence of hardship and fun that evolved into the robust spirit of Texas, she also recognized the importance of preserving it. She wrote in her book of observations on Texas in 1833 that the women's hardy, vigorous constitutions, free spirits, and spontaneous gaiety should be passed as a legacy to their children. Mary's admonishment has been heard.

The nineteenth-century women who helped forge the spirit of Texas produced heirs who did not fritter it away, seeking refinement at the expense of risk. They married rowdy men who added to their ranches, or wildcatters who discovered oil under land that wasn't fit for livestock.

The nineteenth-century legacy produced twentieth-century

leaders in every field. Women started businesses, became doctors and lawyers, raised money for museums and the arts, were elected to run cities, counties, courts, and state agencies, and promoted quality education. And they didn't take no for an answer.

I am reminded of a time years ago, before I ran for the U.S. Senate, when I called a local Dallas business leader to ask for a contribution for breast cancer research. He said, "Kay, I'd rather run into the Dallas Cowboys line than say no to you. How much do you want?"

Versions of this conversation have been going on in Texas for more than 175 years, and because the seeds were planted by these early strong women, I have complete confidence that it will always be so. And the Texas spirit will never die nor be buried in mediocrity.

Appendix:
Family Trees

Taylor-Shindler Family
Hall-Sharp Family
Austin Family
Parker Family
Houston Family
Lea Family
Bunton-Johnson Family
King Family

TAYLOR-SHINDLER FAMILY TREE
partial

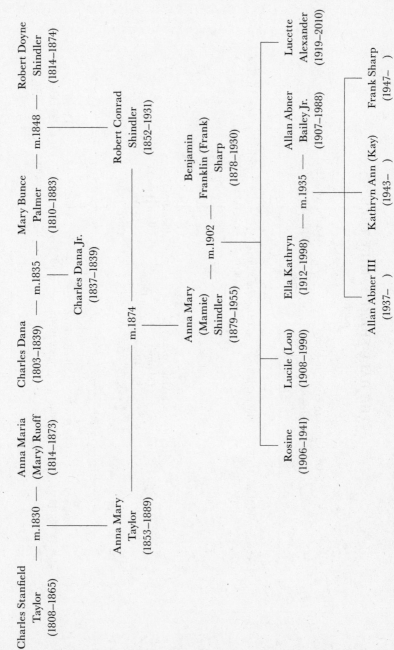

THE HALL-SHARP FAMILY TREE
partial

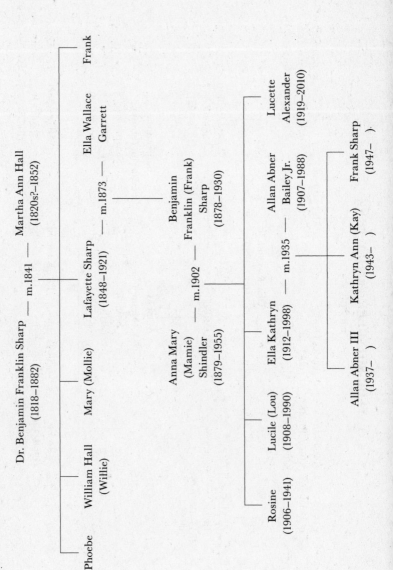

THE AUSTIN FAMILY TREE

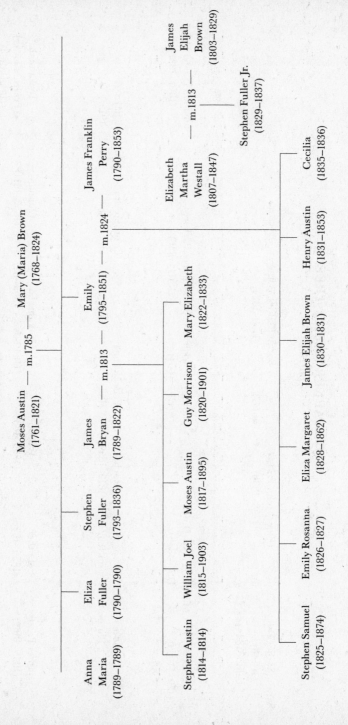

THE PARKER FAMILY TREE
partial

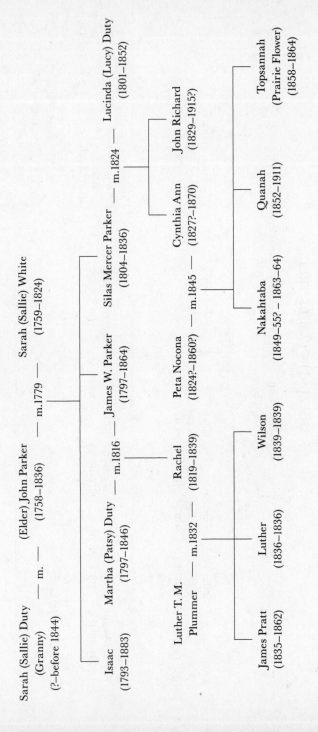

Sarah (Sallie) Duty (Granny) (?–before 1844) — m. — (Elder) John Parker (1758–1836) — m.1779 — Sarah (Sallie) White (1759–1824)

Isaac (1793–1883)

Martha (Patsy) Duty (1797–1846) — m.1816 — James W. Parker (1797–1864)

Silas Mercer Parker (1804–1836) — m.1824 — Lucinda (Lucy) Duty (1801–1852)

Luther T. M. Plummer — m.1832 — Rachel (1819–1839)

Peta Nocona (1824?–1860?) — m.1845 — Cynthia Ann (1827?–1870)

John Richard (1829–1915?)

James Pratt (1835–1862)

Luther (1836–1836)

Wilson (1839–1839)

Nakahtaba (1849–55? – 1863–64)

Quanah (1852–1911)

Topsannah (Prairie Flower) (1858–1864)

THE HOUSTON FAMILY TREE

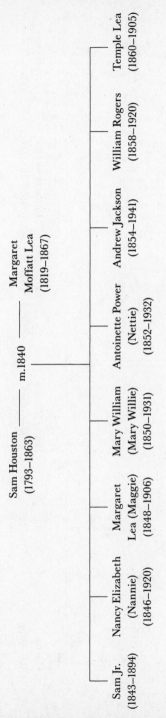

Sam Houston —— m.1840 —— Margaret
(1793–1863)   Moffatt Lea
                                   (1819–1867)

Sam Jr.
(1843–1894)

Nancy Elizabeth
(Nannie)
(1846–1920)

Margaret
Lea (Maggie)
(1848–1906)

Mary William
(Mary Willie)
(1850–1931)

Antoinette Power
(Nettie)
(1852–1932)

Andrew Jackson
(1854–1941)

William Rogers
(1858–1920)

Temple Lea
(1860–1905)

THE LEA FAMILY TREE

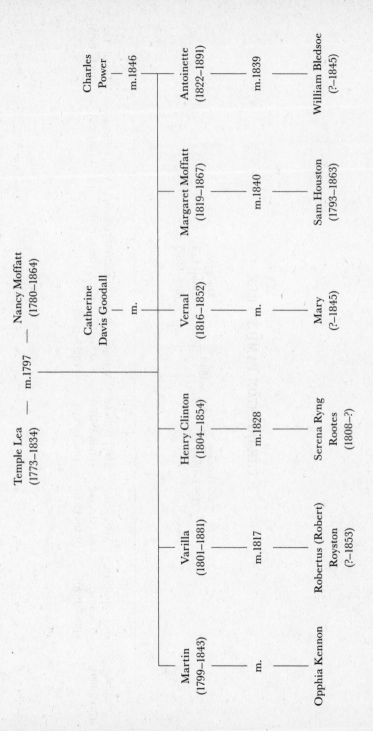

THE BUNTON-JOHNSON
FAMILY TREE
partial

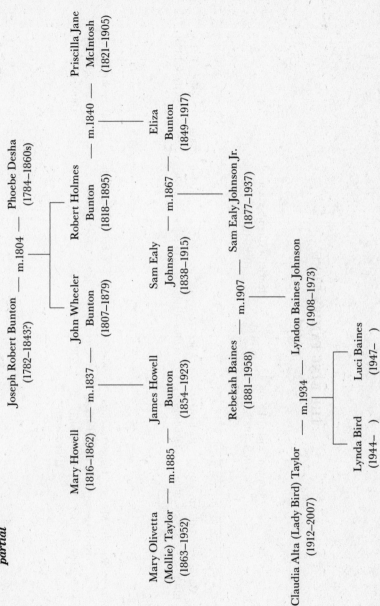

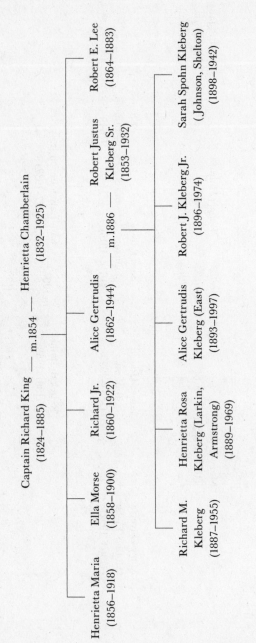

THE KING FAMILY TREE
partial

Captain Richard King — m.1854 — Henrietta Chamberlain
(1824–1885)   (1832–1925)

Henrietta Maria
(1856–1918)

Ella Morse
(1858–1900)

Richard Jr.
(1860–1922)

Alice Gertrudis
(1862–1944) — m.1886 — Robert Justus
Kleberg Sr.
(1853–1932)

Robert E. Lee
(1864–1883)

Richard M.
Kleberg
(1887–1955)

Henrietta Rosa
Kleberg (Larkin,
Armstrong)
(1889–1969)

Alice Gertrudis
Kleberg (East)
(1893–1997)

Robert J. Kleberg Jr.
(1896–1974)

Sarah Spohn Kleberg
(Johnson, Shelton)
(1898–1942)

Suggestions for Further Reading

General Texas History

Randolph B. Campbell. *Gone to Texas: A History of the Lone Star State*. New York: Oxford University Press, 2003.

T. R. Fehrenbach. *Lone Star*. New York: Macmillan, 1968.

Ben Procter and Archie P. McDonald, eds. *The Texas Heritage*. 4th ed. Wheeling, IL: Harland Davidson, 2003.

The Handbook of Texas Online. http://www.tshaonline.org/handbook/online. Published by the Texas State Historical Association.

Texas Women's History

Evelyn Carrington, ed. *Women in Early Texas*. Austin: Jenkins, 1975.

Bruce Glasrud and Merline Pitre, eds. *Black Women in Texas History*. College Station: Texas A&M University Press, 2008.

Kay Bailey Hutchison. *American Heroines: The Spirited Women Who Shaped Our Country*. New York: William Morrow, 2004.

Ann Patton Malone. *Women on the Texas Frontier: A Cross-Cultural Perspective*. El Paso: Texas Western Press, 1983.

Donald Willett and Stephen Curley, eds. *Invisible Texans: Women and Minorities in Texas History*. Boston: McGraw-Hill, 2005.

Brief Biographies

Ann Fears Crawford and Crystal Sasse Ragsdale. *Women in Texas*. Burnet, TX: Eakin Press, 1982. Includes chapters on Jane Long,

Dilue Rose Harris, Margaret Houston, Henrietta King, Molly Goodnight, and Lizzie Johnson Williams.

Jo Ella Powell Exley. *Texas Tears and Texas Sunshine*. College Station: Texas A&M University Press, 1985. Includes chapters on Dilue Rose Harris and Rachel Parker Plummer.

Women of Texas. Waco: Texian Press, 1972.

My Heritage

Mary Shindler

Mary Dana Shindler. *A Southerner Among the Spirits*. Memphis, TN: Southern Baptist Publication Society, 1877. Reprinted, Whitefish, MT: Kessinger, 2009.

Linda Sundquist. *The Poetess of Song: The Life of Mary Shindler*. Livermore, CA: WingSpan Press, 2006.

Jane Long, The Mother of Texas

Neila Petrick. *Jane Long of Texas: 1798–1880*. Gretna, LA: Pelican, 2000.

Martha Anne Turner. *The Life and Times of Jane Long*. Waco: Texian Press, 1969.

Anne A. Brindley. "Jane Long." *Southwestern Historical Quarterly* 56 (October 1952), 211–38.

The Texas Revolution: The Alamo, the Runaway Scrape, San Jacinto

Mary L. Scheer, ed. *Women and the Texas Revolution*. Denton: University of North Texas Press, 2012.

Susanna Dickinson

C. Richard King. *Susanna Dickinson: Messenger of the Alamo*. Austin: Shoal Creek, 1976.

Crystal Sasse Ragsdale. *The Women and Children of the Alamo*. Austin: State House Press, 1994.

Gale Hamilton Shiffrin. *Echoes from Women of the Alamo*. San Antonio: AW Press, 1999.

Dilue Rose Harris

"Reminiscences of Mrs. Dilue Harris." *Quarterly of the Texas State Historical Association* 4 (October 1900), 85–127; (January 1901), 155–89; and 7 (January 1904), 214–22.

Pamelia Mann

William Ransom Hogan. "Pamelia Mann: Texas Frontierswoman." *Southwest Review* 20 (Summer 1935), 360–70.

Andrew Forest Muir. "In Defense of Mrs. Mann." In *Mexican Border Ballads and Other Lore*, edited by Mody C. Boatright. Austin: Texas Folklore Society, 1946, pp. 113–35.

Emily Austin Bryan Perry

Light Townsend Cummins. *Emily Austin of Texas, 1795–1851.* Fort Worth: TCU Press, 2009.

Marie Beth Jones. *Peach Point Plantation: The First 150 Years.* Waco: Texian Press, 1982.

Anna Raguet Irion

Ever Thine Truly: Love Letters from Sam Houston to Anna Raguet. Austin: Jenkins Garret Press, 1975.

Marquis James. *The Raven: A Biography of Sam Houston.* Indianapolis: Bobbs-Merrill, 1929. Reprinted, New York: Paperback Library, 1967; Atlanta: Mockingbird Books, 1977.

Mary Ann Turner. *Sam Houston and His Twelve Women.* Austin: Pemberton Press, 1966.

Mary "Polly" Rusk

Elizabeth Brooks. *Prominent Women of Texas.* Akron, OH: Werner, 1896.

Mary Whatley Clarke. *Thomas J. Rusk: Soldier, Statesman, Jurist.* Austin: Jenkins, 1971.

Cleburne Houston. *Towering Texan: A Biography of Thomas J. Rusk.* Waco: Texian Press, 1971.

Indian Captives

Rachel Parker Plummer

Rachael Plummer. *Narrative of Twenty-one Months Servitude as a Prisoner Among the Commanchee Indians*, with a preface by Archibald Hanna and an introduction by William S. Reese. Austin: Jenkins, 1977. Facsimile reprint of the 1838 edition.

Cynthia Ann Parker

Paul H. Carlson and Tom Crum. *Myth, Memory, and Massacre: The Pease River Capture of Cynthia Ann Parker.* Lubbock: Texas Tech University Press, 2010.

James T. DeShields. *Cynthia Ann Parker: The Story of Her Capture*. St. Louis: privately printed, 1886. Reprinted, San Antonio: Naylor, 1934.

Jo Ella Powell Exley. *Frontier Blood: The Saga of the Parker Family*. College Station: Texas A&M University Press, 2001.

Margaret Houston and Her Contemporaries

Margaret Houston

Madge Thornall Roberts. *Star of Destiny: The Private Life of Sam and Margaret Houston*. Denton: University of North Texas Press, 1993.

————, ed. *The Personal Correspondence of Sam Houston*. 4 vols. Denton: University of North Texas Press, 1996–2001.

William Seale. *Sam Houston's Wife: A Biography of Margaret Lea Houston*. Norman: University of Oklahoma Press, 1970.

Angelina Eberly

C. Richard King. *The Lady Cannoneer: A Biography of Angelina Belle Peyton Eberly, Heroine of the Texas Archives War*. Burnet, TX: Eakin Press, 1981.

Louis Wiltz Kemp. "Mrs. Angelina B. Eberly." *Southwestern Historical Quarterly* 36 (January 1933), 193–99.

Women Ranchers and Trail Drivers

Brief Biographies

J. Marvin Hunter, ed. *Trail Drivers of Texas*. 2 vols. 4th ed. Austin: University of Texas Press, 1985. Includes recollections by several trail hands about the Reynolds and Matthews cattle operations, Amanda Burks's account of the drive she made with her husband, Bud, in 1871, and separate accounts by William B. Slaughter and his wife, Anna McAdams Slaughter, of their drive to Liberal, Kansas, with fifteen hundred head of cattle.

Sara R. Massey, ed. *Texas Women on the Cattle Trails*. College Station: Texas A&M University Press, 2006. Includes chapters on Kate Malone Medlin, Bettie Matthews Reynolds, Amanda Nite Burks, Hattie Standefer Cluck, Molly Dunn Bugbee, Margaret Borland, Molly Dyer Goodnight, Lizzie Johnson Williams, and Mollie Taylor Bunton.

Thomas Ulvan Taylor. *The Chisholm Trail and Other Routes*. San Antonio: Naylor, 1936. Chapter 10, "Ladies of the Trail," recounts the trail drives of Hattie Standefer Cluck, Amanda Nite Burks, Molly Dyer Goodnight, and Mollie Taylor Bunton.

Henrietta Chamberlain King

Helen Kleberg Groves. *Bob and Helen Kleberg of King Ranch*. Albany, TX: Bright Sky Press, 2004.

Tom Lea. *The King Ranch*. 2 vols. Boston: Little, Brown, 1957.

Jane Clements Monday and Frances Brannen Vick, eds. *Letters to Alice: Birth of the Kleberg-King Ranch Dynasty*. Corpus Christi: Gulf Coast Books, sponsored by Texas A&M University–Corpus Christi, 2012.

Molly Dyer Goodnight

William T. Hagan. *Charles Goodnight: Father of the Texas Panhandle*. Norman: University of Oklahoma Press, 2007.

J. Evetts Haley. *Charles Goodnight*. Norman: University of Oklahoma Press, 1949.

Phoebe Kerrick Warner. "The Wife of a Pioneer Ranchman." *Cattleman*, March 1921, 65–71.

Eliza Bunton Johnson

Robert Caro. *Path to Power*. New York: Knopf, 1982.

Rebekah Baines Johnson. *A Family Album*. New York: McGraw-Hill, 1965.

William C. Pool, Emmie Craddock, and David Eugene Conrad. *Lyndon Baines Johnson: The Formative Years*. San Marcos: Southwest Texas State College Press, 1965.

T. U. Taylor. "Heroines of the Hills." *Frontier Times* 18, no. 1 (October 1940), 15–24.

Mollie Taylor Bunton

Mollie Taylor Bunton. *A Bride on the Old Chisholm Trail in 1886*. San Antonio: Naylor, 1939.

Bettie Matthews Reynolds

Frances Mayhugh Holden. *Lambshead Before Interwoven: A Texas Range Chronicle, 1848–1878*. College Station: Texas A&M University Press, 1982.

Sallie Reynolds Matthews. *Interwoven; a Pioneer Chronicle*. Houston: Anson Jones Press, 1936. Reprinted, Austin: University of Texas Press, 1974.

Janet M. Neugebauer, ed. *Lambshead Legacy: The Ranch Diary of Watt R. Matthews*. College Station: Texas A&M University Press, 1997.

Laura Wilson. *Watt Matthews of Lambshead*. 2nd ed. Austin: Texas State Historical Association, 2007.

Lizzie Johnson Williams

Emily Jones Shelton. "Lizzie E. Johnson: A Cattle Queen of Texas." *Southwestern Historical Quarterly* 50 (January 1947), 355–62.

Master Builders:
A Tale of Two Cities and Two Centuries

Sarah Cockrell

Vivian Anderson Castleberry. *Sarah—the Bridge Builder: Dowager of a Dallas Dynasty*. Dallas: Odenwald Press, 2004.

———. *Daughters of Dallas: A History of Greater Dallas Through the Voices and Deeds of Its Women*. Dallas: Odenwald Press, 1994.

Elizabeth York Enstam. *Women and the Creation of Urban Life: Dallas, Texas, 1843–1920*. College Station: Texas A&M University Press, 1998, pp. 18–22, 34–50, 70–72.

———. "Opportunity Versus Propriety: The Life and Career of Frontier Matriarch Sarah Horton Cockrell." *Frontiers: A Journal of Women's Studies* 6, no. 3 (Autumn 1981), 106–14.

Oveta Culp Hobby

Stephen Fenberg. *Unprecedented Power: Jesse Jones, Capitalism, and the Common Good*. College Station: Texas A&M University Press, 2011.

Robert T. Pando, *Oveta Culp Hobby: A Study of Power and Control*. Tallahassee: Florida State University Press, 2008.

Harry Hurt III. "The Last of the Great Ladies." *Texas Monthly*, October 1978, pp. 142–48, 225–34, 236–38, 240.

Credits

Grateful acknowledgment is made for permission to reproduce the following illustrations and maps:

Photographs

Eva Rosine and Anna Mary Ruoff: Courtesy of City of Nacogdoches Historic Sites Department.

Mary Shindler: Courtesy of Senator Kay Bailey Hutchison.

Jane Long: Courtesy of the George Ranch Historical Park, Richmond, Texas.

Susanna Dickinson: Photograph SC12294, courtesy of the Daughters of the Republic of Texas Library.

Anna Raguet Irion: Courtesy, Irion Family Papers, Special Collections, The University of Texas at Arlington Library, Arlington, Texas.

Emily Austin Bryan Perry: Courtesy of the Brazoria County Historical Commission.

Mary "Polly" Rusk: Courtesy of the East Texas Research Center, R. W. Steen Library, Stephen F. Austin State University, Nacogdoches, Texas.

Cynthia Ann Parker: Courtesy of the Southwest Collection/Special Collections Library, Texas Tech University, Lubbock, Texas.

Margaret Houston, age twenty-one or twenty-two: Courtesy of the Sam Houston Memorial Museum, Huntsville, Texas.

Margaret Houston in middle age (painted posthumously): Courtesy of the Sam Houston Memorial Museum, Huntsville, Texas.

Henrietta King: Courtesy of the General Photograph Collection, MS 362: 088-0231, University of Texas at San Antonio Libraries Special Collections from the Institute of Texan Cultures.

Molly Goodnight: Photograph PA-653, courtesy of Amarillo Public Library.

Bettie Matthews Reynolds: Courtesy of Jennifer Hoy Orton.

Eliza Bunton Johnson: Image courtesy of the United States National Park Service, Lyndon Johnson National Historical Site.

Lizzie Johnson Williams: Courtesy of the General Photograph Collection, MS 362: 075-0539, University of Texas at San Antonio Libraries Special Collections from the Institute of Texan Cultures.

Mollie Taylor Bunton: Photograph number AR.L.011(018), courtesy of the Austin History Center, Austin Public Library.

Sarah Cockrell: Courtesy Dallas Historical Society. Used by permission.

Oveta Culp Hobby: Oveta Culp Hobby Papers, courtesy of Woodson Research Center, Fondren Library, Rice University.

Maps

East Texas map showing Houston and Lea family homes: From *The Personal Correspondence of Sam Houston, Volume 1: 1839–1845*, edited by Madge Thornall Roberts. Copyright © 1996 Madge Thornall Roberts and reprinted by permission of the University of North Texas Press.

Maps courtesy of the Dolph Briscoe Center for American History, University of Texas at Austin:

- Detail map of Mississippi, Louisiana, and East Texas showing Wilkinson/Long family homes.

- Detail map of Texas in 1836.

- Major battles of the Texas Revolution.

- Major cattle trails from Texas to Missouri, Kansas, and Colorado.

Index

BOOKS BY KAY BAILEY HUTCHISON

UNFLINCHING COURAGE
Pioneering Women Who Shaped Texas

Available in Paperback and eBook

The only woman ever to represent Texas in the United States Senate, Kay Bailey Hutchison has been a trailblazer in the Lone Star State. Nevertheless, Hutchison is just one of many women who have embodied what we've come to recognize as the spirit of Texas. In *Unflinching Courage*, Senator Hutchison tells the dynamic history of her home state through the lives of some of these pioneering women and their remarkable achievements.

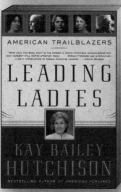

LEADING LADIES
American Trailblazers

Available in Paperback and eBook

Following in the footsteps of her national bestseller, *American Heroines*, Senator Kay Bailey Hutchison celebrates female accomplishment. From the Nobel Prize to the halls of Congress, the trailblazers profiled in these biographical portraits have battled tremendous odds to achieve success in their respective fields. These courageous women have all woven the thin threads of opportunity into sweeping tapestries of achievement.

AMERICAN HEROINES
The Spirited Women Who Shaped Our Country

Available in Paperback and eBook

The indomitable spirit of American women has shaped both the country's history and society. *American Heroines* presents female pioneers in fields as varied as government, business, education and healthcare, who overcame the resistance and prejudice of their times and accomplished things that no woman had done before. Interspersed with the stories of America's historic female leaders are stories of today's women whose successes are clearly linked to those predecessors.